The Azar-Hagen Grammar Series

TEST BANK for

FUNDAMENTALS OF
English
Grammar

FOURTH EDITION

PEARSON
Longman

Kelly Roberts Weibel

Fundamentals of English Grammar, Fourth Edition
Test Bank

Azar Associates: Shelley Hartle, Editor, and Sue Van Etten, Manager

Pearson Education, 10 Bank Street, White Plains, NY 10606

Staff credits: The people who made up the *Fundamentals of
English Grammar, Fourth Edition, Test Bank* team, representing
editorial, production, design, and manufacturing, are, Diane Cipollone,
Dave Dickey, Christine Edmonds, Ann France, Amy McCormick, and
Ruth Voetmann.

Text composition: S4Carlisle Publishing Services
Text font: 10.5/12 Plantin

Printed in the United States of America

ISBN 10: 0-13-707144-2
ISBN 13: 978-0-13-707144-9

11 12—V092—16 15 14

CONTENTS

CHAPTER 4   PRESENT PERFECT AND PAST PERFECT **45**

CHAPTER 5   ASKING QUESTIONS **64**

CHAPTER 6   NOUNS AND PRONOUNS **82**

INTRODUCTION

This test bank accompanies *Fundamentals of English Grammar, Fourth Edition*. Instructors can choose from over 200 quizzes and thirty-two tests to use for assessment. Teachers familiar with the third edition will find a great deal of material has been updated for this fourth edition.

QUIZZES

Each chapter contains a series of quizzes keyed to individual charts in the student book, followed by two chapter tests. The quizzes are intended as quick checks of student understanding for both teacher and student. Mastery of a quiz is a strong indicator that students are ready to progress to the next section.

CHAPTER TESTS

The tests at the end of each chapter are comprehensive, covering as many points from the chapter as possible. The formats of the questions in the chapter tests follow those used in the previous quizzes. The two chapter tests are identical in format so that one may be used as a practice test if desired.

EXAMS

Two midterm exams covering chapters one through seven and two comprehensive final exams are included in this test bank. They can be used in conjunction with the other quizzes and tests or used separately.

FORMAT

Because students bring a variety of learning styles to the classroom, there is a wide selection of test formats, including sentence completion, sentence connection, multiple choice, and error analysis, as well as more open completion. To maximize the use of the answer key, open-ended writing practice has been kept to a minimum. Teachers wishing to incorporate more writing into the tests are encouraged to add their own material at the end of the chapter tests.

ANSWER KEY

An answer key for all quizzes, tests, and exams can be found in the back of the text.

DUPLICATION

The material has been formatted so teachers can easily make copies for their students. Permission is granted to duplicate as many copies as needed for classroom use only.

Acknowledgements

This work wouldn't have been possible without the love and support of my family, who keep me in touch with natural-sounding English and give me valuable feedback. Thanks, guys! I also want to thank my colleagues at Edmonds Community College for their encouragement. Special thanks, once again, to Ruth Voetmann and Stacy Hagen for making this project such a pleasure to work on.

Present Time

Simple Present Tense (Chart 1-1)

Directions: Complete the sentences. Use the simple present form of the verbs in parentheses.

SITUATION: A Weekday Morning

Example: The coffee shop on Sixth Avenue (*serve*) _____*serves*_____ the best coffee in town.

1. Ben (*eat*) _____ breakfast at 6:00 A.M. every morning.

2. Suzie (*eat, not*) _____ any breakfast.

3. Her neighbor, Mrs. Jones, (*enjoy*) _____ her breakfast on her front porch.

4. Many children in our neighborhood (*walk*) _____ to school every day.

5. Some parents (*take*) _____ their younger children to school.

6. A few teenagers (*drive*) _____ themselves.

7. The teacher (*begin*) _____ class at 9:00 A.M. every day.

8. The bell (*ring*) _____ at 8:55 A.M.

9. Several students often (*come*) _____ late.

10. They (*have, not*) _____ a good reason for being late.

Simple Present and Present Progressive (Charts 1-1 and 1-2)

Directions: Complete the chart with the correct forms of the verb **walk**. The first one is done for you as an example.

Simple Present Tense	Present Progressive Tense
I _____*walk.*_____	I _____*am walking.*_____
You _____	You _____
Laura _____	Henri _____
We _____	My husband and I _____
You and your classmates _____	You and your sister _____
They _____	Suzy and Charles _____

A. Directions: Complete the questions with **Is she** or **Does she**.

SITUATION: The Visitor

Examples: _____Is she_____ a tourist?

_____Does she_____ travel often?

1. _____ have a tourist visa or a student visa?

2. _____ speak English?

3. _____ enjoying her time here?

4. _____ have any plans for staying here?

5. _____ happy here?

B. Directions: Make the second sentence in each pair a negative.

Example: It's too hot today.

It _____isn't_____ too cold today.

1. My parents call me every week.

My parents _____ me every day.

2. Paolo is studying international law at Oxford University. .

Paolo _____ computer science.

3. I remember my English teacher's name.

I _____ my science teacher's name.

4. Jonas and Antoine are taking the bus to school.

Jonas and Antoine _____ a taxi to school.

5. Mikael lives in St. Petersburg.

Mikael _____ in Moscow.

A. *Directions:* Complete the sentences. Use appropriate frequency adverbs from the list. More than one answer is possible.

Example: Samantha eats out three times a week.

Samantha ___*often eats out.*___

| always | often | sometimes | rarely | never |

1. Ari is late for work about once a week.

   Ari _____ late for work.

2. Every time I buy something, I use a credit card.

   When I buy something, I _____ a credit card.

3. Every once in a while, my computer printer stops printing in the middle of a page.

   My computer printer _____ printing in the middle of a page.

4. I go running at 5:00 every morning, rain or shine.

   I _____ running in the morning.

5. I see the dentist about once every five years.

   I _____ the dentist.

B. *Directions:* Add the given adverb to each sentence. Make any necessary changes to the sentence.

Example: My dad goes to work at 5:30 A.M. (*always*)

   ___*My dad always goes to work at 5:30 A.M.*___

1. Does Alex go bowling? (*ever*)

   _____

2. We go to the theater more than once a month. (*seldom*)

   _____

3. Abdul is hungry at dinnertime. (*usually*)

   _____

4. I stay out past midnight on weekends. (*never*)

   _____

5. Lee doesn't remember his homework. (*always*)

   _____

QUIZ 5 Simple Present vs. Present Progressive (Charts 1-1 → 1-4)

Directions: Choose the correct completions.

Example: Maria (sleeps), *is sleeping* until noon every day.

1. Right now, Janice (*relax, relaxes, is relaxing*) on her sofa. She (*read, reads, is reading*) a good book.

2. The newspaper usually (*come, comes, is coming*) by 7:00. Frequently it (*get, gets, is getting*) wet because the newspaper carrier (*throw, throws, is throwing*) the paper on the grass.

3. A: The phone (*ring, rings, is ringing*).
   B: I'll get it.
   A: Who (*call, calls, is calling*)?

4. The Wilsons (*work, works, are working*) in their garden right now. They (*clean, cleans, are cleaning*) up their vegetable garden. Sometimes they (*garden, gardens, are gardening*) for several hours on weekends.

QUIZ 6 Non-Action Verbs (Chart 1-6)

Directions: Choose the correct verbs.

Example: That small dog (looks), *is looking* like a cat.

1. The teachers (*need, are needing*) a break. They (*are, are being*) tired.

2. Mrs. Brown (*understands, is understanding*) her students well.

3. I'm sorry. I (*don't remember, am not remembering*) your name.

4. This package (*belongs, is belonging*) to Mr. Johnson.

5. I (*think, am thinking*) about my family now.

6. I (*think, am thinking*) that my parents are wonderful.

7. (*Do you have, Are you having*) a good time?

8. What (*do you know, are you knowing*) about your work schedule for next week?

9. I (*don't have, am not having*) enough money for lunch.

Directions: Complete the sentences with the simple present or the present progressive form of the verbs in parentheses.

Examples: Shhh. Grandma (*sleep*) __is sleeping__ on the couch. She (*need*) ____needs____ some rest.

1. Right now, Professor Kim (*help*) _____ his students individually. He usually (*help*) _____ them the last ten minutes of each class.

2. In addition to Japanese, Tomo (*speak*) _____ four other languages. Right now he (*speak*) _____ to his friends in English. They (*need*) _____ more oral practice.

3. Look! An eagle (*fly*) _____ overhead with a snake in his mouth!

4. Vivian usually (*exercise*) _____ at a fitness center after work. Tonight she (*work*) _____ late. She (*exercise, not*) _____.

5. I love traveling! (*you, like*) _____ to travel?

Directions: Complete the conversation. Use the simple present or present progressive form of the verbs in parentheses. Give short answers to the questions as necessary.

SITUATION: Talking about Pets

Examples: A: (*Karl, have*) _____Does Karl have_____ a cat?

B: No, __he doesn't__. He (*be*) __is__ allergic to cats.

A: (*your neighbors, have*) _____ a dog?

B: Yes, _____. They (*have*) _____ a bulldog.

A: (*he, be*) _____ friendly?

B: Yes, _____. He (*love*) _____ people.

A: (*he, bark*) _____ a lot?

B: Yes, _____. He (*be*) _____ very noisy.

A: (*your parents, be*) _____ planning to get a dog?

B: No, _____.

Directions: Choose the correct completions.

Example: A large car ((*uses*), *is using*) more gasoline than a small car.

1. On Sundays, we usually (*go, are going*) for a drive in the country. It (*does, is*) very relaxing.

2. A: Your homework assignment (*looks, is looking*) long. (*Does, Is*) it hard?
   B: Yes, it (*does, is*). Please be quiet. I (*try, am trying*) to study.

3. This party is a great idea. We (*have, are having*) a wonderful time.

4. A: (*Do, Are*) you need anything at the store? I (*leave, am leaving*) now.
   B: No, I (*don't, am not*). Thanks anyway.

5. My parents (*believe, are believing*) in hard work. They (*own, are owning*) two restaurants.
   They (*work, are working*) seven days a week.

6. A: What (*do you do, are you doing*) right now?
   B: I (*send, am sending*) an email to my teacher.
   A: (*Do you send, Are you sending*) emails often?
   B: No, I (*don't, am not*). Only when I (*have, am having*) to hand my homework in late.

7. Every time it (*snows, is snowing*), our water pipes (*freeze, are freezing*).

Directions: Complete the sentences with the simple present or present progressive form of the verbs in parentheses. Add the frequency adverb where needed.

Examples: Right now, Mike (*play*) _____is playing_____ a game on his computer. He (*play*) _____plays_____ games often.

1. My work day (*begin, usually*) _____ at 8:00 A.M. and (*end*)

   _____ at 5:00 P.M.

2. Listen. The birds in the trees (*sing*) _____. It's beautiful!

3. A: The baby (*cry*) _____.

   B: I know. She (*be, always*) _____ hungry.

4. A: (*you, watch*) _____ this show?

   B: Yes, I _____.

   A: (*you and Sam, want*) _____ to watch a movie later?

   B: No, we _____. We have to do our homework.

5. Ellen (*catch*) _____ the bus every evening at 6:00. Then she (*walk*)

   _____ from the bus stop to her house.

6. The children (*paint*) _____ pictures right now. They are using blue,

   yellow, and red paint.

7. A: Why (*be*) _____ the window open?

   B: I (*know, not*) _____. It (*be*) _____ too cold!

CHAPTER 1 - TEST 1

Part A *Directions:* Circle the correct verbs.

1. Hurry! The bus (*comes, is coming*).

2. I (*don't understand, am not understanding*) Mrs. Brown. She never (*lets, is letting*) her children play outside.

3. A: Where are the children?

   B: Upstairs. They (*watch, are watching*) a video.

4. A: Excuse me. Is this purse yours?

   B: No, it (*doesn't belong, isn't belonging*) to me.

5. A: Let's stop at a cash machine. I (*need, am needing*) some money.

   B: OK. There (*is, are*) a cash machine on the corner.

Part B *Directions:* Complete the sentences with the simple present or the present progressive form of the verbs in parentheses. Add the frequency adverb where needed.

1. Look outside. The sky (*get*) _____ dark. A storm (*come*)

   _____ .

2. Every afternoon after school, Yasuko (*practice*) _____ the violin

   for several hours.

3. John (*go*) _____ to the park every day. He (*play, always*)

   _____ soccer with his friends. Right now, two soccer players

   (*kick*) _____ the ball on the field.

4. Beth (*work*) _____ at a golf course two days a week. She

   (*teach, often*) _____ golf classes to young children. The children

   (*like*) _____ her because she (*be*) _____

   very patient.

5. Abdul (*have*) _____ two summer jobs. He (*pick*)

   _____ apples in the morning. It (*be, not*) _____

   _____ easy work. In the afternoons, he and his friends (*repair*)

   _____ cars. Today, they (*work*) _____

   on a 1940 classic car.

Part C *Directions:* Make the second sentence in each pair a negative.

1. Mr. and Mrs. Billings like to dance the salsa.

   Mr. and Mrs. Billings _____ to dance the waltz.

2. Jeremiah wants a chocolate milkshake.

   Jeremiah _____ a strawberry milkshake.

3. My sister is a college basketball coach.

   She _____ a soccer coach.

4. The doctor sees forty patients a day.

   The doctor _____ 150 patients a day.

5. I am a taxi driver.

   I _____ a bus driver.

Part D *Directions:* Correct the errors.

1. The teacher is yelling never at her students. She is very patient.

2. What time are you leave school every day?

3. The Smiths no have a car. They take the bus everywhere.

4. Is Jonathan own an apartment or a house?

5. Wait. The sandwiches is ready, but not the pizza.

CHAPTER 1 – TEST 2

Part A *Directions:* Circle the correct verbs.

1. Ruth (*cuts, is cutting*) her children's hair once a month. She (*does, is doing*) a good job.

2. Slow down! I (*hear, am hearing*) a siren. An ambulance (*comes, is coming*).

3. Martha (*reads, is reading*) the newspaper on the Internet every morning. She (*doesn't want, isn't wanting*) a lot of newspapers in her house.

4. My sister usually (*goes, is going*) to the supermarket on Fridays.

Part B *Directions:* Complete the sentences with the simple present or the present progressive form of the verb in parentheses.

1. My plants look dry. They (*need*) _____ water.

2. Julie is very talented. She (*play*) _____ several musical instruments well.

3. The classroom (*be*) _____ very quiet right now. Some students (*work*) _____ at their desks. Others (*write*) _____ on the blackboard. Their teacher (*correct*) _____ some papers.

4. My aunt and uncle (*own*) _____ a small farm. Every morning they (*wake*) _____ up before sunrise. My aunt (*feed*) _____ the animals. My uncle (*take*) _____ care of the vegetable garden. They also (*have*) _____ jobs in town. My uncle (*leave*) _____ for work at 8:00. My aunt (*catch*) _____ the bus at 9:00. Today is a holiday, so they (*stay*) _____ home and (*enjoy*) _____ a quiet day off.

Part C *Directions:* Make the second sentence in each pair a negative.

1. I have two cats, a hamster, and a goldfish.
   I _____ a dog.

2. The story is about three little pigs and a big bad wolf.
   The story _____ about three bears and a little girl.

3. Henry and Marie enjoy eating at French restaurants.
   Henry and Marie _____ eating hamburgers.

4. The coffee tastes fresh.
   The coffee _____ stale.

5. We are going to Yellowstone Park.
   We _____ going to the Grand Canyon.

Part D *Directions:* Correct the errors.

1. Are you go to school always by bus?

2. I no like movies with sad endings.

3. Oh no, look! A rat plays in the garbage can.

4. Is Maria go to work on Saturdays?

5. The books is on sale, but not the magazines.

6. Michelle have a beautiful engagement ring from her boyfriend.

7. Mr. Green is elderly, but he isn't want to live with his children.

CHAPTER 2   **Past Time**

Directions: Change the sentences to past time. Use the simple past and *yesterday* or *last*.

Examples: Jan exercises every day before work.

Jan _____ *exercised yesterday before work* _____.

I see my cousins every Sunday.

I _____ *saw my cousins last Sunday* _____.

1. Andrew studies for two hours every day.

   Andrew _____.

2. Mark and Jan go to bed at 10:00 every night.

   Mark and Jan _____.

3. The alarm clock rings at 6:00 every morning.

   The alarm clock _____.

4. My grandparents visit us every month.

   My grandparents _____.

5. I take a nap every afternoon.

   I _____.

6. Dr. Hughes teaches medical students every Tuesday evening.

   Dr. Hughes _____.

7. Victoria buys coffee on her way to work every day.

   Victoria _____.

8. Mr. Wilson shops at the Farmer's Market every Saturday.

   Mr. Wilson _____.

9. Anne calls her best friend every week.

   Anne _____.

10. It rains in Seattle every winter.

    It _____.

Directions: The statements are not correct. Make true statements by using the negative.

Example: Dinosaurs lived in the ocean.

Dinosaurs _____*didn't live*_____ in the ocean. They lived on land.

1. It was 100 degrees Celsius yesterday. It snowed.

   It was 100 degrees yesterday. It _____. It was sunny.

2. Marco Polo was one of the first Europeans to travel in South America.

   Marco Polo _____ in South America. He traveled in Asia.

3. Louis Pasteur developed the chicken pox vaccine.

   Louis Pasteur _____ the chicken pox vaccine. He developed the rabies vaccine.

4. The Beatles' first USA tour was in 1963.

   The Beatles' first USA tour _____ in 1963. It was in 1965.

5. George Lucas made eight *Star Wars* movies.

   George Lucas _____ eight *Star Wars* movies. He made six.

6. Mozart wrote famous literature.

   Mozart _____ famous literature. He composed music.

7. People drove cars in the fifteenth century.

   People _____ cars in the fifteenth century. They rode horses.

8. The 2010 Winter Olympic Games were in Grenoble, France.

   The 2010 Winter Olympic Games _____ in Grenoble. They were in Vancouver, Canada.

9. A tornado damaged San Francisco in 1906.

   A tornado _____ San Francisco in 1906. An earthquake did.

10. In *Alice in Wonderland,* Alice met three bears.

    Alice _____ three bears. She met a white rabbit.

Directions: Complete the sentences with **Did**, **Was**, or **Were**.

Examples: ___Did___ you ride the bus to work today?

___Was___ the bus on time?

SITUATION: At the Grocery Store

1. _____ you go to the grocery store yesterday?

2. _____ the vegetables fresh?

3. _____ the meat expensive?

4. _____ the clerk helpful?

5. _____ the clerk put your groceries in a bag?

SITUATION: At Home

6. _____ you happy to stay home last weekend?

7. _____ you invite your friends over for dinner?

8. _____ you and your friends enjoy it?

9. _____ your family enjoy having company?

10. _____ everyone tired after dinner?

Directions: Write the question and negative forms for each sentence.

Example: The plane arrived on time.

      QUESTION: *Did the plane arrive*   on time?

      NEGATIVE: *The plane didn't arrive*   on time.

1. Ben worked late last night.

      QUESTION: _____ late last night?

      NEGATIVE: _____ late last night.

2. The restaurant was expensive.

      QUESTION: _____ expensive?

      NEGATIVE: _____ expensive.

3. Julie got a promotion at work.

      QUESTION: _____ a promotion at work?

      NEGATIVE: _____ a promotion at work.

4. The nurse took the patient's temperature.

      QUESTION: _____ the patient's temperature?

      NEGATIVE: _____ the patient's temperature.

5. Nina bought a new laptop computer.

      QUESTION: _____ a new laptop computer?

      NEGATIVE: _____ a new laptop computer.

Directions: Complete the conversations with the correct form of the words in parentheses. Add short answers to questions as necessary.

Example: A: (*Beethoven, write*) ___Did Beethoven write___ symphonies?

B: Yes, ___he did___. He (*write*) ___wrote___ nine symphonies.

1. A: (*Julia, eat*) _____ her vegetables last night?

   B: Yes, _____. She (*eat*) _____ peas and carrots.

2. A: (*you, go*) _____ to work on Saturday?

   B: No, _____. I (*be*) _____ on vacation.

3. A: (*a fish, jump*) _____ out of the water a few moments ago?

   B: Yes, _____. It (*jump*) _____ very high.

4. A: (*the Warrens, build*) _____ a new home last summer?

   B: Yes, _____. They (*build*) _____ a vacation home.

5. A: (*you, sleep*) _____ well last night?

   B: No, _____. I (*hear*) _____ noises outside and (*stay*) _____ awake for a long time.

6. A: (*the monster movie, scare*) _____ the children?

   B: No, _____. It (*scare, not*) _____ them. It (*make*) _____ them laugh.

Directions: Write the simple past form of the verbs in **bold**. The first one is done for you.

1. I **want** soup for lunch. ___wanted___
2. I **run** at night. _____
3. Jay **is** a chef. _____
4. It **works** well. _____
5. They **aren't** ready. _____
6. You **understand**. _____
7. Antonio **ties** his shoes. _____
8. Julia **has** many friends. _____
9. The baby **cries**. _____
10. Sue **doesn't yell** at us. _____
11. Your book **isn't** here. _____
12. It **hurts**. _____
13. You **know** them. _____
14. My dad **snores** loudly. _____
15. Ruth **cleans** her room. _____
16. They **don't have** time. _____

Directions: Complete the sentences with the simple past form of the verbs in parentheses.

Example: Mari (*work*) _____worked_____ six days in a row last week.

1. Abdou (*send*) _____ his parents three emails yesterday.

2. Our taxi driver (*take*) _____ a wrong turn on the way to the airport this morning.

3. You (*bring*) _____ home lots of bags and packages. What (*you, buy*) _____ at the store?

4. The ground (*shake*) _____ several times more during the night after the big earthquake.

5. I (*pick*) _____ up lots of books at the sale last week.

6. Jeff (*ask*) _____ his question several times, but the teacher (*hear, not*) _____ him.

7. I (*order*) _____ wild salmon at the restaurant. It (*be*) _____ delicious.

Directions: Complete the paragraph with the simple past form of the verbs in parentheses. The first one is done for you.

SITUATION: Happy birthday to me!

I (*have*) _____had_____ a wonderful birthday last Friday. It (*be*)
                        1

_____ my thirtieth birthday. I (*want, not*) _____
           2   3

a party, so I (*tell, not*) _____ my friends about it. I (*take*)
                               4

_____ the day off from work. I (*wake*) _____ up
           5   6

early and (*decide*) _____ to go shopping. I (*ride*)
                            7

_____ the bus downtown and (*get*) _____ off at
           8   9

Woodland Mall. It (*be, not*) _____ crowded because it (*be*)
                                        10

_____ the middle of a work day. I (*shop*) _____
           11   12

for clothes and (*buy*) _____ a leather jacket and some boots. I (*find*)
                              13

_____ a restaurant with a view of the city and
           14

(order) _____ a delicious lunch. Finally, I (walk)
              15

_____ to a nearby pastry shop and (buy) _____
         16   17

dessert and coffee. I (sit) _____ outside in a small park and (enjoy)
                                    18

_____ my dessert and the beautiful weather. At the end of the day, I
         19

(feel) _____ relaxed and happy. It (be) _____
             20   21

one of my best birthdays ever.

QUIZ 9 **Regular Verbs: Pronunciation of -ed Endings** (Chart 2-5)

Directions: Choose the correct pronunciation. The first one is done for you.

1. ordered	/t/	(/d/)	/əd/		7. buzzed	/t/	/d/	/əd/
2. clapped	/t/	/d/	/əd/		8. washed	/t/	/d/	/əd/
3. questioned	/t/	/d/	/əd/		9. waited	/t/	/d/	/əd/
4. wanted	/t/	/d/	/əd/		10. tried	/t/	/d/	/əd/
5. helped	/t/	/d/	/əd/		11. looked	/t/	/d/	/əd/
6. needed	/t/	/d/	/əd/					

QUIZ 10 **Understanding Past Time** (Charts 2-1 → 2-6)

A. Directions: Match the sentences in Column A with the correct order in Column B.
Write the number on the line. The first one is done for you.

Column A

1. I ended the call. My doorbell was ringing.

2. I ended the call. My doorbell rang.

3. I woke up. My mother smiled at me.

4. I woke up. My mother was smiling at me.

5. I looked out the window. A bird flew by.

6. I looked out the window. A bird was flying by.

Column B

_____ First the bird began flying.
      Then I looked out the window.

_____ First I ended the call.
      Then my doorbell began ringing.

_____ First I woke up.
      Then my mother smiled.

__1__ First my doorbell started to ring.
      Then I ended the call.

_____ First I looked out the window.
      Then the bird started to fly.

_____ First my mother began smiling.
      Then I woke up.

B. Directions: Read each sentence and answer the question.

Example: Jordan was reading the newspaper. He found out about the accident.
Jerry found out about the accident. He read the newspaper.
QUESTION: *Who began to read after he heard about the accident?*   Jordan   (Jerry)

1. Juliette was driving to the bank. Her mother called.
Abby's mother called. She drove to the bank.
QUESTION: *Who got a call when she was in the car?*   Juliette   Abby

2. Peter was doing his homework. He fell asleep.
Max did his homework. He fell asleep.
QUESTION: *Who finished his homework before he fell asleep?*   Peter   Max

3. The boys were jogging. The rain stopped.
The rain stopped. The girls went for a walk.
QUESTION: *Who didn't mind going out in the rain?*   the boys   the girls

4. Jan drank her coffee. She was listening to the news.
Marek drank his coffee. He listened to the news.
QUESTION: *Who began to drink coffee after the news started?*   Jan   Marek

5. Faisal was watching a movie. He ate dinner.
Atsushi watched a movie. He ate dinner.
QUESTION: *Who ate dinner after the movie ended?*   Faisal   Atsushi

---

QUIZ 11   **Simple Past vs. Past Progressive**   (Charts 2-1 → 2-6)

Directions: Complete each sentence using the information in the chart. Use the simple past for one clause and the past progressive for the other. The first one is done for you. More than one answer is possible.

SITUATION: Simone, Linda, and Janet are busy teachers.

Activity in Progress	Simone	Linda	Janet
work in her office	answer the phone	meet with students	check her email
wait for the bus	send a text message	call her son	read a novel
sit at the snack bar	drink a cola	meet an old friend	eat some peanuts

1. While Simone ___*was working in her office, she answered the phone*___.

2. Linda _____ while _____.

3. While Janet _____.

4. Simone _____ while _____.

5. While Linda _____.

6. Janet _____ while _____.

Directions: Complete the sentences with the simple past or the past progressive form of the verbs in parentheses.

Examples: I'm sorry I'm late. I (*hear, not*) _____*didn't hear*_____ the alarm clock. It
(*buzz*) _____*was buzzing*_____ for thirty minutes!

1. Last week my sister and her husband (*decide*) _____ to sell their
   home and move into an apartment.

2. The Norlings (*spend*) _____ last winter in Mexico. While they
   (*live*) _____ there, they (*study*) _____
   Spanish.

3. Our soccer team (*make*) _____ a goal in the last few seconds of
   the game, and we (*win*) _____ the championship.

4. George (*plan*) _____ a retirement party for his office manager,
   and more than 100 people showed up.

5. Melissa's dog (*run*) _____ away from home while she (*travel*)
   _____ in South America last month. She (*try*)
   _____ to find him when she (*return*) _____,
   but she (*have, not*) _____ any luck.

6. Last Tuesday we (*have*) _____ a terrible windstorm. The wind
   (*blow*) _____ and (*howl*) _____ all
   night long. While I (*try*) _____ to sleep, my cats (*become*)
   _____ frightened and (*hide*) _____
   under the bed.

7. Geoff (*live*) _____ in Paris for three months last year. He
   (*speak*) _____ French every day.

Directions: Complete the paragraph with the simple past or the past progressive form of the verbs in parentheses. The first one is done for you.

SITUATION: Dinner in a Foreign Language

Yesterday, while Sara (*walk*) _____*was walking*_____ home from work, she (*see*)
₁

_____*saw*_____ an old friend. While they (*talk*) _____, another friend of
₂   ₃

Sara's (*join*) _____ them. They all (*chat*) _____
        ₄   ₅

for a while and then (*decide*) _____ to have dinner at a new restaurant
                  ₆

nearby. At the restaurant, they (*know, not*) _____ what to order
                          ₇

because the menu (*be*) _____ in another language. They (*ask*)
               ₈

_____ the waiter for suggestions, but he (*be, not*)
        ₉

_____ very helpful. They finally (*point*) _____ to
        ₁₀   ₁₁

some food on the menu and (*hope*) _____ for a tasty meal.
                  ₁₂

Directions: Decide what happens first and what happens second. Write the first and second actions on the lines. The first one is done for you.

SITUATION: Joann decided to bake a cake. . . .

1. Before Joann baked the cake, she found a recipe in her cookbook.

    First action: ___*found a recipe*___ *Second action:* ___*baked the cake*___

2. After she found a recipe she liked, Joann made a shopping list.

    First action: _____ *Second action:* _____

3. Joann shopped until she had everything on her list.

    First action: _____ *Second action:* _____

4. When Joann finished shopping, she went home to bake the cake.

    First action: _____ *Second action:* _____

5. Joann turned on the oven as soon as she got home.

    First action: _____ *Second action:* _____

6. She measured flour, sugar, and salt before she stirred the eggs and milk.

    First action: _____ *Second action:* _____

7. She poured the batter into the pan as soon as she mixed everything together.

    First action: _____ *Second action:* _____

8. Joann took the cake out of the oven when it finished baking.

 First action: _____ *Second action:* _____

9. Joann's family waited patiently until she cut the cake.

 First action: _____ *Second action:* _____

10. As soon as Joann served the cake, her family began to eat.

 First action: _____ *Second action:* _____

11. After they enjoyed the cake, they thanked Joann for the delicious dessert.

 First action: _____ *Second action:* _____

QUIZ 15 Expressing Past Time: Using Time Clauses (Chart 2-7)

Directions: Combine the two sentences into one sentence by using time clauses. Add punctuation where needed.

Example: *First:* Patrick lost a library book. *Then:* He paid for it.
 After _____*Patrick lost a library book, he paid for it*_____.

1. *First:* Donna got a ticket for speeding. *Then:* She drove home very slowly.

 After _____.

2. *First:* Eric got home. *Then:* He took a shower.

 _____ as soon as _____.

3. *First:* Maria and Lucio were exercising. *Then:* Their children played a board game.

 While _____.

4. *First:* Joy's parents drove her to school. *Then:* She got her driver's license.

 _____ before _____.

5. *First:* Rachel was cooking dinner. *Then:* Rick gave the children a bath.

 _____ while _____.

6. *First:* I put on my pajamas. *Then:* I went to bed.

 As soon as _____.

7. *First:* My family lived in Germany. *Then:* My dad got a job in Italy.

 Until _____.

8. *First:* Kevin did his homework. *Then:* He watched a movie.

 Before _____.

9. *First:* The students were nervous. *Then:* The exam began.

 _____ until _____.

10. *First:* The band started to play. *Then:* Everyone started dancing.

 _____ after _____.

Directions: Complete each sentence with *used to* and a verb from the list. The first one is done for you.

be	drink	have	ski	swim	work
chase	✓eat	live	speak	wake up	

1. I ____used to eat____ peanuts for a snack, but now I'm allergic to peanuts.

2. I _____ in the ocean when I was a child, but now the water is too cold for me.

3. My hair _____ long, but now I cut it short every month.

4. I _____ carrot juice, but then my skin began to turn orange.

5. My father _____ six cups of coffee everyday until he had a heart attack.

6. You _____ a lot of homework when you were in high school.

7. The baby _____ several times during the night, but now she sleeps through the night.

8. Mark and Marissa _____ in Chicago, but now they live in Omaha.

9. When I lived in Montana, I _____ every winter. There was a lot of snow.

10. Susan _____ Spanish, but now she doesn't remember much.

11. Our dog _____ cars, but now she just watches them.

Directions: Correct the errors.

1. Joe no walk to work yesterday. He take the bus.

2. Mary was go to the emergency room at midnight last night.

3. While Dr. Hughes listen to his patient, his cell phone rang. He wasn't answer it.

4. Marco no use to swim, but now he does because he was taking swimming lessons.

5. Tua got a new job after he celebrated his success with his friends.

6. When the phone was ringing at 11:00 last night, I was in a deep sleep. I almost not hear it.

Directions: Complete the sentences using the words in parentheses. Use the simple present, present progressive, simple past, or past progressive form of the verbs.

Examples: Jack usually (*pay*) _____pays_____ his telephone bill with a credit card, but last month he (*pay*) _____paid_____ by check.

1. A: What time (*you, get up*) _____ every day?

    B: I usually (*wake up*) _____ before the sun (*rise*)

    _____, but yesterday I (*sleep*) _____ until

    9:00 A.M. It (*feel*) _____ wonderful!

2. At least once a week, the cat (*catch*) _____ a mouse, but last week she

    (*catch*) _____ three mice. While she (*chase*) _____

    one of them, she (*knock*) _____ over the dog's water bowl.

3. Last Saturday, before I (*leave*) _____ for the beach, I (*buy*)

    _____ gas for my motorbike.

4. A: Arnie, why are you on the floor? What (*you, do*) _____?

    B: I (*clean*) _____ the kitchen floor. Your dog (*get*)

    _____ into the garbage last night while we (*sleep*)

    _____. He (*make*) _____ a mess!

5. Every year, the Smiths travel to Africa, but last year they (*travel*) _____

    to Southeast Asia. While they (*travel*) _____, they (*visit*)

    _____ several small villages. They (*stay, not*) _____

    in any big cities. They (*enjoy*) _____ visiting a new continent.

6. The Bentons usually (*watch*) _____ movies on Saturday night, but

    yesterday they (*watch*) _____ their neighbor's children instead.

7. When Jack (*step*) _____ off the train, his wife (*wait*)

    _____ for him on the station platform.

8. We used to (*live*) _____ in Mumbai, but now we (*live*)

    _____ in Delhi. After we (*move*) _____ here, I (*miss*)

    _____ my friends and school in Mumbai very much. Now I (*be*)

    _____ used to Delhi, and I (*like*) _____ it very much.

9. A: (*you, see*) _____ the newspaper this morning?

    B: No, I _____. Why?

    A: There was an article about your former boss. He (*go*) _____ to

    jail for theft.

CHAPTER 2 – TEST 1

Part A *Directions:* Complete the paragraph with the simple past or the past progressive form of the verbs in parentheses.

Last weekend, we (*take*) _____ a day trip in our sailboat. We

(*see*) _____ a small island in the middle of a lake. We (*want*)

_____ to explore it, so we (*leave*) _____ our boat

on the beach on the island. We (*find*) _____ a trail and (*hike*)

_____ around the island. While we (*hike*) _____,

we (*hear*) _____ some strange noises in the bushes. We (*stand*)

_____ on the trail and (*wait*) _____. While we

(*wait*) _____, a small bear (*come*) _____ out of

the woods. He (*eat*) _____ blackberries. After we (*see*)

_____ the bear, we slowly (*walk*) _____

backwards. Fortunately, the bear (*follow, not*) _____ us, and we (*get*)

_____ back to our boat safely.

Part B *Directions:* Complete the conversation with the correct present or past form of the verbs in parentheses.

A: How old were you when you (*learn*) _____ to swim?

B: I (*be, not*) _____ very old, probably three or four. My father first

    (*teach*) _____ me to blow bubbles under water. Then he

    (*show*) _____ me how to kick properly.

A: (*you, like*) _____ to swim now?

B: I (*love*) _____ it!

Part C *Directions:* Circle the correct answers.

1. A: (*Do, Did, Were*) you remember to call the dentist?

    B: Yes. I (*make, made, was making*) an appointment for Tuesday.

2. A: What time (*does, was, did*) Jason leave last night?

    B: I don't know. I (*don't hear, didn't hear, wasn't hearing*) him.

3. A: How are you doing? You (*look, looked, were looking*) tired.

    B: I (*am, was, did*). I (*am not sleeping, wasn't sleeping, didn't sleep*) well last week, and I'm

    still tired.

Past Time **25**

1. Bees use to making honey in a tree next to our house until lightning split the tree in half.

2. Carol no was go to work yesterday because her son sick.

3. Doug and Peter were having a party last weekend. Everyone from our class come.

4. Did you upset with your test results yesterday?

5. After Bill got up, he woke up.

CHAPTER 2 – TEST 2

Part A *Directions:* Complete the paragraph with the simple past or the past progressive form of the verbs in parentheses.

Traffic was very slow yesterday. There (*be*) _____ an accident on
the freeway. I (*sit*) _____ in my car for fifteen minutes and (*go, not*)
_____ anywhere. While I (*sit*) _____ in the car,
I (*watch*) _____ the other drivers. One woman (*talk*)
_____ on her cell phone the entire time. Another driver (*try*)
_____ to entertain her baby. He (*cry*) _____ .
An elderly man (*eat*) _____ an ice-cream cone. He (*look*)
_____ like the only happy driver. Finally, traffic (*begin*)
_____ to move again. After we (*wait*) _____ so
long, we all (*feel*) _____ relieved.

Part B *Directions:* Complete the conversation with the correct present or past form of the verbs in parentheses.

A: Hi, Bill. What (*you, do*) _____?

B: I (*look*) _____ at pictures of my vacation. I (*spend*)
_____ it at my cousins' house.

A: Where (*they, live*) _____?

B: They live on a lake in the country.

A: What (*you, do*) _____ there?

B: One day we (*rent*) _____ a canoe. We (*spend*)
_____ all afternoon fishing and swimming. We also (*take*)
_____ long walks in the woods. Once, while we (*walk*)
_____, we (*see*) _____ some raccoons and a
family of foxes.

A: How long (*you, stay*) _____ there?

B: For a week. I (*want*) _____ to go back there next summer, too.

Part C *Directions:* Circle the correct answers.

1. Tina (*watching, is watching, watched*) her little girl very carefully right now. A few hours ago, while Tina (*talks, was talking, talked*) on the phone, her daughter quietly (*is opening, was opening, opened*) a sack of flour. First, she (*is pouring, was pouring, poured*) it all over the floor. Then, she (*adds, was adding, added*) water to it. What a mess it made! Tina (*cleans, was, cleaned*) it up, and now the floor (*looks, is looking, looked*) fine.

2. A: Where (*are, were, did*) you have lunch yesterday?

   B: I (*am eating, was eating, ate*) at Ellen's new restaurant. I (*am having, was having, had*) chicken and rice.

   A: (*Is, Was, Did*) your meal good?

   B: Yes, it (*taste, was tasting, tasted*) delicious.

Part D *Directions:* Correct the errors.

1. Dr. Martin used to working in a hospital, but now she has a private practice.

2. I was home alone last night. First, I was cooking dinner. Then, I was washing the dishes.

3. Matt busy yesterday. He wasn't go to the party.

4. The Millers buy a restaurant last month. They open for business last week.

5. The baby tryed to crawl a few times, but her legs aren't strong enough yet.

6. Liz and Ron planed to get married last summer, but just before the wedding, Ron is losing his job. Now they are waiting until next summer.

7. Professor Scott no have time to help us with our lab experiment yesterday. Maybe she can today.

8. Ernesto was building a model train set by himself in his basement. He finished it last month.

CHAPTER 3   Future Time

QUIZ 1   **Understanding Present, Past, and Future**   (Chapters 1, 2, and 3)

Directions: Choose the correct time word.

Example: Zach drove to work in bad traffic.   every day   (yesterday)

1.	Niko is going to clean his apartment.	yesterday	tomorrow
2.	Bill will celebrate his birthday.	yesterday	tomorrow
3.	Do you work in the city?	every day	yesterday
4.	Susan woke up early.	every day	yesterday
5.	Does Ming take the bus to school?	every day	yesterday
6.	Sara broke her leg.	every day	yesterday
7.	Will you be here?	yesterday	tomorrow
8.	The mail comes at 1:00 P.M.	every day	yesterday
9.	Is Alexa going to visit us?	yesterday	tomorrow
10.	Dr. Hayashi saw two patients at the hospital.	every day	yesterday

QUIZ 2   *Will and Be Going To*   (Charts 3-1 → 3-3)

Directions: Complete the sentences with *will* and *be going to* and the verbs in parentheses.

Example: (*depart*) The plane _____*will depart*_____ soon.

            The plane _____*is going to depart*_____ soon.

1. (*have*)   We _____ a party tomorrow.

            We _____ a party tomorrow.

2. (*meet*)   Our book club _____ tomorrow night.

            Our book club _____ tomorrow night.

3. (*return*)   I _____ the library books tomorrow morning.

            I _____ the library books tomorrow morning.

4. (*be*)   Hurry up! You _____ late!

            Hurry up! You _____ late!

5. (*leave*)   The Wilsons _____ for their trip next Saturday.

            The Wilsons _____ for their trip next Saturday.

Directions: Write questions with *will* and *be going to*.

Examples: you/study

      Will you study   tomorrow?

      Are you going to study   tomorrow?

1. the cat/catch

   _____ the mouse?

   _____ the mouse?

2. Dr. Brown/retire

   _____ next month?

   _____ next month?

3. your family/be

   _____ at the wedding?

   _____ at the wedding?

4. our team/win

   _____ the game?

   _____ the game?

5. Mr. and Mrs. Bell/find

   _____ their lost puppy?

   _____ their lost puppy?

QUIZ 4 *Be Going To* (Charts 3-1 and 3-2)

Directions: Complete the conversations with *be going to* and the words in parentheses.

Examples: A: What (*you, do*) _____*are you going to do*_ next Saturday?

           B: I (*shop*) _____*am going to shop*_____ for a wedding gift for my niece.

1. A: When (*we, leave*) _____ for the airport?

   B: We (*leave*) _____ in about fifteen minutes.

2. A: (*you, go*) _____ to the market after work?

   B: Yes, I (*buy*) _____ some fresh vegetables.

3. A: My mother (*visit, not*) _____ us during the holidays

   this year.

   B: I'm sorry to hear that. What (*she, do*) _____?

   A: She (*spend*) _____ the holidays in Florida.

4. A: Josh and Joy (*go*) _____ to a jazz concert next

    weekend.

   B: That sounds great! Who (*perform*) _____?

   A: Jazz Connection.

   B: They are really good. I'm sorry I (*be, not*) _____ able

    to go.

QUIZ 5 *Will* (Charts 3-1 and 3-3)

Directions: Complete the conversation with *will* and the words in parentheses.

SITUATION: Visiting Vancouver, Canada

Example: Kevin and his dad (*travel*) <u>will travel</u> from Seattle to Vancouver tomorrow.

KEVIN: Dad, how long is the trip to Vancouver?

DAD: We (*drive*) _____ for about three hours, but crossing the border
                                        1

        into Canada (*take*) _____ at least thirty minutes.
                                 2

KEVIN: Maybe the traffic (*be, not*) _____ too bad because it's a weekday.
                                      3

     I (*listen*) _____ to music to make the time pass quickly.
                     4

DAD: I think the weather in Vancouver (*be*) _____ terrible this week.
                                               5

     The weather report says it (*rain*) _____.
                                     6

KEVIN: That's OK, Dad. I (*bring*) _____ my raincoat with me.
                                   7

DAD: That's a good idea. We (*take*) _____ an umbrella, too.
                                       8

KEVIN: (*go, we*) _____ to Stanley Park while we are there?
                  9

DAD: Sorry, but we (*have, not*) _____ enough time. Maybe we can go
                                 10

     next time.

Contractions with *Will* and *Be Going To* (Charts 3-2 and 3-3)

Directions: Write the contractions for the <u>underlined</u> words.

SITUATION : Lunch Time!

Example: <u>I will</u> help you make lunch. _____I'll_____

1. <u>We are</u> going to fix cheese sandwiches. _____

2. First <u>we will</u> slice the cheese. _____

3. Then <u>I am</u> going to butter the bread. _____

4. <u>You are</u> going to prepare the lettuce and tomatoes. _____

5. Clara and Kathy <u>are not</u> going to have tomatoes on their sandwiches. _____

6. Richard is very hungry. <u>He is</u> going to eat two sandwiches. _____

7. <u>He will</u> have mayonnaise and mustard on his sandwiches. _____

8. <u>You will</u> slice some fruit and open a bag of chips. _____

9. We <u>will not</u> have any dessert. _____

10. <u>We are</u> going to enjoy a delicious lunch! _____

QUIZ 7 **Certainty About the Future** (Chart 3-4)

Directions: Decide if the speaker is 100% sure, 90% sure, or 50% sure. Put a check (✓) in the box. The first one is done for you.

SITUATION: A New Hotel

	100%	90%	50%
1. The new hotel is not going to open next month.	✓		
2. Maybe it will open the month after that.			
3. Many people will probably be upset about the change.			
4. The hotel may give them discounts for future stays.			
5. The owners will refund travelers their money.			

SITUATION: Amanda's Problem

	100%	90%	50%
6. Amanda isn't going to pass her classes.			
7. She won't be surprised about her poor grades.			
8. She'll probably be a little upset.			
9. Amanda's parents may be very upset.			
10. Maybe they will be strict with her.			
11. Amanda probably won't be able to go out with her friends.			

Directions: Use the given words to make two predictions about each situation. Include the words in parentheses. Use *will* or ***be going to*** where needed. More than one answer is possible.

Example: SITUATION: Kelly drank too much coffee.

she \ not \ be able to sleep (*probably*)

_____*She probably isn't going to be able to sleep.*_____

she \ lie \ awake all night (*maybe*)

_____*Maybe she will lie awake all night.*_____

1. SITUATION: Tom's cat has a bad scratch.

   Tom \ take \ the cat to the vet tomorrow (*probably*)

   _____

   the vet \ give \ the cat some medicine (*may*)

   _____

2. SITUATION: Max doesn't like his boss.

   Max \ quit \ his job (*maybe*)

   _____

   Max's boss \ be \ not \ upset (*probably*)

   _____

3. SITUATION: Yujung speaks Korean, Chinese, and English.

   Yujung \ get \ a job in international business (*may*)

   _____

   she \ earn \ a good salary with her language skills (*maybe*)

   _____

4. SITUATION: The Shepherds are planning their vacation.

   they \ go skiing \ not \ this year (*probably*)

   _____

   they \ spend \ a week on the Mediterranean (*may*)

   _____

5. SITUATION: My children enjoy watching movies.

   they \ go \ not \ to a movie theater this weekend (*probably*)

   _____

   they \ watch \ a movie on DVD at home this weekend (*maybe*)

   _____

Directions: Read the conversations. Think about the meaning of the *italicized* verbs. Decide if the speaker is making a prediction, has a prior plan, or decides or volunteers at the moment of speaking.

Example: A: My mom probably *is going to call* today. (prediction)   prior plan   decide/volunteer

           B: Tell her hello from me.

1. A: Mary has a beautiful singing voice!
   B: I think she *will be* a famous singer someday.   prediction   prior plan   decide/volunteer

2. A: Do you have anything planned for the weekend?
   B: No. We*'re going to stay* home and relax.   prediction   prior plan   decide/volunteer

3. A: The sink is full of dishes.
   B: I *will wash* them for you.   prediction   prior plan   decide/volunteer

4. A: The sky is really dark and cloudy.
   B: I think it*'s going to rain.*   prediction   prior plan   decide/volunteer

5. A: It's almost midnight. I have to hurry!
   B: Your parents *will be* really angry if you are late.   prediction   prior plan   decide/volunteer

6. A: Where is your appointment?
   B: Downtown. I*'m going to take* the bus.   prediction   prior plan   decide/volunteer

7. A: The movie starts at 7:30.
   B: OK. I *will meet* you at the theater.   prediction   prior plan   decide/volunteer

8. A: Do you have any pets?
   B: No, but we *are going to get* a dog next month.   prediction   prior plan   decide/volunteer

9. A: We want to go to Spain in October.
   B: That *will be* a wonderful trip!   prediction   prior plan   decide/volunteer

10. A: What are we having for dinner?
    B: I guess I *will cook* some chicken and vegetables.   prediction   prior plan   decide/volunteer

Directions: Complete the conversations with *be going to* or *will*.

Example: A: What are you doing this afternoon?
B: Maggie and I <u>are going to</u> go to a movie.
A: I <u>'ll</u> go with you if it is OK with you.
B: Sure!

1. A: I just spilled some milk.
   B: Don't worry. I _____ clean it up.

2. A: Why did Greg rent a truck?
   B: He _____ pick up a new refrigerator and stove.

3. A: What are your plans for the weekend?
   B: We _____ to paint our living room.

4. A: How does this dress look?
   B: I think it's a little too short.
   A: OK. I guess I _____ get the other one.

5. A: Does Joan have a new phone number yet?
   B: Yes. It's in my purse. I _____ get it.

6. A: There's a potluck dinner at Scott's this weekend.
   B: I know. Tony and I _____ make a spicy chicken dish.

7. A: This box is too heavy!
   B: Put it down. You _____ hurt your back.
   I _____ carry it for you.

8. A: Pat is at the hardware store. He _____ buy a new drill.
   B: Really? Why?
   A: We _____ fix our fence. It blew down in the storm last weekend.
   B: That's too bad.

Directions: Use the given verbs to complete the sentences. Give a future meaning to the sentences.

Example: buy a new car / earn enough money

As soon as Matt ___*earns enough money*___ , he ___*will buy a new car*___ .

1. pick up their airplane tickets / fly to Thailand

   Before the Smiths _____, they

   _____.

2. get dressed / go to work

   As soon as Sonya _____, she _____.

3. feel better / stay home

   Chris _____ until he _____.

4. wash her hands / make lunch

   Before Ellen _____, she _____.

5. get a driver's license / take the driving test

   After Mr. Hill _____, he _____.

6. get a new phone / call us

   When the Thompsons _____, they _____.

7. win a lot of money / quit her job

   If Janice _____, she _____.

8. go to the staff meeting / go home

   David _____ after _____.

9. mail the letter / buy a stamp at the post office

   Before Antonio _____, he _____.

10. be in bed by midnight / finish his homework

    Josh _____ if he _____.

A. *Directions:* Rewrite the sentences. Use the present progressive to express the future.

Example: The restaurant is going to close for one week.

The restaurant _____*is closing*_____ for one week.

1. I am going to change schools.

   I _____ schools.

2. The Andersons are going to remodel their house.

   The Andersons _____ their house.

3. Liz is going to join a hiking club.

   Liz _____ a hiking club.

4. Dr. Allen is going to take a leave of absence.

   Dr. Allen _____ a leave of absence.

5. Are you going to move to New Jersey?

   _____ you _____ to New Jersey?

B. *Directions:* Choose all the correct time expressions to complete each sentence.

Example: The Moores are going to stay home ⟨tomorrow.⟩ ⟨tonight.⟩ yesterday. ⟨now.⟩

1. Po is cooking dinner   tonight. right now. every day. all next week.
2. Carl is going to graduate   today. tomorrow. tonight. next week. every day.
3. The clinic is opening   today. in one hour. next week. every day. next year.
4. I am going to work   now. in 10 minutes. tomorrow. next week.
5. I am going to go to work   tomorrow. last week. in a few minutes. soon.

Directions: Choose all the possible completions.

Example: We (*watch*, (*are watching*), (*are going to watch*)) a news program after dinner.

A. Carmen (*goes, is going, is going to go*) to Mexico City next week. She

¹

   (*visits, is visiting, is going to visit*) her grandparents. Her plane (*leaves, is leaving, is going to leave*)

² ³

   at 8:00 A.M. Saturday. She (*stays, is staying, is going to stay*) with her grandparents for two

⁴

   weeks.

B. A: What time does Simone's birthday party start tomorrow night?

   B: The party (*starts, is starting, is going to start*) at 7:30.

¹

   A: I (*bring, am bringing, am going to bring*) a chocolate cake.

²

   B: She'll love that!

C. The department store (*has, is having, is going to have*) a big sale tomorrow. In fact, the

¹

   store (*opens, is opening, is going to open*) at 6:00 A.M. Many shoppers

²

   (*go, are going, are going to go*) shopping early tomorrow morning. The store

³

   (*closes, is closing, is going to close*) at 10:00 P.M. tomorrow night.

⁴

Directions: Choose all the correct sentences. The first one is done for you.

1. ⓐ I'm planning to travel this
   summer.
   ⓑ I'm traveling this summer.
   c. I travel this summer.
   ⓓ I will travel this summer.
   ⓔ I'm going to travel this summer.

2. a. Beth is retiring next June.
   b. Beth retired next June.
   c. Beth will retire next June.
   d. Beth is going to retire next June.

3. a. School ends on Friday.
   b. School will end on Friday.
   c. School is ending on Friday.
   d. School is going to end on Friday.

4. a. Dinner will be ready in ten minutes.
   b. Dinner is going to be ready in ten minutes.
   c. Dinner is being ready in ten minutes.
   d. Dinner ready in ten minutes.

5. a. It snows tomorrow.
   b. It is going to snow tomorrow.
   c. It will snow tomorrow.
   d. It snowed tomorrow.
   e. It was snowing snow tomorrow.

6. a. The new manager is arriving in a few
      minutes.
   b. The new manager is going to arrive in a
      few minutes.
   c. The new manager will arrive in a few
      minutes.
   d. The new manager arrives in a few minutes.

Directions: Correct the errors.

am going to paint

Example: Tomorrow I ~~paint~~ the kitchen.

1. After I am going to feed the children, I will start dinner for the rest of us.

2. If I will have time, I will help you.

3. You're getting a ticket if you continue to drive so fast.

4. Tina washes the windows this afternoon.

5. Ms. Reed will intend to help you with your expense report.

6. I plan go to a conference on early childhood learning.

7. Shhh. The baby about to go to sleep.

8. When are we gonna leave?

9. In two years, I will quit my job and sailing around the world.

10. Charlie and Kate will getting married next summer.

Directions: Correct the errors. The first one is done for you.

SITUATION: A Week in the Mountains

to

1. Next week, I plan ∧ take a vacation in the mountains.

2. I am hiking and going to climb for several days.

3. At night, when I will get tired, I will find a place to set up my tent.

4. I will building a campfire and cooking my food.

5. Then I am looking at the stars through my small telescope.

6. I will probably tired, so I go to bed early.

7. I will sleeping very hard because my muscles are going be very tired.

8. When I will wake up in the morning, I will going to feel much better.

9. It will going to be a wonderful vacation.

Directions: Complete the sentences with a form of the words in parentheses. Read carefully for time expressions.

Examples: When the pizza (*come*) ___comes___ , let's eat. I (*get*) ___am getting___ hungry.

1. As soon as the weather (*clear*) _____, the plane (*take off*)

   _____. I hope we (*have*) _____

   a smooth flight.

2. Last week our teacher (*give*) _____ us a surprise quiz. We

   (*be*) _____ very unhappy.

3. I have a busy day tomorrow. First, I (*take*) _____ the children

   shopping for back-to-school clothes. Then we (*meet*) _____

   friends for a quick lunch. As soon as we (*finish*) _____ lunch,

   we (*go*) _____ home to bake cookies.

4. A: Who's at the door?

   B: I (*check*) _____ . . . . It's your newspaper carrier. She

      has a bill.

   A: OK. I (*come*) _____ right now.

5. A: (*you, watch*) _____ the soccer match with us later?

   B: No, thanks. I (*work*) _____ on my essay for history

      class. I have to turn it in tomorrow.

6. A: Ms. Martin, can we go outside?

   B: No, Johnny. You can't leave until the bell (*ring*) _____.

   A: When (*the bell, ring*) _____?

   B: In five minutes.

7. Tomorrow after work, I (*pick up*) _____ the dog at the vet

   and (*take*) _____ her home. Then I (*eat*)

   _____ dinner. After dinner, my friend and I (*watch*)

   _____ a new movie.

CHAPTER 3–TEST 1

Part A *Directions:* Complete the conversations with *will* and the words in parentheses.

1. A: I don't understand these directions.

   B: I (*help*) _____ you.

2. A: I'm depressed. I'm not learning English quickly enough.

   B: Don't worry. You (*see, probably*) _____ a lot of improvement

   soon.

3. A: Don't forget to pick up the clothes at the cleaners.

   B: No problem. I (*forget, not*) _____.

4. A: Does anyone want to go to the store with me?

   B: Rachel (*go*) _____ with you. (*you, get*)

   _____ some milk?

   A: Sure.

B. *Directions:* Complete the conversations with *be going to* and the words in parentheses.

5. A: What (*you, do*) _____ on your summer break?

   B: I (*visit*) _____ some friends in Oregon. They live near

   the ocean.

   A: (*you, stay*) _____ there the entire time?

   B: No, I (*be, probably*) _____ there a few weeks. After

   that, (*look*) _____ for a part-time job. I want to earn

   some money for college.

C. *Directions:* Complete the conversations with *will* or *be going to* and the verbs in
   parentheses. If there is a plan, use *be going to*.

6. A: I can't find my keys, and I'm in a hurry.

   B: I (*help*) _____ you look for them.

7. A: Do you plan to buy your lunch at school?

   B: No, I (*make*) _____ it. It's much less expensive.

8. A: Why are you looking at wedding rings?

   B: I (*ask*) _____ Julie to marry me.

   A: What (*she, say*) _____?

   B: I hope (*she, say*) _____ yes!

Part B *Directions:* Circle all the possible completions.

1. Anne loves soccer! She (*is going to play, plays, is playing*) soccer next summer.

2. I think her team (*is winning, is going to win, will win*) many games. They are good!

3. Bart (*starts, will start, is going to start*) his new job on Monday. He is looking forward to it!

4. In a couple of hours we (*will meet, are meeting, are going to meet*) our friends at the new Italian restaurant on Meridian Street.

5. I think I (*order, will order, am going to order*) seafood.

Part C *Directions:* Complete the conversations with the correct form of the words in parentheses. Use present, past, or future.

1. A: Oh no!

   B: What's the matter?

   A: My computer just (*crash*) _____ .

   B: (*you, lose*) _____ all your work?

   A: I don't know. As soon as I (*make*) _____ some repairs, I

   (*check*) _____ .

2. A: What time (*your flight, arrive*) _____ tomorrow?

   B: I'm not sure.

Part D *Directions:* Check (✓) the correct sentences. Correct the incorrect sentences.

1. _____ After we will get married, we will buy a house.

2. _____ The train leaves at 6:45 tomorrow morning.

3. _____ Julia will sing in the choir and going to play the piano at her school concert next week.

4. _____ I go downtown tomorrow with my friends.

5. _____ My husband and I are will not use our credit card so much next month.

6. _____ If Eric call me, I am going tell him I am not available to work this weekend.

7. _____ School ends next week.

8. _____ Tomorrow when John is going to get home, he will help you plant your vegetable garden.

9. _____ Toshi maybe will quit his job soon.

10. _____ Yoko is crying when she hears my news.

CHAPTER 3 – TEST 2

Part A *Directions:* Complete the conversation with *will* and the words in parentheses.

1. A: What's the weather forecast for the rest of the week?

   B: Tomorrow it (*rain*) _____ all day, but after that it (*be*)
   _____ dry. We (*have, probably*) _____
   _____ sun for several days. I believe it (*rain, not*) _____
   again until next week.

   A: Great! Let's go to the beach later this week. I (*bring*) _____
   a picnic lunch.

   B: That sounds like fun!

B. *Directions:* Complete the conversation with *be going to* and the words in parentheses.

2. A: What (*you, do*) _____ with those beautiful flowers in
   your garden?

   B: I (*take*) _____ some of them to work and (*put*)
   _____ them on my desk. I (*give, probably*)
   _____ the rest to my coworkers and
   neighbors.

   A: I'm sure they (*like*) _____ that.

C. *Directions:* Complete the conversations with *will* or *be going to* and the verbs in parentheses. If there is a plan, use *be going to*.

3. A: Do you want to wash the dishes or dry?

   B: I (*dry*) _____.

4. A: Why are you wearing a bathing suit?

   B: I (*go*) _____ swimming.

   A: No! It's too cold out.

   B: Don't worry. I (*swim*) _____ indoors, not outdoors!

5. A: Mmmm. Those cookies sure smell good.

   B: Don't touch! We (*sell*) _____ them. There's a bake sale
   at school tomorrow.

6. A: That was a delicious dinner.

   B: How about some dessert?

   A: Sure. But sit down. I (*get*) _____ it.

Part B *Directions:* Circle all the possible completions.

SITUATION: Our Vegetable Garden

1. Next weekend my husband and I (*are planting, are going to plant, plant*) our garden.

2. First, we (*are going to pull, are pulling, pull*) out all of the weeds.

3. After that, we (*will dig up, are going to dig up, digs up*) the soil, and then we (*are deciding, are going to decide, will decide*) what to plant.

4. My husband (*will die, is going to die, is dying*) when he sees all the work he has to do!

Part C *Directions:* Complete the conversations with the correct form of the words in parentheses. Use present, past, or future.

1. A: Help! A bee (*buzz*) _____ near me.

   B: Calm down! Sit still!

   A: If I (*sit*) _____ still, it (*sting*) _____

   me.

   B: Look. It just (*fly*) _____ away.

   A: Thank goodness.

2. A: Where (*you, be*) _____ last night?

   B: Sorry. I (*be*) _____ at the office. I (*need*)

   _____ to finish a project.

   A: (*you, work*) _____ late again tonight?

   B: No. I plan to leave by 6:00. If I (*need*) _____ to work late,

   I (*call*) _____ you.

Part D *Directions:* Check (✓) the correct sentences. Correct the incorrect sentences.

1. _____ Michelle starts her vacation tomorrow afternoon.

2. _____ The business office will closing for one week next month.

3. _____ Dinner is almost ready. The oven timer about go off.

4. _____ Fortunately, our teacher not gonna give us a quiz tomorrow.

5. _____ Next Saturday, Boris will stay home and cleaning out his garage.

6. _____ I have to hurry. We leave for our trip in an hour.

7. _____ Masako buy a new truck next week. She plans to drive it to work.

8. _____ Our electric bill is going maybe to increase next month.

9. _____ The plane is going to arrive an hour late. There were delays at the airport.

10. _____ Tomorrow when Pierre will get to work, he interview several candidates for the

   assistant manager position.

Present Perfect and Past Perfect

Present Perfect with *Since* and *For* (Chart 4-2)

Directions: Complete each sentence with the present perfect form of the given verb. The first one is done for you.

SITUATION: Alicia is a travel writer.

For almost seven years, Alicia . . .

1. live   _____has lived_____ in New York City.

2. be   _____ a professional writer.

3. work   _____ at *Travel World* magazine.

4. meet   _____ people from every continent through her work.

5. love   _____ her work.

Since she began her job at Travel World, *Alicia . . .*

6. visit   _____ the Taj Mahal.

7. go   _____ hiking in the Swiss Alps.

8. eat   _____ sushi in Japan.

9. drink   _____ wine in France.

10. see   _____ the Great Wall of China.

11. travel   _____ by boat through the Amazon.

Directions: Complete each sentence with the present perfect form of the verbs in parentheses. The first one is done for you as an example.

SITUATION : Selena's Favorite Books

Selena is fifteen years old, and she likes to read. She (*read*)

_____ *has read* _____ many books since she was a little girl. She (*enjoy*)

1

_____ both novels and true-life books. For the last two years,

2

her favorites (*be*) _____ the books in the *Traveling Pants* series.

3

Since she read the first book, she (*become*) _____ a big fan of the

4

girls in the stories. She (*visit*) _____ the books' Web site many

5

times, and she (*write*) _____ several emails to the books' author.

6

Two years ago she started decorating her own jeans like the girls in the stories did. For

the last two years, she (*add*) _____ a new decoration every time

7

she (*have*) _____ a new and interesting experience. Since she

8

started decorating the jeans, she (*sew*) _____ or (*stick*)

9

_____ on a rainbow, a music note, a soccer ball, a starfish, and a

10

heart. She (*find*) _____ pleasure in this project since she began

11

doing it. She reads other books, too, but she still enjoys these stories about the girls and

their unusual jeans.

Directions: Complete the sentences with **since** or **for**.

Examples: Kathleen has lived in Dublin . . .

    since   2006.

    for   her entire life.

Macey has had a part-time job . . .

1. _____ almost two months.

2. _____ April.

3. _____ a few weeks.

4. _____ last week.

5. _____ several days.

6. _____ the beginning of school.

7. _____ school started.

8. _____ she moved to the city.

9. _____ a long time.

10. _____ about one year.

QUIZ 4 *Since vs. For* (Chart 4-2)

Directions: Complete the sentences with **since** or **for.**

Sɪᴛᴜᴀᴛɪᴏɴ : People in My Neighborhood

Example: Pam has played the violin in the school orchestra ____*for*____ two years.

1. Mr. and Mrs. Nelson have lived in a retirement home _____ June. They have

   been there _____ five months.

2. Carmen has been a nurse _____ fifteen years. She has had a job at

   the local hospital _____ a few weeks.

3. Leo hasn't worked _____ 2009. He has been out of work

   _____ the factory closed.

4. Carl has been in bed _____ three days. He has felt ill

   _____ he ate seafood last weekend.

5. Nathan has been a chef at a hotel _____ he graduated from cooking

   school. He took a summer off and worked on a fishing boat _____ a

   few months. He hasn't worked on a boat _____ then.

QUIZ 5 Time Clauses with *Since* (Chart 4-2)

Directions: Choose the correct completions.

Example: The weather (*is*, (*has been*)) very cold since it snowed last week.

1. I have known how to read since I (*was, have been*) three years old.

2. Toshi has loved baseball since his father (*took, has taken*) him to his first game.

3. Ted and Joanne (*were, have been*) together since they met in high school.

4. Dr. Amadi has wanted to work abroad since she (*received, has received*) her medical degree.

5. The baby (*had, has had*) a fever since she woke up this morning.

6. Our families have been friends since they (*met, have met*) on a vacation in the Bahamas.

7. Luke has wanted to be a writer since he (*took, has taken*) a creative writing class.

8. My car hasn't run well since I (*drove, have driven*) it in the desert.

9. Marty (*rode, has ridden*) his bike to work every day since he started his new job.

10. I haven't seen David since he (*came, has come*) to my office last Tuesday.

QUIZ 6 Present Perfect Negatives (Chart 4-3)

Directions: Complete the sentences with the given verbs. Use the negative form of the present perfect.

Example: Karen (*visit*) _____ *hasn't visited* _____ us yet.

1. The rain (*stop*) _____ yet.

2. Max and Rosa (*met*) _____ yet.

3. Sue (*finish*) _____ her degree yet.

4. You (*pass*) _____ your driving test yet.

5. The game (*start*) _____ yet.

6. The Wilsons (*call*) _____ yet.

7. We (*buy*) _____ our new car yet.

8. Mr. Adams (*go*) _____ to the supermarket yet.

9. They (*come*) _____ yet.

10. I (*get*) _____ the flu yet.

QUIZ 7 Negatives, Questions, and Short Answers in the Present Perfect (Chart 4-3)

Directions: Complete the conversations. Use the present perfect form of the verbs in parentheses.

Example: A: (*you, eat*) _____Have you eaten_____ lunch?

B: Yes, we _____have_____. We (*eat*) _____have eaten_____ lunch.

1. A: (*Cara and Jenn, finish*) _____ their shopping?

   B: No, they _____. They (*finish, not*) _____

   their shopping yet.

2. A: (*you, ever, go*) _____ to Hawaii?

   B: Yes, I _____. I (*be*) _____ to Maui three

   times.

3. A: (*Adam, ever, play*) _____ in an orchestra?

   B: No, he _____. He (*play, never*) _____

   in an orchestra.

4. A: (*the museum, have*) _____ many visitors this month?

   B: Yes, it _____. Over 5,000 people (*visit*) _____

   _____ the special exhibit this month.

5. A: (*Natalia, ever, make*) _____ crêpes flambées?

   B: No, she _____. She (*try, never*) _____

   to cook French food.

Directions: Look at Miriam's day planner. Write present perfect questions using the given words. Then write answers to the questions. Make complete sentences with ***yet*** and ***already***. The first one is done for you.

Tuesday, December 15	
8:30	*drop kids off at school*
9:00	*exercise class*
11:00	*meet electrician*
2:00	*haircut appointment*
3:30	*pick up kids at school*
6:00	*dinner with the Costas*

It is 1:30 P.M. right now.

1. Miriam \ drop \ her kids off at school \ already?

   _____ Has Miriam already dropped her kids off at school? _____

   _____ Yes, she has already dropped her kids off at school. _____

2. Miriam \ pick up \ her kids at school \ yet?

   _____

   _____

3. Miriam \ go \ to her exercise class \ yet?

   _____

   _____

4. Miriam \ have \ dinner with the Costas \ already?

   _____

   _____

5. Miriam \ meet \ with the electrician \ yet?

   _____

   _____

6. Miriam \ get \ a haircut \ yet?

   _____

   _____

Directions: Choose the correct completion for each sentence.

Example: My parents ____ married twenty-three years ago.
    (a.) got   b. have gotten

1. Carol ____ a pet snake when she was a child.
    a. had   b. has had

2. Brian ____ insurance for twenty years. He still enjoys it.
    a. sold   b. has sold

3. I ____ in the rainforest twice and plan to go again next year.
    a. hiked   b. have hiked

4. Khalid ____ the keys to his car yet. He's still looking.
    a. didn't find   b. hasn't found

5. I ____ a toothache since this morning.
    a. has had   b. have had

6. Leo ____ any bananas at the supermarket. They were sold out.
    a. didn't find   b. hasn't found

7. Ellen ____ afraid of spiders since one fell from the ceiling into her hair.
    a. was   b. has been

8. Mr. Perez ____ golf until he had a stroke at the age of eighty-five.
    a. played   b. has played

9. We ____ from Jack since he moved to Toronto.
    a. didn't hear   b. haven't heard

10. I didn't know you lived here! How long ____ here?
    a. did you live   b. have you lived

Directions: Complete the sentences with the simple past or present perfect form of the verbs in parentheses.

Example: I really like the new *Crime Fighters* movie! I (*see*) ____*have seen*____ it three times.

1. Asher (*drink*) _____ three cups of coffee already. He (*sleep, not*) _____ well last night, and he is trying to stay awake.

2. A: (*Oscar, be, ever*) _____ to South America?

   B: Yes, he _____. He (*go*) _____ to Chile on business last February.

3. I (*eat, not*) _____ breakfast yet. I (*be, not*) _____ hungry when I got up this morning.

4. Two months ago we (*go*) _____ to a Chinese restaurant. We (*have, not*) _____ Chinese food since then.

5. Last year Katarina (*win*) _____ a prize for being the top student in her class. In fact, she (*win*) _____ it several times since she started school.

A. Directions: Write the present progressive and present perfect progressive forms of the verbs. The first one is done for you.

	present progressive	**present perfect progressive**
1. He *rides* the bus.	*is riding*	*has been riding*
2. I *read* my email.		
3. You *don't work* hard.		
4. Isabella *teaches* Italian.		
5. They *dance* the samba.		
6. Josh *doesn't study* history.		
7. We *practice* karate.		
8. Students *do* homework.		

B. *Directions:* Complete the conversations. Use the present progressive or present perfect progressive form of the verbs in parentheses.

Examples: A: Do you watch *Starcrosser?* I (*watch*) _____ *have been watching* _____ it every week
since the program first started.
B: I (*see, not*) _____ *haven't seen* _____ it yet. Is it good?

1. A: It's almost time for dinner. Where's Kate?

   B: She (*do*) _____ her homework at the library. She (*study*)

   _____ at the library since noon.

2. A: Hi! What (*do, you*) _____?

   B: I (*watch*) _____ a movie. I (*watch*)

   _____ it for ten minutes. Do you want to join me?

3. A: Where (*go, you*) _____?

   B: I'm on my way to the grocery store. Do you need anything?

QUIZ 12 **Present Perfect Progressive** (Chart 4-6)

A. *Directions:* Complete the conversations with the present perfect progressive form of the verbs in parentheses.

Example: A: Where's Linda?
B: She's in her bedroom. She (*talk*) _____ *has been talking* _____ on the phone since
she woke up.

1. A: What's the matter?

   B: Your dog (*bark*) _____ since you left this morning. You

   need to do something.

2. A: I hear a noise.

   B: It's my cell phone. It (*beep*) _____ all morning because

   the battery is dead.

3. A: I'm so bored.

   B: I know. Professor Adams (*speak*) _____ on the same

   subject for more than an hour. Will he ever stop?

4. A: I think we're lost.

   B: Let's ask for directions. We (*drive*) _____ around for

   almost an hour. That's long enough.

5. A: What's that?

   B: It's my new MP3 player. I (*download*) _____ music

   from the Internet for the past twenty minutes. I'm almost finished.

B. Directions: Make complete sentences. Use the given words and the present perfect progressive.

Example: the baby \ cry \ for an hour _____*The baby has been crying for an hour.*_____

1. how long \ you \ stand \ here?

   _____

2. I \ work \ since 10:00 A.M.

   _____

3. it \ snow \ for two days

   _____

4. how long \ they \ study \ for the test?

   _____

5. the taxi \ wait \ for ten minutes

   _____

QUIZ 13 **Present Perfect Progressive vs. Present Perfect** (Chart 4-7)

Directions: Complete the sentences with the present perfect or present perfect progressive form of the verbs in parentheses.

Example: A: Are you going anywhere during the semester break?
B: Maybe, but I (*decide*) _____*haven't decided*_____ yet.

1. Peter (*go*) _____ to the dentist several times this month. He's having problems with his teeth.

2. I need to use a different shampoo. I (*comb*) _____ my hair for fifteen minutes, and it's still tangled.

3. A: How is your mother? I (*talk, not*) _____ to her since we played bridge last month.
   B: She is fine, thank you.

4. Look at all the food on the table. It looks like you (*cook*) _____ all day.

5. Mark is afraid of flying. He (*fly, never*) _____ on an airplane.

6. A: Did you hear that Alex is quitting management?
   B: Yes. I (*know*) _____ about it for a few weeks.

7. Can't you sit down and rest for a minute? You (*work*) _____ nonstop.

8. A: I'm sorry I'm late for work. I overslept.

   B: I (*hear*) _____ that excuse from you too many times.
   You need to be more responsible.

9. Mr. Hale (*work*) _____ in his garden for hours. It looks
beautiful!

10. A: Our neighbor has to move out. He (*pay, not*) _____
   the rent for six months.

   B: Oh, that's too bad.

QUIZ 14 Past Perfect (Chart 4-8)

Directions: Identify which action in the past took place first (1st) and which action took
place second (2nd).

Example: Josh turned in his research paper when he had finished writing it.
   a. *2nd* Josh turned in his research paper.
   b. *1st* Josh finished writing his research paper.

1. Pat quickly threw his fishing line into the water. A fish had jumped 20 feet from shore.

   a. _____ Pat threw his fishing line into the water.

   b. _____ A fished jumped.

2. After Bill had recovered from his surgery, he felt better than ever.

   a. _____ Bill recovered from his surgery.

   b. _____ He felt better than ever.

3. I offered Cathy a cup of coffee, but she didn't want any. She had already drunk two cups
of coffee.

   a. _____ I offered Cathy a cup of coffee.

   b. _____ Cathy drank two cups of coffee.

4. The soccer players hugged each other and cheered their coach. Their teammate had
scored the winning goal.

   a. _____ The teammate scored the winning goal.

   b. _____ The players hugged each other.

5. I tried to give Mary my address on the phone, but she had already hung up.

   a. _____ I tried to give Mary my address.

   b. _____ Mary hung up.

Directions: Complete the sentences with the words in parentheses. Use the past perfect.

Example: As soon as I got home from France, I gave Julia her gift. I (*promise*)
_____had promised_____ to bring her some perfume from Paris.

1. I got off work late. By the time I got to the bus stop, the bus (*leave, already*) _____
_____.

2. We (*think, not*) _____ of moving until we found out that the
schools in the other district were much better.

3. Chris and Diane asked me to join them for dinner, but I (*eat, already*) _____
_____.

4. We wanted to build a campfire when we got to our campsite, but the camp ranger (*put up,*
already) _____ a sign saying "No Fires."

5. Pedro planned to get an autograph from one of the baseball players, but when he arrived,
the players (*start*) _____ the pre-game practice.

6. My parents were interested in buying the Clarks' house on Fifth Street, but when they
went to look at it, it (*sell, already*) _____.

7. Ken was about to pay his credit card bill when he saw that his wife (*pay, already*)
_____ it.

8. Jan was going to talk to her assistant about the importance of arriving at work on time,
but her manager (*meet, already*) _____ with him.

9. Hannah sat down on the sofa and began to read the mystery novel. After a few pages, she
realized she (*read, already*) _____ it.

10. Our electric bill was very high this month because we (*leave*) _____
_____ some lights on in the house while we were away on vacation.

Directions: Correct the errors.

SITUATION: Rita's Trips to the Philippines

has
Example: Rita lives in Seattle. She ~~had~~ lived in the U.S. for twenty years.

1. Rita has left two weeks ago to visit her family in the Philippines.

2. Rita's parents live in Manila. She hadn't been visiting them for two years.

3. Her sister and brother-in-law have been lived in Manila for many years, too.

4. Rita likes to visit Rizal Park when she is in Manila. She had been there many times already.

5. Rizal Park had some beautiful Japanese and Chinese gardens.

6. Every time she has gone to Manila, she has been taking her niece to the Star City Amusement Park.

7. Last year a new aquarium, Manila Ocean Park, opened. Rita haven't visited it yet.

8. Since the Manila Baywalk was renovated several years ago, it had become Rita's favorite place in Manila.

9. The Baywalk has many outdoor restaurants, cafés and bars. Rita has been gone there many times in the evenings.

10. Rita's parents had come to the U.S. several times, but Rita always enjoys going "home" to the Philippines.

Directions: Choose the correct completions.

Example: I can't come with you. I need to stay here. I _____ for a phone call.
    a. wait   b. will wait   (c.) am waiting   d. have waited

1. I _____ my glasses three times so far this year. One time I dropped them on a cement floor. Another time I sat on them. And this time I stepped on them.
    a. broke   b. was breaking   c. have broken   d. have been breaking

2. Kate reached to the floor and picked up her glasses. They were broken. She _____ on them.
    a. stepped   b. had stepped   c. was stepping   d. has stepped

3. Sarah gets angry easily. She _____ a bad temper ever since she was a child.
    a. has   b. will have   c. had   d. has had

4. Now, whenever Sarah starts to lose her temper, she _____ a deep breath and _____ to ten.
    a. takes . . . counts   c. took . . . counted
    b. has taken . . . counted   d. is taking . . . counting

5. Nicky, please don't interrupt me. I _____ to Grandma on the phone. Go play with your trucks so we can finish our conversation.
    a. talk   b. have talked   c. am talking   d. have been talking

6. We _____ at a hotel in Miami when the hurricane hit southern Florida last month. As soon as the hurricane moved out of the area, we left and went back home.
    a. had stayed   b. stay   c. were staying   d. stayed

7. Now listen carefully. When Aunt Martha _____ tomorrow, give her a big hug.
    a. arrives   b. will arrive   c. arrived   d. is going to arrive

8. My cousin _____ with me in my apartment for the last two weeks. I'm ready for him to leave, but he seems to want to stay forever. Maybe I should ask him to leave.
    a. is staying   b. stayed   c. was staying   d. has been staying

9. Mrs. Larsen discovered a bird in her apartment. It was in her living room. It _____ into her apartment through an open window.
    a. was flying   b. had flown   c. has flown   d. was flown

10. The phone rang, so I _____ it up and _____ hello.
    a. picked . . . had said   c. was picking . . . said
    b. picked . . . said   d. was picking . . . had said

11. My mother began to drive when she was fourteen. Now she is eighty-nine, and she still drives. She _____ for seventy-five years.
    a. was driving   b. drives   c. drove   d. has been driving

12. Since prehistoric times, people in every culture _____ jewelry.
    a. wear   b. wore   c. have worn   d. had worn

13. It _____ when I left the house this morning, so I wore my hat and mittens.
    a. snowed   b. had snowed   c. is snowing   d. was snowing

14. Australian koala bears are interesting animals. They _____ practically their entire lives in trees without ever coming down to the ground.
    a. are spending   b. have been spending   c. have spent   d. spend

15. The teacher is late today, so class hasn't begun yet. After she _____ here, class will begin.
    a. will get   b. is going to get   c. gets   d. is getting

16. It's raining hard. It _____ an hour ago and _____ yet.
    a. had started . . . doesn't stop   c. started . . . hasn't stopped
    b. has started . . . didn't stop   d. was starting . . . isn't stopping

17. Alex's bags are almost ready for his trip. He _____ for Syria later this afternoon. We'll say good-bye to him before he _____
    a. left . . . went   c. is leaving . . . goes
    b. leaves . . . will go   d. has left . . . will go

18. I heard a slight noise, so I walked to the front door to investigate. I looked down at the floor and saw a piece of paper. Someone _____ a note under the door to my apartment.
    a. had pushed   b. is pushing   c. has pushed   d. pushed

19. I walked slowly through the market. People _____ all kinds of fruits and vegetables. I studied the prices carefully before I decided what to buy.
    a. have sold   b. sell   c. had sold   d. were selling

20. I really like my car. I _____ it for six years. It runs beautifully.
    a. have   b. have had   c. had   d. have been having

CHAPTER 4–TEST 1

Part A *Directions:* Write the past participle form of the verbs.

1. pay _____   6. grow _____

2. swim _____   7. leave _____

3. know _____   8. cut _____

4. wait _____   9. begin _____

5. study _____   10. eat _____

Part B *Directions:* Complete the sentences with **since** or **for**.

Rosa has worked as a project manager . . .

1. _____ two years.

2. _____ January.

3. _____ Monday.

4. _____ a few months.

5. _____ last week.

6. _____ such a long time.

Part C *Directions:* Complete the sentences with the words in parentheses. Use the simple past or the present perfect.

Situation: A New Town

1. We (*move*) _____ here three years ago. Since then I (*meet*) _____ many nice people.

2. I go to Franklin High School. Since I started high school, I (*have*) _____ some good teachers and some terrible teachers. Last year my favorite teacher (*be*) _____ Mr. Freeman, my chemistry teacher.

3. I (*play*) _____ the drums in our school marching band since my first year of high school. It's exciting!

Part D *Directions:* Complete the conversations with the words in parentheses. Use the present perfect or the present perfect progressive.

1. A: (*you, try, ever*) _____ to make homemade candy?

   B: No, I _____. But I (*make*)

      _____ chocolate sauce several times. It was delicious.

2. A: (*you, finish*) _____ your homework yet?

   B: Yes, we _____. We just finished.

3. A: The dog (*scratch*) _____ at the door for five minutes.

   B: I think she wants to go outside.

4. A: (*Anna, drive*) _____ the car alone yet?

   B: No, she _____. She's still learning to drive.

5. A: Your eyes are red. (*you, cry*) _____?

   B: No, I have dust allergies.

Part E *Directions:* Choose the correct completions.

1. Look! The storm ____ branches from the trees onto our lawn. It will take a long time to clean up.
   a. has blown   b. had blown

2. Susie was upset. Another child ____ her toy train. She found it on the floor in several pieces.
   a. has broken   b. had broken

3. I ____ really tired all week. I've been getting enough sleep, so maybe I should see a doctor.
   a. have felt   b. had felt

4. Dina didn't need a ride home. She ____ to work.
   a. has driven   b. had driven

5. When Mark arrived at the station, the train wasn't there. It ____ already.
   a. has left   b. had left

Part F *Directions:* Correct the errors.

1. Gary is at work since 5:00 this morning.

2. Steve have enjoyed listening to Mozart since he took a music class in high school.

3. Nadia hadn't finished her dinner yet. She can't have dessert until she does.

4. It has been raining on my birthday every year for the last ten years.

5. Already I have decided to major in marine biology.

Part A *Directions:* Write the past participle form of the verbs.

1. visit _____
2. speak _____
3. think _____
4. write _____
5. stand _____

6. buy _____
7. win _____
8. read _____
9. teach _____
10. sell _____

Part B *Directions:* Complete the sentences with **since** or **for**.

Mariko has been trying to lose weight . . .

1. _____ a year.
2. _____ several months.
3. _____ she had a baby.
4. _____ April.
5. _____ a long time.
6. _____ last summer.

Part C *Directions:* Complete the sentences with the words in parentheses. Use the simple past or the present perfect.

SITUATION: Retirement

1. Greg and Sharon Smith were teachers for many years. Five years ago, they (*quit*)
   _____ their jobs. They (*travel*) _____
   to many countries since they retired.

2. The Smiths (*be*) _____ to Asia several times. Last year, they
   (*visit*) _____ Vietnam and Thailand.

3. During the past five years, they (*enjoy*) _____ seeing so many
   different parts of the world.

Part D *Directions:* Complete the conversations with the words in parentheses. Use the present perfect or the present perfect progressive.

1. A: (*you, wear, ever*) _____ a tuxedo?

   B: No, I _____. They don't look very comfortable.

2. A: Billy, your clothes are all dirty. (*you, jump*) _____ in mud puddles?

   B: Yes, I _____. I'm sorry, Mommy.

3. A: This bee (*fly*) _____ around me for ten minutes.

   B: Why don't we go inside?

4. A: (*you, get, ever*) _____ a speeding ticket?

   B: Yes, I _____. I (*get*) _____ two tickets.

5. A: (*you, do*) _____ the wash yet?

   B: Yes, I _____. I just finished.

Part E *Directions:* Choose the correct completions.

1. I woke up tired, but I didn't take a nap because I _____ for ten hours.
   a. have already slept   b. had already slept

2. Jason _____ without a lifejacket. He's going to try tomorrow.
   a. has never swum   b. had never swum

3. Dennis _____ his ankle again. He needs to be more careful when he plays soccer.
   a. has hurt   b. had hurt

4. I wanted to buy some new dishes, but I decided I _____ too much money on clothes yesterday.
   a. have spent   b. had spent

5. Dr. Brooks treats patients, and she _____ two medical devices that help people with heart disease.
   a. has invented   b. had invented

Part F *Directions:* Correct the errors.

1. Sandy have been trying to call you. Did she reach you yet?

2. Ted hadn't called yet. I wonder if he lost our phone number.

3. Andy is on vacation since Saturday.

4. I have been knowing about those problems for a few weeks.

5. Chris has been starting his Ph.D. thesis several times. He's not sure about his topic.

CHAPTER 5   Asking Questions

Yes/No Questions and Short Answers (Chart 5-1)

Directions: Choose the correct verbs.

Examples: ((Is), *Does*) that your new fishing rod? Yes, it ((is), *does*).

SITUATION: Going Fishing

1. (*Is, Does*) Pat like to catch fish? Yes, he (*is, does*).

2. (*Is, Does*) he going fishing tomorrow? Yes, he (*is, does*).

3. (*Are, Do*) you going to go also? Yes, I (*am, do*).

4. (*Are, Do*) you like to go fishing? Yes, I (*am, do*).

5. (*Are, Do*) you good at catching fish? No, I (*am, do*) not.

6. (*Have, Were*) you ever caught a fish before? No, I (*haven't, wasn't*).

7. (*Are, Do*) there clouds in the sky right now? No, there (*aren't, doesn't*).

8. (*Will, Is*) the weather be nice tomorrow too? Yes, it (*will, is*).

9. (*Is, Are*) there a good place to fish near here? Yes, there (*is, are*).

10. (*Are, Do*) you and Pat plan to catch lots of fish? Yes, we (*are, do*).

QUIZ 2 **Yes/No Questions and Short Answers** (Chart 5-1)

Directions: Use the information in parentheses to make yes/no questions. Complete each conversation with an appropriate short answer. Do not use a negative verb in the question.

Example: A: _____*Do you know my sister?*_____

B: No, ____*I don't.*____ (*I don't know your sister.*)

1. A: _____?

   B: No, _____. (*I'm not hungry.*)

2. A: _____?

   B: Yes, _____. (*Dinner is ready.*)

3. A: _____?

   B: No, _____. (*It didn't rain last night.*)

4. A: _____?

   B: Yes, _____. (*John is sending a text message.*)

5. A: _____?

   B: Yes, _____. (*The mail has already come.*)

6. A: _____?

   B: No, _____. (*Mr. and Mrs. Jennings won't be at the wedding.*)

7. A: _____?

   B: Yes, _____. (*They are going to be here soon.*)

8. A: _____?

   B: Yes, _____. (*I am in a hurry.*)

9. A: _____?

   B: No, _____. (*The movie hasn't started yet.*)

10. A: _____?

    B: Yes, _____. (*You already told me that.*)

QUIZ 3 *Where, Why, When, and What Time* (Charts 5-2 and 5-3)

Directions: Choose the correct question words. The answers to the questions are in parentheses.

Example: _____ do you usually go to bed? (*Around midnight.*)
     a. Where   b. Why   ⓒ What time

1. _____ does the party start? (*At 9:30.*)
   a. What time   b. Where   c. Why

2. _____ will the party be? (*At Sam's.*)
   a. What time   b. Where   c. Why

3. _____ can I find out my test results? (*Tomorrow morning.*)
   a. When   b. Where   c. Why

4. _____ did Jeff quit his job? (*Because he wanted more of a challenge.*)
   a. What time   b. Where   c. Why

5. _____ is a good place for us to meet? (*At the Mountain View Café.*)
   a. When   b. Where   c. Why

6. _____ shall we meet? (*10:00 A.M.*)
   a. What time   b. Where   c. Why

7. _____ are you leaving? (*Because I have a class in ten minutes.*)
   a. When   b. Where   c. Why

8. _____ did Dr. Smith call? (*About an hour ago.*)
   a. When   b. Where   c. Why

9. _____ are you going on vacation? (*On Friday.*)
   a. What time   b. Where   c. When

10. _____ does Yasuko live? (*On Fourteenth Avenue West.*)
    a. Where   b. When   c. Why

Directions: Write two questions using the information from each sentence.

SITUATION: A Trip to Greece

Examples: Sven and Erik are going to the airport at 9:30.
   What time _____*are Sven and Erik going to the airport?*_____
   Where _____*are Sven and Erik going at 9:30?*_____

1. Sven and his brother, Erik, are going to Greece on June twenty-eighth.

   Where _____?

   When _____?

2. Their flight will arrive in Athens on June twenty-ninth at about 1:00 P.M.

   What time _____?

   When _____?

3. Sven wants to go to Athens because he wants to see the Acropolis.

   Where _____?

   Why _____?

4. Erik was in Greece five years ago because he was a student there.

   Why _____?

   When _____?

5. Sven and Erik will return home on July fifteenth because they have to go back to work.

   Where _____?

   Why _____?

Directions: Complete the conversations with **who** or **what**. Some sentences may have more than one correct completion.

Example: A: _____Who_____ is at the door?

B: It's our neighbor.

1. A: _____ did you buy?

   B: We bought a new kitchen table.

2. A: _____ did Neil forward the email to?

   B: He sent it to his boss.

3. A: _____ is that?

   B: It's a honeydew melon.

4. A: _____ did you eat lunch with?

   B: I ate with Alison.

5. A: _____ do the kids wear to school?

   B: They wear blue and white uniforms.

6. A: _____ lives next door to you?

   B: The Johnsons live there.

7. A: _____ was the call from?

   B: It was from my sister.

8. A: _____ does Norita eat for breakfast?

   B: She usually has toast and coffee.

9. A: _____ is your doctor?

   B: His name is Dr. Griggs.

10. A: _____ baked this delicious apple pie?

    B: My husband.

Directions: Make questions with *who* or *what*. Use the same verb tense that is used in the parentheses.

Example: ___Who painted the picture___? Picasso. (*Picasso painted the picture.*)

1. _____?

   Henry. (*Bill saw Henry.*)

2. _____?

   Roberto. (*Roberto saw the fox.*)

3. _____?

   The clerk. (*Marcella paid the clerk.*)

4. _____?

   A hamburger. (*Charles ordered a hamburger.*)

5. _____?

   Kim. (*Kim rides a motorcycle.*)

6. _____?

   Mr. Brown. (*Mr. Brown came late.*)

7. _____?

   A dog. (*Ruth brought home a dog.*)

8. _____?

   Lee's toy train. (*Lee's toy train broke.*)

9. _____?

   Sue. (*Tara called Sue.*)

10. _____?

    Juan's parents. (*Juan's parents won a contest.*)

Directions: Make questions with ***what*** + a form of ***do*** to complete the conversations. Use the same verb tense that is used in the parentheses.

Example: A: _____*What did you do*_____ yesterday afternoon?
B: Went hiking. (*I went hiking yesterday afternoon.*)

1. A: _____?
   B: They study rocks. (*Geologists study rocks.*)

2. A: _____ when you turn sixty-five?
   B: Retire. (*I will retire when I turn sixty-five.*)

3. A: _____ to help you?
   B: Dries the dishes. (*Anne usually dries the dishes to help me.*)

4. A: _____ when his car broke down?
   B: Called a tow truck. (*Carl called a tow truck when his car broke down.*)

5. A: _____ if it snows?
   B: Stay home. (*We will stay home if it snows.*)

6. A: _____?
   B: Trying to catch a butterfly. (*Caroline is trying to catch a butterfly.*)

7. A: _____?
   B: Go to the art museum. (*We are going to go to the art museum tomorrow.*)

8. A: _____?
   B: Study for his final exams. (*David is going to study for his final exams this weekend.*)

9. A: _____ when you heard the siren?
   B: Stopped my car. (*I stopped my car when I heard the siren.*)

10. A: _____ when your baby cries?
    B: Sing to her. (*I sing to my baby when she cries.*)

Directions: Complete the conversations with *which* or *what*.

Example: A: Can I please have a soda?
 B: We have cola and orange. ____*What*____ kind do you want?
 A: A cola, please.

1. A: There are three different kinds of soup on the menu.

 B: _____ one do you want?

 A: I think I'll have vegetable soup, please.

2. A: Dad, at _____ temperature does water boil?

 B: 100° Celsius or 212° Fahrenheit.

3. A: I want to get Ramon a DVD for his birthday. _____ kind of

 movies does he like?

 B: He enjoys comedies.

4. A: I know you can write with both your left and right hands, but

 _____ do you prefer to use?

 B: My left hand.

5. A: Tom has lost a lot of weight!

 B: Yeah, he has. I don't know _____ size he wears now.

6. A: _____ kind of pasta should we have for dinner?

 B: Let's make spaghetti carbonara. It's my favorite.

7. A: I like all of these dresses.

 B: All four dresses look nice on you. I don't know _____ one you

 should buy.

 A: I think I'll get the black one.

8. A: _____ color eyes do you have? They seem to change color with

 the clothes you wear.

 B: They are blue, but sometimes they look green.

9. A: There are several Web sites with local news. _____ one is the

 best?

 B: I often read ShorelineAreaNews.org. It's very up-to-date.

10. A: _____ score did you get on your driving test?

 B: I don't know exactly, but I passed!

Who vs. *Whose* (Chart 5 - 7)

Directions: Choose the correct question words.

Situation: At the Office

Example: ((Who), Whose) works here?

1. (*Who, Whose*) told you about my new job?
2. (*Who, Whose*) answers the phone?
3. (*Who, Whose*) papers are on your desk?
4. (*Who, Whose*) desk is by the window?
5. (*Who, Whose*) manages that project?
6. (*Who, Whose*) boss is the nicest?
7. (*Who, Whose*) took my lunch from the refrigerator?
8. (*Who, Whose*) wrote this email?
9. (*Who, Whose*) is going to help you with the report?
10. (*Who, Whose*) laptop computer is on the table?

QUIZ 10 *Who's* vs. *Whose* (Chart 5-7)

A. *Directions:* Complete the questions with **Who's** or **Whose**.

Situation: Questions About Your Family

Example: ___Who's___ the oldest person in your family?

1. _____ not married yet?
2. _____ still living in your hometown?
3. _____ children are in college?
4. _____ job is the most interesting?
5. _____ your favorite relative?

B. Directions: Write complete questions using **Who's** or **Whose**. Use the same verb tense that is used in the parentheses.

SITUATION: Our Neighbors

Example: A: _____ *Who's the woman next door?* _____
B: Ms. Bell. (*Ms. Bell is the woman next door.*)

1. A: _____?

   B: Beth. (*Beth is the new neighbor.*)

2. A: _____?

   B: Mary's. (*Mary's dog always barks at the mailman.*)

3. A: _____?

   B. The Johnsons'. (*The Johnsons' car is parked across the street.*)

4. A: _____?

   B: Mr. Babcock. (*Mr. Babcock is working in his garden.*)

5. A: _____?

   B: Everyone. (*Everyone is coming to the barbecue.*)

QUIZ 11 **Questions with *How*** (Chart 5-8)

Directions: Match each question with the best response. The first one is done for you.

1. _f_ How tired are you?   **a.** Very interesting.

2. ___ How old is the baby?   **b.** By car.

3. ___ How tall is your father?   **c.** In ten minutes.

4. ___ How big is your apartment?   **d.** Three months.

5. ___ How far away is the airport?   **e.** 75 percent.

6. ___ How good is that book?   **f.** Very sleepy.

7. ___ How did you do on the test?   **g.** Four rooms.

8. ___ How soon will this movie end?   **h.** I'm starving.

9. ___ How hungry are you?   **i.** Six feet.

10. ___ How well do you speak English?   **j.** Twenty miles.

11. ___ How do you get to work?   **k.** Not very well.

Directions: Complete the conversation questions with ***often***, ***far***, or ***long***.

Example: SUZANNE: How ____*long*____ have you lived here?
             LUCIO: About 25 years.

1. ELENA: Sara, how _____ do you see your grandchildren?

   SARA: About once a week.

   ELENA: How _____ away do they live?

   SARA: About thirty-five miles.

   ELENA: How _____ does it take to get to their house?

   SARA: If traffic isn't heavy, it takes about an hour.

2. GIL: Max, how _____ do you exercise?

   MAX: Three to four times a week. I work out at the gym, and I run.

   GIL: How _____ do you spend at the gym?

   MAX: Usually an hour.

   GIL: How _____ do you run?

   MAX: Just a few kilometers.

3. KENTO: Hiro, how _____ is it from your apartment to your office?

   HIRO: About ten miles.

   KENTO: How _____ does it take you to get to work by car?

   HIRO: About forty-five minutes.

   KENTO: How _____ do you take the bus to work?

   HIRO: A few times a week.

   KENTO: How _____ is it from the bus stop to your office?

   HIRO: About three blocks.

Directions: Make complete questions with ***how*** for the given answers. The information in *italics* will help you.

Example: This water is *very cold*. You can't swim in it.
<u>   How cold is this water?   </u>

1. It took me about *thirty minutes* to check my email.

   _____

2. *E - L - E - P - H - A - N - T.*

   _____

3. We go to the movies about *three times a month*.

   _____

4. I came here *by bus*.

   _____

5. Our school is just *two blocks* away.

   _____

6. We need to leave *in ten minutes*.

   _____

7. "Ms." is an easy word *to pronounce*. You say "mizz."

   _____

8. Jon's birthday was yesterday. He's *twenty*.

   _____

9. I'm feeling *great*!

   _____

10. Mr. Wang speaks English *perfectly*. He sounds like a native speaker.

    _____

A. *Directions:* Emily is at a job interview. Write the questions the interviewer asks her. Use *where, what, who, why, how,* or *how long*. The information in *italics* will help you. The first one is done for you.

1. INTERVIEWER: Good morning. ___How are you doing today___ ?

   EMILY: *I'm doing fine,* thank you.

2. INTERVIEWER: _____?

   EMILY: I want to work here *because this is a good company.*

3. INTERVIEWER: _____?

   EMILY: Now I work *at KRW Enterprises* as a computer programmer.

4. INTERVIEWER: _____?

   EMILY: I have worked there *for five years.*

5. INTERVIEWER: _____?

   EMILY: My favorite project was *writing a program to help students learn English.*

6. INTERVIEWER: _____?

   EMILY: My supervisor is *Joshua Smith.*

B. *Directions:* A teacher is asking her students questions about their summer vacation. Write the questions she asks. Use *how, when, whose, how far,* or *how often.* The information in *italics* will help you.

1. TEACHER: _____?

   SUE: *Ian's vacation* was the most exciting. He rode a camel in Morocco!

2. TEACHER: _____?

   IAN: We rode *for about ten kilometers.*

3. TEACHER: _____?

   IAN: *It felt strange* at first, but then it was fun!

4. TEACHER: _____?

   JILL: We go to the beach almost *every summer.*

5. TEACHER: _____?

   JILL: We went to the beach *in July.*

Directions: Complete the tag questions with the correct verbs.

SITUATION: A Rainy Day

Example: The weather is terrible today, __*isn't*__ it?

1. You are going out, _____ you?

2. You're not sick, _____ you?

3. You have a coat on, _____ you?

4. You are dressed warm enough, _____ you?

5. It's not snowing, _____ it?

6. You don't want to walk, _____ you?

7. Pam is going with you, _____ she?

8. Your dog doesn't want to go out, _____ he?

9. The Petersons are out walking in the rain, _____ they?

10. They don't have an umbrella, _____ they?

Directions: Complete the tag questions with the correct verbs.

SITUATION: World Travelers

Example: The Jamison's traveled a lot this year, __*didn't*__ they?

1. They've been around the world twice, _____ they?

2. They haven't been to New Zealand, _____ they?

3. One trip was canceled, _____ it?

4. They had to change their plans, _____ they?

5. They didn't go to Italy, _____ they?

6. They are in China now, _____ they?

7. They sent you a postcard, _____ they?

8. You haven't talked to them recently, _____ you?

9. You are a little jealous of them, _____ you?

10. It's been a good year for them, _____ it?

Directions: Correct the errors.

Example: You don't eat much meat, ~~don't~~ ^{do} you?

1. Who's cell phone is that, mine or yours?

2. I was right about the price of the computer, didn't I?

3. What kind ethnic food you like to cook?

4. When your plane arrives from Paris?

5. Whom helped you prepare the dinner?

6. Why you leave without me?

7. Who you did take to work?

8. How much often do you see your family?

9. His name is Henri, isn't he?

10. How many time a week do you exercise?

Part A   *Directions:*   Complete the questions. Use *what, who, when, whose, why, which, how, how far, how long, how soon,* or *how often*.

1. A: _____ do you like this town?

    B: We love it.

2. A: Traffic was terrible this morning. _____ did it take you to get to

    work?

    B: An hour.

3. A: _____ lunch is this?

    B: It's Pam's. She'll be right back.

4. A: _____ is picking you up from school this afternoon?

    B: My older brother.

5. A: _____ are you going to leave?

    B: In about an hour.

6. A: These are the two bookcases we can afford. _____ one would be

    better?

    B: The shorter one.

7. A: _____ is Billy crying?

    B: He fell down and cut his knee.

8. A: _____ do you go to the post office?

    B: About twice a week.

9. A: _____ are you doing?

    B: I'm trying to fix my glasses.

10. A: _____ is it from here to downtown?

    B: About six kilometers.

Part B *Directions:* Write complete questions. Use the information in *italics* to help you.

SITUATION: Sara Is a Runner

1. Sara trains *one hour a day.*

   _____?

2. She runs *thirty km. a week.*

   _____?

3. She runs *very* fast.

   _____?

4. She is going to run in a marathon *next week.*

   _____?

5. She will run with *several coworkers.*

   _____?

6. She plans *to win.*

   _____?

7. She spells her name *S - A - R - A, not S - A - R - A - H.*

   _____?

Part C *Directions:* Complete the tag questions with the correct verbs.

1. You work outdoors, _____ you?

2. It didn't rain last night, _____ it?

3. Jane's been very busy, _____ she?

4. We aren't going to attend the meeting, _____ we?

5. Sam had to go to the doctor again, _____ he?

6. Your dog is friendly, _____ it?

Part D *Directions:* Correct the errors.

1. What you know about the new department manager?

2. That dog is barking so loudly. Whose it belong to?

3. What means "besides"?

4. Marta changed jobs last month, wasn't she?

5. Which movie you see last night, *Monsters* or *Dragons*?

6. How far does it take from Paris to London?

7. Who did tell you about the party?

CHAPTER 5 – TEST 2

Directions: Complete the questions. Use *what, who, when, whose, why, which, how, how far, how long, how soon,* or *how often.*

SITUATION: Interview with a University Student

1. A: _____ are you living right now?

   B: In an apartment near campus.

2. A: _____ is it from here to your apartment?

   B: About three miles.

3. A: _____ does it take you to get here?

   B: Twenty minutes.

4. A: _____ did you come here?

   B: I wanted to study at a university.

5. A: _____ do you go back home?

   B: About once a month.

6. A: _____ do you like it here?

   B: I love it!

7. A: _____ is helping you pay for school?

   B: My parents.

8. A: _____ do you plan to graduate?

   B: In two years.

9. A: I've forgotten. _____ major did you decide on, math or business?

   B: Business.

10. A: _____ homework is this?

    B: It's mine.

Part B *Directions:* Write complete questions. Use the information in *italics* to help you.

SITUATION: Jill Has a New Job

1. Jill got a new job *last week*.

   _____?

2. She works *at an Internet firm*.

   _____?

3. She is going to *develop marketing plans* for the company.

   _____?

4. She plans to be there for *at least two years*.

   _____?

5. She drives to work *three times a week*.

   _____?

6. She goes to work *by bus* on the other days.

   _____?

7. She works *sixty hours* a week.

   _____?

Part C *Directions:* Complete the tag questions with the correct verbs.

1. You got home late last night, _____ you?

2. It isn't raining right now, _____ it?

3. We don't have to leave yet, _____ we?

4. Dr. Wilson had to leave early, _____ she?

5. Otto is going to pay me back, _____ he?

6. They're not lost, _____ they?

7. You don't like this movie, _____ you?

Part D *Directions:* Correct the errors.

1. What means "anyway"?

2. How you feel about the talk you had with Jeff yesterday?

3. Whose left their dirty dishes on the table?

4. What kind soup you want for lunch?

5. Sonya needs more time, isn't she?

6. How long it takes to get from here to your home?

CHAPTER 6   Nouns and Pronouns

Pronunciation of Final -s/-es (Chart 6-1)

Directions: Circle the correct pronunciation. The first one is done for you.

1. hands   /s/   (/z/)   /əz/
2. bridges   /s/   /z/   /əz/
3. mistakes   /s/   /z/   /əz/
4. emails   /s/   /z/   /əz/
5. boys   /s/   /z/   /əz/
6. cats   /s/   /z/   /əz/
7. boxes   /s/   /z/   /əz/
8. cups   /s/   /z/   /əz/
9. computers /s/   /z/   /əz/
10. desks   /s/   /z/   /əz/
11. dishes   /s/   /z/   /əz/

QUIZ 2 **Plural Forms of Nouns** (Chart 6-2)

Directions: Write the singular or plural form of the given words. The first one is done for you.

1. one table   many ____tables____
2. a mouse   six _____
3. one _____   a lot of leaves
4. a city   two _____
5. one _____   several tomatoes
6. a box   some _____
7. a woman   a lot of _____
8. a _____   two deer
9. one tooth   several _____
10. one child   many _____
11. a business   two _____

Directions: Complete each diagram with the correct subject, verb, and object. Write (*none*) if there is no object.

Examples: The woman found some sunglasses.

The woman	found	some sunglasses
subject	verb	object of verb

My little brother was tired.

My little brother	was	(none)
subject	verb	object of verb

1. Steve asked a question.

subject	verb	object of verb

2. His question wasn't clear.

subject	verb	object of verb

3. The phone rang three times.

subject	verb	object of verb

4. I answered the phone.

subject	verb	object of verb

5. Hanifa loves animals.

subject	verb	object of verb

6. She has had many pets.

subject	verb	object of verb

7. The police stopped several cars.

subject	verb	object of verb

8. The drivers looked surprised.

subject	verb	object of verb

9. My daughter goes to college.

subject	verb	object of verb

10. She is studying anthropology.

subject	verb	object of verb

Directions: If the word in *italics* is used as a noun, circle "N." If the word in *italics* is used as a verb, circle "V."

Examples: I usually *cook* breakfast on Sunday mornings. N Ⓥ
  My sister is a terrible *cook*. Ⓝ V

1. Seattle is famous for *rain*. N V

2. It's going to *rain* all weekend. N V

3. I didn't *reply* to the email. N V

4. I didn't send a *reply* to the email. N V

5. Romance movies often *end* happily. N V

6. The *end* of the story was sad. N V

7. There is a bus *stop* about two blocks away. N V

8. Careful drivers always *stop* at red lights. N V

9. The boys *play* basketball after school every day. N V

10. We saw a very good *play* at the theater. N V

Directions: Read the sentences. Identify any prepositions with *"P"* and objects of prepositions with *"Obj. of P."*

SITUATION: Snowy Winter

  P   Obj. of P
Example: The little boy slid quickly down the snowy hill.

1. Days are short during the winter. The sun rises late and sets early in the winter months.

2. Children love to play outside in the snow. They throw snowballs at each other and make snowmen.

3. Snowboarding is popular with many people. It's challenging and fun to balance on a snowboard.

4. Winter sports can sometimes be dangerous. It's important to be careful on ice and snow.

5. Last winter, two teenagers fell into a frozen pond near their home. Rescuers found them beneath the ice and pulled them to safety.

Directions: Complete the sentences with *in, at,* or *on.* The first one is done for you.

The earthquake occurred . . .

1. _____*at*_____ midnight.

2. _____ 12:00.

3. _____ Saturday.

4. _____ May 24th.

5. _____ May.

6. _____ 2009.

7. _____ the twenty-first century.

8. _____ Saturday night.

9. _____ the spring.

10. _____ the early morning.

11. _____ a weekend.

QUIZ 7 Subject and Verb Agreement (Chart 6-7)

Directions: Choose the correct verbs.

Example: There ((*is*), *are*) only one library in my hometown.

1. Every student at the university (*lives, live*) in the dorm for the first year.

2. The snow on the trees (*is, are*) sparkling in the sunlight.

3. Here (*is, are*) some used computers for sale.

4. Do you think that everyone (*needs, need*) a cell phone?

5. Some spellings in English (*doesn't, don't*) seem to make sense.

6. People everywhere (*uses, use*) the Internet to get information.

7. The mountains in the distance (*is, are*) popular with climbers.

8. Parents of teenagers (*has, have*) many worries and many joys.

9. (*Does, Do*) your brother and sister both have college degrees?

10. There (*is, are*) at least twenty-eight moons around Jupiter.

Directions: Underline the adjectives.

SITUATION: Movie Night at Home

Example: I enjoy watching old movies.

1. The TV and DVD player are new.
2. Let's stay home and watch a funny movie.
3. We can sit on our comfortable sofa.
4. I'll make some hot, buttery popcorn.
5. Some refreshing, cold drinks will taste great with the popcorn.
6. The movie is long. It will be late when it ends.

Directions: Add the given adjectives to each sentence to make a logical sentence. Rewrite the complete sentence.

Example: old, busy   The man crossed the street.
          _____The old man crossed the busy street_____.

1. *tall, dirty*   He used a ladder to wash the windows.

   _____

2. *clean, lower*   Nan put the clothes into the drawer.

   _____

3. *interesting, sad* The book told the story of the Great Chicago Fire of 1871.

   _____

4. *worried, angry*   The manager looked at the workers.

   _____

5. *happy, new*   The child played with her toy.

   _____

Directions: Correct the errors.

vegetable
Example: The vegetables at the ~~vegetables~~ market are always fresh.

1. Your flowers garden has many unusual flowers.

2. The mosquitos were really bad on our camping trip. I got a lot of mosquitos bites.

3. There is customers parking in front of the store. The customers are happy about that.

4. I see three spiders webs in the bathroom. I hate spiders!

5. All the computers printers in the library are new, but the computers are old.

6. Three people in our office are celebrating their birthdays tomorrow. There will be a lot of birthdays cake to eat.

7. Don't throw away the eggs cartons. We will put the hard-boiled eggs in them.

8. I love all the noodles in this soup. It's great noodles soup.

9. My doctor gave me an exercises plan. I have to do my exercises every day.

10. Collin lives in a two-bedrooms apartment. The bedrooms are quite large.

Directions: Complete the sentences with the subject or object pronouns: ***she, her, they, them, we, us,*** or ***it.*** The first one is done for you.

SITUATION 1: Anniversary Party

Mr. and Mrs. Walters celebrated their fiftieth wedding anniversary. Their children had a

party for _____*them*_____. More than 100 people came to celebrate with

                1

_____. _____ enjoyed sharing this special occasion

        2   3

with their friends.

SITUATION 2: Twin Brothers

My twin brother and I are very similar. _____ have the same friends

                                                     4

and enjoy the same activities. _____ wear the same style of clothes.

                                        5

Sometimes our friends and teachers get _____ mixed up.

                                                 6

_____ have a good time fooling _____.

        7   8

SITUATION 3: Sara's Accident

Sara got a new car last week. _____ planned to drive to a friend's

                                        9

house, but on the way a tree branch fell on _____. The roof of the car was

                                            10

damaged. Sara was sad but also very happy that the branch didn't hit _____.

                                                          11

Possessive Nouns (Chart 6-11)

Directions: Use the correct possessive form of the given nouns to complete the sentences.

Example: Earth   The _____Earth's_____ orbit around the sun takes 366 days in a leap
year.

1. teachers   The _____ mailboxes are near their classrooms.

2. Brown   Let's see if we can stay at the _____ summer house during
vacation.

3. wife   My _____ brother is doing research in the Sahara desert.

4. children   The _____ names all start with "A"—Anna, Andy, and Abe.

5. theater   The movie _____ sound system was terrible.

6. woman   It was hard to hear the _____ voice.

7. grandson   We will be attending our _____ graduation next week. We are
so proud!

8. students   The teacher handed back the _____ papers. She was pleased
with their work.

9. hospitals   The _____ nurses have voted against twelve-hour workdays.

10. city   The _____ mayor promised to improve public transportation.

Possessive Pronouns and Adjectives (Chart 6-12)

Directions: Choose the correct words to complete the sentences.

Example: Austen forgot ((*his*), *he's*) cell phone at home.

1. Could I borrow your pen? (*My, Mine*) is out of ink.

2. Ingrid left (*hers, her*) car at school last night, and it was gone this morning.

3. A friend of (*my, mine*) sent flowers to my office today.

4. You have (*your, yours*) opinion, and we have (*our, ours*).

5. The cat carried a mouse in (*its, it's*) mouth.

6. Matt says the smoke is from a forest fire, but I think (*its, it's*) actually from burning trash.

7. Newlyweds Simone and Andre work at the same company in the same department.
(*Their, There, They're*) desks are next to one another. (*Their, There, They're*) happy to be so
close. Friends of (*their, theirs*) wonder about this, but Simone and Andre think (*its, it's*)
good for (*their, there, they're*) relationship.

8. A: Look at this wonderful dessert! Kelly made it for (*our, ours*) party tonight.
   B: I know. (*Its, It's*) very rich. I think it has three kinds of chocolate in (*it, its*).

Directions: Complete the sentences with *myself, yourself, himself, herself, itself, ourselves, yourselves,* or *themselves.*

Example: You got 100 percent on the exam. You should be proud of ___*yourself*___.

1. Luis works sixty-hour weeks. He needs to take care of _____.

2. You two have a good time at the party. Enjoy _____!

3. When Yoko was cutting vegetables, she accidentally cut _____ with the paring knife.

4. My dream is to own my own company and work for _____.

5. When little Ella wakes up from her nap, she likes to play in her room and talk to _____.

6. Before we begin the meeting, let's all introduce _____.

7. Jin looked at _____ in the mirror and saw that he needed to comb his hair.

8. The cat is licking _____ clean.

9. The children played by _____ in the park while their mothers watched.

10. Tasha, you need to have more confidence. You need to believe in _____.

Directions: Choose the correct word(s) to complete the sentences.

Example: I have two brothers. One is named David and (*another,* (*the other*)) is named Michael.

1. I didn't understand that math problem. Could you show us (*another, the other*) one?

2. This is a dangerous intersection. Last night there was (*another, the other*) car accident.

3. We added the charges on the bill twice. The first result seemed incorrect, but (*another, the other*) looked OK.

4. The boots I bought weren't comfortable, so I took them back and got (*another, the other*) pair.

5. We can't decide what to name our baby. We really like two names. One is Hannah, and (*another, the other*) is Rosemary. I like one name, and my husband likes (*another, the other*).

6. Benito has experienced three earthquakes. One was in Turkey, (*another, the other*) was in Italy, and (*another, the other*) was in Japan.

7. We had a bad windstorm yesterday, and the weather forecast says there will be (*another, the other*) one tomorrow.

8. This word has four definitions. I understand the first three, but not (*another, the other*) one.

QUIZ 16 *Other(s) vs. The Other(s)* (Chart 6-15)

Directions: Complete the sentences with **other**(s) or **the other**(s).

Example: Lena, Ann, and May are friends. Lena is in third grade, but _____*the other*_____ girls are fourth graders.

1. I had five homework assignments for the weekend. I've finished two, but now I have to complete _____ before school tomorrow.

2. Juan speaks Portuguese and Spanish. Does he speak any _____ languages?

3. There is only one baked potato left. All of _____ were eaten at lunch.

4. Scientists have discovered a dinosaur fossil in this area. They are looking for _____.

5. The morning flight to London is booked, but two _____ flights are open in the afternoon.

6. Some animals have stripes, but _____ have spots.

7. There are four pears in the dish. Two of them aren't ripe yet, but _____ ones are good.

8. The Italian flag has three colors. One color is red, and _____ are green and white.

9. The teacher caught five students cheating. One student seemed embarrassed, but _____ didn't.

10. Plants need different environments to grow in. For example, some plants prefer shade and lots of water, while _____ grow best in full sun and a dry climate.

Directions: Complete the sentences with the correct form of *other*: **another, other, others, the other,** or **the others**.

Example: My favorite sport is tennis, but ____*another*____ one I enjoy is badminton.

1. Let's order two pizzas. One will be vegetarian. What shall we put on

   _____ one?

2. Oh, no. Look! I found _____ gray hair on my head!

3. Out of all the vegetables I planted this spring, only the peas did well. _____

   died.

4. These jeans have a small hole in them. Do you have any _____ in

   this size?

5. The bus I was waiting for broke down, so I had to catch _____ one.

6. Some people need eight hours of sleep, but _____ need less.

7. I burned your hamburger. I'll make you _____ one.

8. The dog ran away with my only pair of dress shoes. I found one in the garden and

   _____ under the front porch.

9. You have one idea about how to solve the problem, and I have _____ .

   Since we can't agree, let's keep looking for _____ ideas.

Directions: Correct the errors.

teeth

Example: My son lost two ~~tooths~~ last year.

1. There are thirty day in the month of April.

2. Our apartments manager is out of town this week.

3. The bird has brought some worms to feed it's young.

4. She was born in September 8, 1993.

5. I broke my right hand, so I need to write with the another one.

6. The cars in the city produces a lot of pollution.

7. One hundred people are waiting in the rain to buy ticket for the concert. Everyone seem patient, but cold.

8. The childrens swimming pool in the city is open to all children aged three to seven.

9. Mr. Lee company recycles old computers.

10. The dancers practiced all morning in the studio their dance steps.

CHAPTER 6 – TEST 1

Part A   *Directions:*   Make the nouns plural where appropriate. You may need to make some words possessive. Do not change the verbs.

1. I have two children. My children name are Emma and Ellen.

2. People at the lecture thought the speaker idea were fascinating.

3. My new computer aren't working properly. The instruction aren't clear.

4. Beth computer is similar to mine. She's going to let me use hers.

5. There are several article on woman in today newspaper.

Part B   *Directions:*   Circle the correct pronouns.

1. Hamid called the company and asked to speak with (*his, him*) manager.

2. A: Which notebook is (*your, yours*)?
   B: (*My, Mine*) is the one with the star on the cover.

3. Toshi is proud of (*his, him*) daughters. They did well in school, and now each one has (*she, her*) own company and works for (*herself, herselves*).

4. A: Are these sunglasses (*your, yours*)?
   B: No, they're (*hers, she's*).

5. The Bakers invited Graciela and (*I, me*) to a piano concert in the city. (*Their, There, They're*) going to pick us up in (*their, there, they're*) car and drive us (*their, there, they're*). (*It's, Its*) going to be fun.

6. The city bus was so full that it couldn't pick up my brother and (*I, me*). (*We, Us*) had to wait an hour for another one.

Part C   *Directions:*   Complete the sentences with correct forms of *other*: **another, other, others, the other,** or **the others.**

1. Alex found several colorful shells on the beach. He brought one home, but left

   _____ on the sand.

2. After the Blakes got a kitten, they decided they needed _____ one so
   it would have a playmate.

3. We're sorry we can't attend your party. We have _____ plans.

4. Some people prefer traveling by train, but _____ prefer driving.

5. Three of my friends have unusual pets. One has an iguana. _____
   has a python snake. _____ one has a baby alligator.

Directions: Correct the errors.

1. Tony was born in April 2, 1998.

2. The bird's nest have several eggs in it.

3. Several languages schools offer university preparation.

4. In the morning, I like to take in the park long walks.

5. Every students in the class are working hard and making progress.

6. The doctor is busy in the moment. You will have to wait.

7. Nancy's flowers garden has many roses in it.

8. Yesterday morning we saw three deers drinking water from the lake.

9. Many word in French is difficult for me to pronounce.

10. My sister husband is a really funny guy. He always tell jokes.

Part A *Directions:* Make the nouns plural where appropriate. You may need to make some words possessive. Do not change the verbs.

1. Our dog had three puppy last night.

2. My sister has twins. Her baby name are Tyler and Spencer.

3. Professor Browns math class are very difficult.

4. The two other math teacher course are easier.

5. The university main computer is having technical problem, so student cannot register at this time.

Part B *Directions:* Circle the correct pronouns.

1. Did you know that the Smiths are cousins of (*me, mine*)?

2. (*Your, Yours*) hand is bleeding. How did you cut (*you, yourself*)?

3. The baby bird is chirping in (*its, it's*) nest, waiting for (*its, it's*) mother. (*Its, It's*) hungry.

4. My husband works at home. (*His, Him*) office is in the basement. (*He, His*) built it (*himself, itself*). Having a quiet work space makes (*he, him*) more productive now. (*His, Him*) manager is happy with this, too.

5. Luis and (*I, me*) are vacationing in Mexico next month. We are staying at (*his, he's*) parents' house in Mazatlán.

6. A: Whose seats are these?
   B: Those people over (*their, there, they're*). (*Their, There, They're*) waiting in line for popcorn.

Part C *Directions:* Complete the sentences with correct forms of **other**: **another, other, others, the other**, or **the others**.

1. My school offers instruction in several different sports. Golf is one, and swimming is

   _____.

2. So far, your suggestions have been very helpful. What _____ ideas do you have?

3. If Matt gets _____ failing grade, he'll have to repeat the class.

4. My friends have given me three surprise birthday parties in the past. I was surprised by the first, but not by _____.

5. Some people are early risers, and _____ like to sleep until noon.

6. The window washers only need to wash the windows on the front of the building. _____ windows are clean.

Part D *Directions:* Correct the errors.

1. We rented for one month a cabin in the mountains.

2. What are you doing in Thursday evening?

3. My apartments building is small. It has only eleven unit.

4. Your appointment is scheduled for Monday at the afternoon.

5. There is several car in our driveway. Who do they belong to?

6. The table have scratches on it from the children toys.

7. In the future, every students will need to turn in typed assignments.

8. I fell asleep nine o'clock last night.

9. The wedding will be on May.

10. The apples in the box was rotten, so we didn't eat them.

QUIZ 1 The Form of Modal Auxiliaries (Chart 7-1)

Directions: Add the word *to* where necessary. If *to* is not necessary, write Ø.

Examples: The weather reporter says it ___Ø___ will be sunny for several days.
Do we have ___to___ leave right now?

1. The delivery driver couldn't _____ find our house.

2. Stan is able _____ ride his bike ten miles to work every day.

3. You must not _____ drive too fast. The speed limit is 70 miles per hour.

4. I have got _____ get my hair cut. It's so long.

5. Shelley might _____ help if she has time.

6. I can _____ see much better with my new glasses.

7. You may _____ borrow my car if you are back by 6:00 P.M.

8. You ought _____ try this dessert. It's delicious.

9. John isn't here. He must _____ be stuck in traffic.

10. Mr. Daly had better _____ build a stronger fence. Some cows escaped from his field.

QUIZ 2 Expressing Ability (Chart 7-2)

A. *Can* and *Can't*

Directions: Complete the sentences with *can* or *can't*.

Example: Bees ___can___ see many colors, but they ___can't___ see the color red.

1. Newborn babies _____ walk, but newborn horses _____ .

2. Snakes _____ talk to people, but they _____ hiss.

3. Dogs _____ chase cars, but they _____ drive them.

4. Computers _____ think, but they _____ help people solve problems.

5. Spiders _____ make webs, but they _____ make honey.

B. *Could* and *Be Able To*

Directions: Complete the sentences with **could, couldn't, be able to,** or **not be able to.**
More than one answer is possible.

Example: Three years ago, Jean-Pierre _____couldn't_____ understand spoken English, but
now he can.

1. When I was a teenager, I _____ eat a whole pizza by myself, but I
   can't now.

2. Joshua _____ speak Spanish, but his mother was.

3. My dad called me over the Internet. I _____ hear him fine, but I
   _____ see him because my webcam didn't work.

4. Alexander Graham Bell was the first person to talk on a telephone. When he said,
   "Watson, come here," his assistant Thomas Watson _____ hear him.

QUIZ 3 Possibility vs. Permission (Chart 7-3)

Directions: Decide if the modal verbs express *possibility* or *permission*. The first one is done
for you.

	permission	possibility
1. We *may have* hot chocolate later.		✓
2. You *may leave* now.		
3. I *might need* some help.		
4. You *can go* home early.		
5. I *may need* extra time.		
6. You *might not get* a seat in the theater.		
7. You *may not sit* there.		
8. You *can't eat* that candy.		
9. It *may be* nice tomorrow.		
10. We *can begin* work tomorrow.		
11. The bus *may* be late.		

Directions: Rewrite the sentences with the words in parentheses.

Example: It might rain tomorrow. (*maybe*)
        <u>Maybe it will rain tomorrow</u>.

1. Maybe we'll go away this weekend. (*might*)

   _____

2. It might snow tomorrow. (*maybe*)

   _____

3. Our baseball team may win the championship. (*maybe*)

   _____

4. Joan may be in the hospital. (*might*)

   _____

5. David might take the driving test tomorrow. (*may*)

   _____

6. Maybe Sara will meet with us this afternoon. (*might*)

   _____

7. James may be late for the meeting. (*maybe*)

   _____

8. Maybe my keys are in my backpack. (*may*)

   _____

9. We might go to a movie tonight. (*may*)

   _____

10. The car might be ready later this afternoon. (*maybe*)

    _____

Directions: Decide if **could** expresses *past, present,* or *future.* Then decide if it expresses *ability* or *possibility.* The first one is done for you.

	past	present	future	ability	possibility
1. Just think! You *could* graduate in one year!			✓		✓
2. I *could* touch my toes when I was younger.					
3. Traffic is a little heavy. There *could* be an accident.					
4. Mr. Chu *could* speak fluent English a few years ago, but he's forgotten some now.					
5. You *could* help me with the dishes after dinner.					
6. There *could* be some good bargains at the mall.					
7. I *could* be at work late. I've got a project to finish.					
8. Katherine *could* tell time when she was three years old.					
9. We *could* go on a picnic this afternoon if the weather is nice.					
10. What *could* be the problem with your computer?					
11. Claire *could* be a professional actress someday. She's very good!					

Directions: Complete the conversations with *could* or *might* + a verb to suggest possibilities. More than one answer is possible.

Examples: A: I don't know where Rick is? Do you?

B: I'm not sure. He ___*could be*___ at the grocery store, but he ___*might be*___ studying at the library.

1. A: What is the weather going to be like tomorrow?

B: I haven't heard the weather forecast, but it looks like it _____.

2. A: Hmm . . . I'm not sure what to cook for dinner tonight. Any ideas?

B: We _____ some pasta, or we _____ chicken.

3. A: I need a new computer, but I don't have much money.

B: You _____ at the new computer discount store, or you

_____ the big warehouse store. They usually have good deals on

computers.

4. A: Martin looks pale. Is he OK?

B: I'm not sure. He _____ sick.

5. A: Our manager didn't come to work today.

B: She _____ out of town, or she _____ on

vacation.

6. A: What are you going to do on Saturday night?

B: Something relaxing! We _____ a movie, but we

_____ home.

Directions: Read the conversations. Check (✓) *all* the correct modals for each polite request.

Example: A: Do you understand how this computer program works?

B: Sort of, but not really. _____ you explain it to me one more time, please?
_____ May   __✓__ Could   __✓__ Can   __✓__ Would   __✓__ Will

1. A: Mr. Andrews, I have a headache. _____ I leave early, please?
   B: Of course, Ms. Ochoa. I hope you feel better tomorrow.

   _____ May   _____ Could   _____ Can   _____ Would   _____ Will

2. A: Mom, I finished my homework. _____ you check it?
   B: Sure. I'd be happy to.

   _____ May   _____ Could   _____ Can   _____ Would   _____ Will

3. A: The copy machine is out of paper. _____ you refill it?
   B: I'll take care of it in a few minutes.

   _____ May   _____ Could   _____ Can   _____ Would   _____ Will

4. A: Hi, Mr. Martin. It looks like you have your hands full. _____ I help you carry your groceries?
   B: That would be great, Jim. Thanks a lot!

   _____ May   _____ Could   _____ Can   _____ Would   _____ Will

5. A: This rice is delicious. _____ I have another bowl?
   B: Of course! I'm so happy you like it.

   _____ May   _____ Could   _____ Can   _____ Would   _____ Will

6. A: Excuse me. I need to check my email. _____ you let me know when you are finished with the computer?
   B: Sure. I'll be finished soon.

   _____ May   _____ Could   _____ Can   _____ Would   _____ Will

7. A: Good morning. _____ I help you find something in the store?
   B: No thank you. I'm just looking around.

   _____ May   _____ Could   _____ Can   _____ Would   _____ Will

8. A: Mikael, _____ you hand me the phone, please?
   B: Sure, Dad.

   _____ may   _____ could   _____ can   _____ would   _____ will

9. A: Excuse me. _____ I sit here?
   B: I'm sorry, but this seat is already taken. My friend is coming right back.

   _____ May   _____ Could   _____ Can   _____ Would   _____ Will

10. A: _____ you please tell me what happened?
    B: No. I'm too embarrassed to talk about it.

    _____ May   _____ Could   _____ Can   _____ Would   _____ Will

A: *Directions:* Rewrite the sentences using ***should*** or ***shouldn't***.

SITUATION: Traveling to a Different Country

Example: It's a good idea to try learn about the culture.
Travelers _____*should try*_____ to learn about the culture.

1. It's a good idea to be careful with your passport and other travel documents.

   You _____ careful with your passport and other travel documents.

2. It's a good idea to learn to say "please" and "thank you" in the local language.

   People _____ to say "please" and "thank you" in the local language.

3. It's not a good idea to expect everything to be the same as at home.

   Travelers _____ everything to be the same as at home.

4. It's a bad idea to be impatient if someone doesn't understand you.

   You _____ impatient if someone doesn't understand you.

5. It's a good idea to try food that is different from food in your country.

   You _____ food that is different from food in your country.

B: *Directions:* Read the problem. Give some advice using ***should*** or ***ought to***. More than one answer is possible.

Example: A: I'm sleepy.
B: _____*You should/ought to go to bed early tonight*_____.

1. A: My computer keeps crashing.
   B: _____.

2. A: My foot hurts. It has been hurting for several days.
   B: _____.

3. A: I'm so hungry. I didn't have time for breakfast.
   B: _____.

4. A: Henry is so depressed. He failed his chemistry test.
   B: _____.

5. A: My coffee is cold.
   B: _____.

A. *Directions:* Complete the sentences using ***should / ought to*** or ***had better***. Some sentences are negative.

Examples: The boys _____<u>had better not</u>_____ play soccer in the house. They might break something.

You _____<u>should</u>_____ try on this hat. It's cute.

1. You _____ leave early for the airport. That way you won't have to rush.

2. You _____ lose your passport.

3. We _____ put away the game. It's almost time for bed.

4. A: My horse is limping.

   B: Oh? You _____ call the vet. It could be something serious.

5. You _____ be late to your wedding!

B. *Directions:* Make suggestions with ***should, had better,*** or ***ought to***. More than one answer is possible.

Examples: Billy is walking on the carpet with wet shoes. His mother is upset.

   _____<u>Billy should take off his shoes</u>_____. OR
   _____<u>Billy ought to take off his shoes</u>____. OR
   _____<u>Billy had better take off his shoes</u>___.

1. You just touched a hot pan and burned your finger.

   I _____.

2. There is a snake in front of your door, and you need to leave your house.

   I _____.

3. It's raining, and there's a leak in Suzette's roof. Water is coming into her apartment.

   She _____.

4. Mr. Sato finishes dinner at a restaurant and discovers that he has no money with him.

   He _____.

5. I just tripped on your carpet and almost fell! There's a hole in it.

   You _____.

Directions: Choose the correct modals.

Example: Tomorrow I ((have to), had to) go to the dentist.

SITUATION: In Class

1. Yesterday, our teacher (*must, had to*) leave school early.

2. We (*had got to, had to*) work quietly by ourselves until the end of class.

3. Why did she (*have to, had to*) leave early?

SITUATION: At the Airport

4. Everyone (*must, have to*) have a ticket to go to the gate.

5. We usually (*has to, have got to*) wait in a long line.

6. Did you (*have to, had to*) check your luggage?

SITUATION: Going to a Party

7. I (*have got to, had to*) get ready for the party. It starts in fifteen minutes.

8. We (*must, had to*) be on time for this party. We were late for the last one.

9. I didn't have anything nice to wear. I (*have to, had to*) buy a new dress for this party.

10. My sister (*has got to, have got to*) finish her homework before we leave.

Directions: Complete the sentences with **don't / doesn't have to** or **must not**.

SITUATION: Using the Internet

Example: Students ___must not___ surf the Internet when they are in class.

1. You _____ be an expert to use the Internet effectively.

2. People _____ download music or movies illegally.

3. Sometimes you can get music or movies for free. You _____ pay for them.

4. Be careful! You _____ give out too much personal information.

5. Wireless Internet access is so fast! I _____ wait long for pages to load.

6. On some blogs, you _____ be a member. Anyone can write on them.

7. My sister _____ use a computer to check her email; she uses her cell phone.

8. When people chat online, they _____ be so careful with grammar.

9. You _____ believe everything you read online. Some of it isn't true!

10. Parents _____ allow their children to spend too much time online.

Directions: Decide if **must** expresses *logical conclusion* or *necessity*. The first one is done for you.

	logical conclusion	necessity
1. You must be Faisal's son. You look just like your father.	✓	
2. You must wash your hands with warm water and soap.		
3. Ellen must know about the accident. She's a police officer.		
4. You don't look well. You must sit down for a minute.		
5. We must feed the animals before we leave for work.		
6. Julie must like school. She's ready an hour early every morning.		
7. I see lightning in the distance. There must be a storm coming.		
8. Children, you must stay in your seats until the bell rings.		
9. You got 100 percent on the exam! You must feel wonderful.		
10. Your grades are low. You must not study much.		
11. I'm sorry that your mom is so sick. You must be worried.		

Directions: Complete the conversations with **must** or **must not**.

Example: A: Jose isn't here yet.
B: The traffic _____*must*_____ be really bad today.

1. A: Wow! You're shivering! You _____ be cold.

   B: I am. I hope I'm not getting sick.

2. A: Sue has tried on three dresses, but she isn't going to buy any of them.

   B: She _____ like them.

3. A: A car just parked in front on our house.

   B: That _____ be Rudy. He's picking me up.

4. A: The Nelsons' son is getting married next month.

   B: They _____ be very excited about the wedding!

5. A: Lucy skips class at least twice a week.

   B: She _____ care about getting a high grade.

6. A: I have tried to reach Josh on his cell phone, but he won't answer.

   B. He usually answers his phone. He _____ have it with him today.

7. A: There are a lot of bees flying around outside our bedroom window.

   B: Uh-oh! There _____ be a beehive nearby.

8. A: John and Yuko are leaving for Tokyo on Saturday.

   B: They _____ have a lot of packing to do.

9. A: The cat won't eat the fish I gave her.

   B: She _____ like it.

10. A: Nancy practices piano for two hours every day.

    B: She _____ be serious about becoming a professional musician.

QUIZ 14 **Tag Questions with Modals** (Chart 7-12)

Directions: Complete the tag questions.

Example: Derek can speak Turkish, _____*can't*_____ he?

1. You have to study for semester exams, _____ you?

2. Children should get lots of fresh air and exercise, _____ they?

3. Harriet can't cook Vietnamese food, _____ she?

4. Pat wouldn't like this movie, _____ he?

5. You will help me with my project, _____ you?

6. I shouldn't worry so much, _____ I?

7. They would rather stay home, _____ they?

8. We'll be late for school today, _____ we?

9. You couldn't find the information you were looking for, _____ you?

10. He doesn't have to work on the weekend, _____ he?

A. *Directions:* Complete the sentences with the imperative.

SITUATION: Baking a Cake

Example: You have to buy flour, sugar, butter, and eggs.
    ___Buy___ flour, sugar, butter, and eggs.

1. You need to prepare a cake pan.

    _____ a cake pan.

2. It's a good idea to measure flour, sugar, and butter carefully.

    _____ flour, sugar, and butter carefully.

3. You have to mix the butter, sugar, eggs, and milk.

    _____ the butter, sugar, eggs, and milk.

4. After that, you should carefully add the flour, baking powder, and salt.

    _____ the flour, baking powder, and salt.

5. Then you need to pour the cake batter into the pan.

    _____ the cake batter into the pan.

6. You have to bake the cake for 25-30 minutes.

    _____ it for 25-30 minutes.

7. After 25 minutes, you should test the cake to see if it's done.

    After 25 minutes, _____ the cake to see if it's done.

8. When the cake is done, you have to let it cool for ten minutes.

    When the cake is done, _____ it cool for 10 minutes.

9. After that, you can remove it from the pan.

    After that, _____ it from the pan.

10. When the cake is completely cool, you can decorate it.

    When the cake is completely cool, _____ it.

Directions: Complete the sentences with the correct verb form of **prefer, like,** or **would rather**.

Example: Kelly _____*prefers*_____ a laptop to a desktop computer.

1. Dr. Quinn _____ see his hospital patients in the morning than in the evening.

2. Joanne _____ smaller cars better than bigger ones.

3. The Petersons _____ warmer climates to cooler ones.

4. I _____ leave now than later.

5. Monique _____ fish to red meat.

6. Kristof _____ read the news on the Internet than in the newspaper.

7. My father _____ reading novels to watching TV.

8. Scott and Jeff _____ to swim in salt water better than fresh water.

9. I _____ pens to pencils.

10. We _____ spend our vacations with our grandchildren than travel.

Directions: Choose the correct completions. The first one is done for you.

1. I'm not feeling well. ____ I lie down for a while on your sofa?
   (a.) Could   b. Would   c. Must

2. You ____ drive more slowly or you are going to get another speeding ticket.
   a. could   b. ought to   c. had to

3. ____ I borrow your pencil? Mine just broke.
   a. Would   b. Ought   c. May

4. You ____ finish your dinner. I gave you a lot to eat.
   a. must not   b. don't have to   c. couldn't

5. Jessica doesn't look healthy. She ____ see a doctor.
   a. should   b. can   c. would

6. ____ you help me lift this box? It's heavier than I thought.
   a. Will   b. May   c. Should

7. I just heard a car door. Dad ____ be home.
   a. would   b. can   c. must

8. Our dog ____ count! Listen to him bark as I say the numbers.
   a. should   b. can   c. must

9. You ____ be Sally. Mary told me you would be coming at 12:00.
   a. can   b. will   c. must

10. ____ you still be here when I get back?
    a. Will   b. Would   c. May

11. What can we do about Grandma? She ____ drive anymore. She's dangerous.
    a. doesn't have to   b. might not   c. shouldn't

12. I already paid the electric bill by phone. You ____ write a check.
    a. don't have to   b. shouldn't   c. can't

13. ____ you turn down the heat, please?
    a. Could   b. Should   c. May

14. When Kara was two years old, she ____ recognize letters and numbers.
    a. could   b. should   c. might

15. We ____ use our credit card at the store because their computers weren't working.
    a. shouldn't   b. wouldn't   c. couldn't

16. ____ you please repeat that?
    a. Could   b. May   c. Should

17. Your lips are blue, and you're shivering! You ____ be freezing.
    a. ought to   b. must   c. will

18. You ____ turn off the TV right now. You need to finish your homework, or you won't be ready for your exam tomorrow.
    a. had better   b. don't need to   c. would

19. I'm bored. ____ to the mall?
    a. Let's go   b. Why don't we go   c. Go

20. ____ we will come home from our vacation early. We haven't decided.
    a. May be   b. Might   c. Maybe

21. Jim never drinks coffee. He ____ like it.
    a. should not   b. could not   c. must not

Part A *Directions:* Read each conversation. Then circle the best completion.

1. A: Ouch! I cut my hand!
   B: You _____ clean it well and put a bandage on it.
   a. will   b. had better   c. may

2. A: Does this pen belong to you?
   B: No. It _____ be Diana's. She was sitting at that desk.
   a. had better   b. will   c. must

3. A: Let's go to a movie this evening.
   B: That sounds like fun, but I can't. I _____ finish this report before I go to bed tonight.
   a. have got to   b. would rather   c. ought to

4. A: We _____ hurry. The store closes in thirty minutes.
   B: I'll finish my shopping quickly.
   a. should   b. will   c. may

5. A: I did it! I did it! I got my driver's license!
   B: Congratulations, Michelle. I'm really proud of you.
   A: Thanks, Dad. Now _____ I have the car tonight? Please?
   B: No. You're not ready for that quite yet.
   a. will   b. should   c. may

6. A: What do you want to do on our vacation this summer?
   B: I _____ go camping than spend time in a big city.
   a. could   b. would rather   c. prefer

7. A: Are you going to the conference in Atlanta next month?
   B: I _____. I'm not sure yet.
   a. will   b. have to   c. might

8. A: What shall we do after the meeting this evening?
   B: _____ pick Jan up and all go out to dinner together.
   a. Why don't   b. Let's   c. Should

9. A: Have you seen my denim jacket? I _____ find it.
   B: Look in the hall closet.
   a. may not   b. won't   c. can't

10. A: Bye, Mom! I'm going out to play soccer with my friends.
    B: Wait a minute, young man! You _____ do your chores first.
    a. had better not   b. have to   c. would rather

Part B *Directions:* Complete the sentences with **can, could,** or **might**. In some cases, more than one answer is possible.

1. Look at little Ben! He _____ walk!

2. I don't know where Ivona is. She _____ be shopping.

3. When I was younger, I was in great shape. I _____ run for an hour.

4. Turn on the TV. There _____ be news about the accident.

5. Hannah _____ play the piano when she was twelve, but now she can't.

Part C *Directions:* Answer the questions. Write complete sentences. Use the modal in *italics* in your answer.

1. What is something you *had to* do yesterday?

   _____

2. What is something you *must* do before you can drive a car?

   _____

3. What is something that children *shouldn't* do?

   _____

4. What is something you *should* do when you don't feel well?

   _____

5. What is something you *have to* do every morning?

   _____

Part D *Directions:* Correct the errors.

1. I'm feeling hot. I ought take my temperature.

2. Would I borrow your pen? Mine isn't working.

3. I don't feel like cooking. Let's we order a pizza.

4. We'll be free on Saturday. We could to meet then.

5. Look at the sky. It could snow tomorrow, could it?

6. Thomas is late. He can have car trouble again.

7. Children don't have to play with matches. They can start fires.

8. Why we don't go for a walk after dinner? It's such a nice evening.

9. I don't want to stay home this weekend. I rather go hiking.

10. Jenny have to be more careful with her glasses. She has broken them twice.

CHAPTER 7 – TEST 2

Part A *Directions:* Read each conversation. Then circle the best completion.

1. A: Do you think Majed will quit his job?
   B: I don't know. He ____. He'll wait a few weeks to decide.
      a. must   b. may   c. will

2. A: The swimming pool has towels. You ____ bring one.
   B: Okay. I'll just bring my swimsuit.
      a. don't have to   b. must not   c. couldn't

3. A: I heard that Bill was seriously ill.
   B: Really? Well, he ____ be sick now. I just saw him riding his bike to work.
      a. doesn't have to   b. won't   c. must not

4. A: Henry should be here soon, ____ he?
   B: Yes. His plane arrives in ten minutes.
      a. should   b. shouldn't   c. doesn't

5. A: Did you climb to the top of the Statue of Liberty when you were in New York?
   B: No, I didn't. My knee was very sore, and I ____ climb all those stairs.
      a. might not   b. couldn't   c. must not

6. A: Rick, ____ work for me this evening? I'll take your shift tomorrow.
   B: Sure. I was going to ask you to work for me tomorrow anyway.
      a. should you   b. would you   c. do you have to

7. A: What do you want to do with the dog this weekend?
   B: ____ we take him with us?
      a. Why don't   b. Let's   c. Will

8. A: You ____ attend the meeting tomorrow morning. It's important.
   B: OK. I'll be there.
      a. could   b. will   c. must

9. A: I have to pay bills today.
   B: That's good. You ____ forget to pay your credit card bill, or you will have a late fee.
      a. mustn't   b. couldn't   c. don't have to

10. A: Don't wait for me. I ____ late.
    B: OK.
       a. maybe   b. may to be   c. may be

Part B *Directions:* Complete the sentences with **can, could,** or **might**. In some cases, more than one answer is possible.

1. These new glasses are much better. I _____ see much more clearly.

2. When I lived in Paris, I _____ speak fluent French.

3. I don't know why the Martins aren't here. They _____ have another party to go to.

4. I don't know if we have enough help. We _____ need to call more people.

5. When Dr. Kim was in medical school, he _____ work for days with very little sleep.

Directions: Answer the questions. Write complete sentences. Use the modal in *italics* in your answer.

1. What is something you *must* do today?

_____

2. What is something you *should* do when you are at school?

_____

3. What is something that people *shouldn't* do?

_____

4. What is something you *have to* do before you go to bed tonight?

_____

5. What is something you *had to do* last week?

_____

Directions: Correct the errors.

1. My grades are low. I had to better study more.

2. May you please open the window? It's hot in here.

3. I want to stay home tonight. Let invite some friends over.

4. We can't to come to your party. We will be out of town.

5. Susan maybe has a solution to the problem.

6. Jackie isn't here. She can be at home in bed.

7. You mustn't to walk in mud puddles.

8. Why we don't go out for dinner tonight?

9. You have to study tonight, haven't you?

10. I need to make a call. Would I borrow your phone for a minute?

CHAPTER 8 Connecting Ideas

QUIZ 1 Punctuating with Commas and Periods (Chart 8-1)

Directions: Add commas and periods where appropriate. Capitalize as necessary.

SITUATION: Beth's Party

Example: Beth had a party with her friends, neighbors, and roommates.

1. Beth planned to serve pizza green salad and ice-cream at the party
2. Sam Jeff and Ellen helped with the decorations Bob picked up the pizza and drinks
3. The party started at 6:00 several guests were late
4. A few people talked others played soccer and several people danced
5. Everyone had a wonderful time no one wanted to go home
6. Beth thanked everyone for coming and promised to have another party then she told everyone good night

QUIZ 2 Connecting Ideas with *And, But,* and *Or* (Charts 8-1 and 8-2)

Directions: Complete the conversations with **and, but,** or **or**. Add commas as necessary. The first one is done for you.

1. A: Do you want to order dinner now _____*or*_____ later?

   B: Let's order now. I'd like rice, chicken _____ vegetables, please.

2. A: I mailed the letter two weeks ago _____ Pierre hasn't received it.

   B: Did you put one _____ two stamps on it?

   A: Two.

3. A: What do you like to do for fun?

   B: My favorite hobbies are gardening, bicycling _____ bird watching. How about you?

   A: I enjoy playing golf _____ it is an expensive sport. I don't play often.

   B: My favorite sports are soccer _____ swimming. They are more affordable.

4. A: Nicky, you can have spaghetti _____ a grilled cheese sandwich. Which do you want?

   B: I'd like a grilled cheese sandwich _____ a glass of milk, please.

5. A: How was the camping trip?

   B: Too cold! We slept in the tent _____ we got cold in the middle of the night. Then I tried to start a campfire _____ the wood was too wet. It didn't burn.

Directions: Complete the sentences with *so* or *but*.

Example: Norma likes oranges, _____*but*_____ I don't.

1. The soccer game was on TV, _____ I didn't watch it.

2. The basketball game wasn't on TV, _____ I listened to it on the radio.

3. Liz began to cry, _____ I hugged her.

4. Liz began to cry, _____ she wouldn't tell me why.

5. My father is sick, _____ I will stay with him for a few days.

6. My father is sick, _____ he doesn't want me to stay with him.

7. Twenty people were invited to the party, _____ only ten came.

8. The library closes in fifteen minutes, _____ we need to go there now.

9. I can't find my car keys, _____ you'll have to drive.

10. I don't have my library card, _____ Renee has hers.

QUIZ 4 Using Auxiliary Verbs after *But* (Chart 8-4)

Directions: Complete the sentences with the correct auxiliary verbs.

Example: The peas in my garden are ripe, but the corn _____*isn't*_____ .

1. Sara wants to buy a used car, but her husband _____ .

2. Fred isn't ready, but I _____ .

3. Khalid has finished his test, but the other students _____ .

4. Most of our class will graduate this year, but a few students _____ .

5. I haven't read that book, but most of my friends _____ .

6. These lights have fluorescent bulbs, but those lights _____ .

7. We aren't going to work this weekend, but a few coworkers _____ .

8. You won't have to wait, but other passengers _____ .

9. I heard from my parents, but the rest of the family _____ .

10. The children don't want to go to bed, but I _____ .

Directions: Read about the Sweet family. Then complete the sentences with the correct auxiliary verbs. The first one is done for you.

The Sweet family has five people: the parents, two girls, and one boy. Natalie, the mom, owns a coffee shop, and the dad, Will, is a carpenter. They work while their kids are at school. The girls are Laura and Janey. Their brother's name is Aaron. They are students at Ravenswood High School. They love music and sing in the choir. Laura and Aaron are also in the Drama Club. Janey isn't in the Drama Club. She likes painting and drawing, so she is in the Art Club. Natalie and Will are proud of their children.

1. Natalie works, and so _____*does*_____ Will.

2. Natalie works at her coffee shop, but Will _____.

3. Natalie has three kids, and Will _____ too.

4. Laura is a girl, and so _____ Janey.

5. Janey is in high school, and Laura and Aaron _____ too.

6. Laura and Janey sing in the choir, and Aaron _____ too.

7. Aaron likes music, and so _____ Laura and Janey.

8. Laura and Aaron are in the Drama Club, but Janey _____.

9. Janey likes drawing and painting, but Aaron and Laura _____.

10. Janey is in the Art Club, but Laura and Aaron _____.

11. Natalie is proud of the kids, and so _____ Will.

Directions: Read the facts about two brothers, Joe and Sam. Complete the sentences using *so, too, either,* or *neither* and the correct auxiliary verb. Make true statements. The first one is done for you.

Joe ...	Sam ...
is thirty-five years old	is thirty-three years old
is a math teacher	is a sports trainer
is married	is married
has two daughters	has two daughters
lives in Los Angeles	lives in San Francisco
is a vegetarian	is a vegetarian
has been to London	has been to London
is learning French	is learning Chinese

1. Joe is in his thirties, and _____*so is*_____ Sam.

2. Joe will turn forty in a few years, and Sam _____.

3. Joe isn't a music teacher, and Sam _____.

4. Joe is married, and Sam _____.

5. Joe isn't single, and _____ Sam.

6. Joe has two daughters, and _____ Sam.

7. Joe doesn't have any sons, and Sam _____.

8. Joe lives in California, and Sam _____.

9. Joe doesn't eat meat, and _____ Sam.

10. Joe has been to London, and _____ Sam.

11. Joe is studying a foreign language, and Sam _____.

QUIZ 7 Connecting Ideas with *Because* (Chart 8-6)

Directions: Combine each pair of sentences in two different orders. Use ***because***. Punctuate carefully.

Examples: Andy is going to go shopping. His favorite store is having a sale.
_____ *Andy is going to go shopping because his favorite store is having a sale.* _____
_____ *Because Andy's favorite store is having a sale, he is going to go shopping.* _____

1. I had a high fever. I went to the doctor.

   _____

   _____

2. Cindy failed the class. She didn't study.

   _____

   _____

3. We went to the beach. It was a beautiful day.

   _____

   _____

4. I need to get new jeans. My old jeans have holes in them.

   _____

   _____

5. My car is making strange noises. I feel uncomfortable driving.

   _____

   _____

A. Directions: Check (✓) the correct sentences.

Examples: _____ So the page torn, I can't read it.
_✓_ Because the page is torn, I can't read it.
_✓_ The page is torn, so I can't read it.

1. _____ Because it was hot, I jumped in the cool water.

_____ I jumped in the cool water, so it was hot.

_____ It was hot, so I jumped in the cool water.

2. _____ I took off my uncomfortable shoes, so my feet hurt.

_____ Because my feet hurt, so I took off my uncomfortable shoes.

_____ My feet hurt, so I took off my uncomfortable shoes.

3. _____ Oscar began coughing because the restaurant was smoky.

_____ The restaurant was smoky because Oscar began coughing.

_____ The restaurant was smoky, so Oscar began coughing.

B. Directions: Complete the sentences with *because* or *so*.

Example: I wore my sunglasses _____*because*_____ the sun was shining.

1. Yesterday I had a fever, _____ I didn't go to work.

2. _____ my mother's birthday is tomorrow, I am going to buy her some flowers.

3. Harry is nervous about meeting his girlfriend's parents _____ he wants to marry her.

4. Dave plays in a jazz group, _____ he is often busy on Saturday nights.

5. Campers in Yellowstone Park have to put away their food _____ there are bears nearby.

A. *Directions:* Choose the correct sentence in each pair.

Example: (a.) Because the page is torn, I can't read it.
   b. Even though the page is torn, I can't read it.

1. a. The skaters practice every day because they hope to skate in the Olympics.
   b. The skaters practice every day although they hope to skate in the Olympics.

2. a. Even though Antoine quit smoking, he doesn't have any matches.
   b. Because Antoine quit smoking, he doesn't have any matches.

3. a. Although we try to save money, we always seem to spend more than we have.
   b. Because we try to save money, we always seem to spend more than we have.

4. a. The store is open at night even though it doesn't have many customers.
   b. The store is open at night because it doesn't have many customers.

5. a. Although the police could smell gas, they couldn't find a gas leak.
   b. Because the police could smell gas, they couldn't find a gas leak.

B. *Directions:* Choose the best completion for each sentence.

Example: The students stayed indoors at school because _____
      a. they wanted to play soccer.
      (b.) there were storm clouds in the area.

1. Because our car was low on gas, _____
   a. we stopped at the gas station.
   b. we didn't stop for gas before we left town.

2. Nora didn't go to the dentist even though _____
   a. she had a toothache.
   b. she didn't have a toothache.

3. The kitchen smells delicious because _____
   a. we burned a pizza.
   b. we have been making cookies.

4. Although Alan _____, he has difficulty getting up on time.
   a. has two alarm clocks
   b. stays up late

5. Even though my teacher told us about the test, _____
   a. I studied hard.
   b. I didn't study at all.

Directions: Add commas where necessary.

Example: Even though I like eggplant, I rarely eat it.

1. Even though the roads were crowded we got home on time.

2. Alice can't eat peanut butter because she is allergic to nuts.

3. Because the students felt the building shake they got under their desks.

4. Erica can't figure out this puzzle even though she did it once before.

5. Brad's computer is slow even though he just upgraded the memory.

6. Although this TV is new the picture isn't very clear.

7. A lot of people are working even though it's a holiday.

8. Although it was raining we stood in line to get tickets for the concert.

9. It's difficult for me to do crossword puzzles even though I love word games.

10. Because my parents were celebrating twenty-five years of marriage they had a big party.

QUIZ 11 Chapter Review

Directions: Correct the errors.

Example: Clothing is getting more expensive, and ~~neither~~ is food.
                                              so

1. I enjoy science my favorite subjects are physics math and chemistry.

2. Julia doesn't participate in sports. Either her friends.

3. Our baseball team lost the game. Because not enough players showed up.

4. The downstairs phone isn't working properly and this one doesn't either.

5. I wore a hat and sunglasses so the sun was so bright.

6. My mother is Australian, my father is Brazilian.

7. Even though you're upset now, but you'll understand our decision in a few days.

8. So our parents both work, my brothers and I sometimes cook dinner.

9. I have never been to Hawaii, and so hasn't my husband.

10. The photographs turned out wonderfully, but the video isn't.

CHAPTER 8 – TEST 1

Part A *Directions:* Add commas, periods, and capital letters as appropriate. Don't change any words or the order of the words.

SITUATION: An Afternoon at the Beach

Elena decided the weather was too nice to stay at home so she packed a picnic lunch and drove to the beach even though it was crowded she found a place to sit she spread out her blanket and opened her lunch inside was a sandwich potato chips and an apple because she was still full from breakfast she ate only a little and saved the rest for later she took out a book and opened it minutes later she was asleep and she woke up just as the sun was going down

Part B *Directions:* Complete the sentences with *and, but, or, so, because,* or *even though*.

SITUATION: Bryan and Cathy's Wedding

1. Bryan and Cathy are getting married next month, _____ they are very excited.

2. _____ there is a lot to do to get ready for the wedding, Bryan doesn't seemed stressed.

3. The invitation list looked long, _____ it didn't take long to write them all.

4. _____ Cathy's aunt has a large home, she has invited all their relatives for a wedding party.

5. We can buy their gift online today, _____ we can go shopping next Saturday.

6. The bridesmaids will wear beautiful yellow dresses, _____ the groomsmen will wear tuxedos.

7. _____ the wedding is next month, Cathy hasn't bought a wedding dress yet.

8. Who's going to sing at the wedding, Mary _____ someone else?

9. They love chocolate, _____ they'll have a chocolate wedding cake.

10. Bryan's boss won't be able to come to the wedding _____ he'll be away on business.

Part C *Directions:* Complete the sentences using *so, too, either* or *neither* and the correct auxiliary verb.

SITUATION: Students in My English Class

1. Nini likes learning English, and _____ Kay.

2. Dao is from Vietnam, and Boon _____.

3. Johannes isn't from Asia, and Martin _____.

4. Jacob doesn't speak Chinese, and _____ Masaki.

5. Max speaks German, and _____ I.

6. Bashir speaks Russian, and Andre _____.

7. Shirley hasn't been in the US long, and _____ Julien.

8. Erik will go to Disneyland over spring break, and Vincent _____.

9. Mona is from Saudi Arabia, and _____ Majed and Ibrahim.

10. The teacher enjoys this class, and the students _____.

Part D *Directions:* Correct the errors.

1. I study hard even my classes are very easy.

2. After the accident, my left arm hurt and too my right shoulder.

3. Blackberries, strawberries, blueberries. They all grow in our garden.

4. Because taxes were so high, and people refused to pay.

5. We were excited about the concert, but we got there early to get good seats.

CHAPTER 8 – TEST 2

Part A *Directions:* Add commas, periods, and capital letters as appropriate. Don't change any words or the order of the words.

SITUATION: Ron's Future

Ron needs to decide if he is going to go to graduate school or if he is going to get a job he will finish business school in a few months although he has enjoyed being a student he wants to start earning his own money his parents want him to get a Master's degree they have said they will pay for it so they think he should agree to stay in school Ron appreciates their generosity but he also wants to be more independent at this time in his life

Part B *Directions:* Complete the sentences with *and, but, or, so, because,* or *even though*.

1. Which would you like, fried _____ boiled eggs?

2. _____ the birds in the trees make a lot of noise in the morning, Joyce wakes up early.

3. Sometimes my parents take their early morning walk in the park, _____ sometimes they go to the mall.

4. I fell asleep at the train station, _____ I missed my train.

5. _____ Peter read the chapter several times, he still couldn't remember the important details.

6. _____ her son is in the hospital, Mrs. Davis has decided to take time off from work.

7. We went to several stores, _____ we couldn't find a birthday gift for Nathan. He's difficult to shop for.

8. _____ Melissa slept eight hours, she still felt tired in the morning.

9. Melissa slept eight hours, _____ she still felt tired in the morning.

10. The owner wanted too much money for his truck, _____ we decided not to buy it.

Part C *Directions:* Complete the sentences using *so, too, either,* or *neither* and the correct auxiliary verb.

SITUATION: Visiting the Zoo

1. I am at the zoo, and _____ my daughter.

2. The penguins seem happy, and the otters _____.

3. The zebras live in the "savannah," and _____ the giraffes.

4. A big elephant is having a bath, and a small one _____.

5. The monkeys are eating, and _____ the gorillas.

6. The lions will get food later, and _____ the bears.

7. Elephants don't eat meat, and gorillas _____.

8. We ate lunch at the Zoo Café, and _____ many other people.

9. My daughter likes the birds, and I _____.

10. She doesn't like the hyenas, and _____ I.

Part D *Directions:* Correct the errors.

1. People couldn't describe the accident. Because it happened so quickly.

2. Even Nadia is a new student, but she has made many friends.

3. So a storm was approaching the sailors decided to go into shore.

4. You can either pay by cash and check. Which do you prefer?

5. Maria didn't understand the lecture. Neither I did too.

Comparisons

Comparisons with *As ... As* (Chart 9-1)

A. *Directions:* Compare the temperatures of the cities. Use ***just as ... as, almost as ... as***, or ***not as ... as***. The first one is done for you.

Yesterday's weather:	Vienna	68°F / 20°C	Hong Kong	75°F / 24°C
	Vancouver	70°F / 21°C	Athens	90°F / 32°C
	Paris	70°F / 21°C	Dubai	104°F / 40°C

1. Paris _____*was not as warm as*_____ Athens.

2. Athens _____ Dubai.

3. Vienna _____ Paris and Vancouver.

4. Vancouver _____ Paris.

5. Vienna and Paris _____ Athens.

6. Hong Kong _____ Athens and Dubai.

B. *Directions:* Compare the ages of the people. The first one is done for you.

Jim	27	Max	40
Susan	28	Paulo	43
Lacey	28	Maria	45

1. Susan is as old as _____*Lacey*_____ .

2. Paulo is almost as old as _____.

3. Max is not quite as old as _____.

4. Lacey is just as old as _____.

5. Jim is nearly as old as _____.

6. Paulo is not as old as _____.

Directions: Using the given words, complete the sentences with *just as . . . as* or *not as . . . as*. Give your own opinions.

Example: a sunrise / a sunset

_____*A sunrise is just as*_____ beautiful _____*as a sunset*_____ .

1. light chocolate / dark chocolate

   _____ delicious _____

   _____ .

2. spring / fall

   _____ colorful _____

3. sending email / text messaging

   _____ easy _____

   _____ .

4. a hard pillow / a soft pillow

   _____ comfortable _____

   _____ .

5. a poisonous snake / a non-poisonous snake

   _____ scary _____

   _____ .

6. eating / sleeping

   _____ important _____ .

7. China / England

   _____ large _____ .

8. a sports car / a school bus

   _____ fast _____ .

9. soccer / basketball

   _____ popular _____ .

10. the Winter Olympics / the Summer Olympics

    _____ exciting _____

    _____ .

Directions: Complete the sentences with the correct comparative form (*-er / more*) of the given adjectives.

Example: The Taj Mahal is (*old*) __older__ than the Blue Mosque.

1. The Sahara desert is (*large*) _____ than the Kalahari desert.

2. Brown rice is (*health*) _____ than white rice.

3. Which is (*dangerous*) _____: ice climbing or bungee jumping?

4. A hardcover book is (*heavy*) _____ than a paperback book.

5. An essay is (*long*) _____ than a paragraph.

6. Small grocery stores are usually (*expensive*) _____ than supermarkets.

7. Paying bills online can be (*easy*) _____ than writing checks.

8. Fast food restaurants serve food (*quick*) _____ than sit-down restaurants.

9. I find classic movies (*interesting*) _____ than current ones.

10. Riding a bike with a helmet is (*safe*) _____ than riding without one.

Directions: Make comparison sentences with *-er* / *more* and the given adjectives.

Example: a turtle / a rabbit (*fast*)

_____*A rabbit is faster than a turtle*_____.

1. summer / winter (*warm*)

   _____

2. Mexico City / New York City (*big*)

   _____

3. a work day / a holiday (*enjoyable*)

   _____

4. air / rocks (*heavy*)

   _____

5. snow / ice (*soft*)

   _____

6. ice cream / lemons (*tasty*)

   _____

7. a newspaper / a book (*expensive*)

   _____

8. vegetables / butter (*healthy*)

   _____

9. a DVD player / a DVD (*cheap*)

   _____

10. a month / a year (*long*)

    _____

Directions: Complete the sentences with *farther* and/or *further*. Use both if possible.

Example: The bank is _____ farther / further _____ from here than the post office.

1. If you need to discuss these matters _____, give me a call.

2. The bus station is _____ from our house than the train station.

3. We're almost home. We just have a little _____ to go.

4. If you don't get our plumbing fixed now, it may cause _____ problems later.

5. I was surprised we hiked all the way to the lake. We went _____ than we had planned.

6. If you need more information, please contact my lawyer. I have nothing _____ to say.

7. My grandparents like their new retirement community, but it's _____ from town than they realized.

8. Since my surgery, I've begun taking walks. Every day, I try to walk a little _____ .

9. You'll need to take a train from the airport to your hotel. The airport is _____ from the city than the travel brochures tell you.

10. You can go now. We have no _____ need of your services.

Directions: Complete the sentences. Use pronouns in the completions. The first one is done for you.

SITUATION: The Smith Family

1. You don't know the Smiths well. I know them better than _____*you do*_____.

2. Dr. Gary Smith is thirty-three years old. His wife, Annie, is thirty. I am twenty-nine. Gary and Annie are older than _____. I am younger than

   _____.

3. The Smiths have four children. I have only two children. Their family is bigger than

   _____.

4. The Smith's son, Jared, can count to one hundred in Spanish. The other children in his class can only count to twenty. Jared can count better than _____.

5. Annie doesn't enjoy cooking. Her husband loves to cook. His cooking is better than

   _____.

6. Gary can run a mile in ten minutes. Annie can run a mile in eight minutes. Annie can run faster than _____.

7. We bought a two-bedroom house. The Smiths bought a four-bedroom house. The Smiths bought a larger house than _____.

8. Dr. Smith isn't an expensive dentist. The other dentists in the city are more expensive than _____.

9. The Smith's daughter, Beth, loves to swim. Her brothers and sisters don't like to swim that much. Beth likes swimming more than _____.

Directions: Complete the sentences with *very, much, a lot,* or *far.* More than one answer may be correct.

Example: Channel 8 has ____*a lot*____ more international news than other TV stations.

1. This fish is not _____ good. You don't have to eat it.

2. My mother is _____ more active than my father.

3. It's starting to snow. It must be _____ cold outside.

4. Barbara has a sunny personality. She is _____ happier than most people I know.

5. For me, math is _____ more difficult than a foreign language.

6. You look _____ tired. Are you getting enough sleep?

7. Tasha's _____ excited about school. She will be in kindergarten this year.

8. This painting is _____ prettier than I remembered. It's also _____ more expensive than I remembered.

9. Janice is _____ older than her husband.

Directions: Choose the correct answer. In some cases, both answers may be correct.

Example: Gorillas are ((*less intelligent than*), (*not as intelligent as*)) chimpanzees.

1. Green peppers are (*less sweet than, not as sweet as*) red peppers.

2. A shower is (*less relaxing than, not as relaxing as*) a bath.

3. High heels are (*less comfortable than, not as comfortable as*) slippers.

4. Vegetables are (*less fattening than, not as fattening as*) sweets.

5. Taking a bus is usually (*less fast than, not as fast as*) taking a train.

6. This test is (*less difficult than, not as difficult as*) the last one.

7. My pillow is (*less soft than, not as soft as*) yours.

8. The fish from the grocery store is (*less fresh than, not as fresh as*) the fish from the fish market.

9. The air in the countryside is (*less polluted than, not as polluted as*) the air in the city.

10. Arithmetic is (*less hard than, not as hard as*) calculus.

Directions: Complete the comparisons. Use the words in parentheses and **-er** / **more** as needed.

Example: I collect dolls. I have (*dolls*) _____*more dolls*_____ than my sisters.

1. A top-loading washing machine uses (*water*) _____ than a front-loading machine.

2. Shelley runs (*fast*) _____ than the rest of the track team.

3. You have ten minutes left. Is that enough, or do you need (*time*) _____?

4. The reading in our literature class is (*difficult*) _____ than I expected.

5. The weather is (*sunny*) _____ today than yesterday.

6. This car has (*miles*) _____ on it than the salesperson told me.

7. The last math test was pretty hard. I hope the next one is (*easy*) _____.

8. The plants outside are so dry. We need (*rain*) _____ than we had last month.

9. The children like cold weather (*well*) _____ than their parents do.

10. The children are working (*quiet*) _____ today than they were yesterday.

Directions: Complete the answers by repeating the comparatives in *italics*.

Example: Charles is so *tall*. He has really grown! He is getting _____*taller and taller*_____.

1. The weather will get *hot* in the next few days. In fact, the weather reporter says it will get

   _____.

2. My teacher can't explain geometry problems very well. I get *confused*. I don't ask for
   further explanations because I just get _____.

3. When we began our hike, it was raining a little. As we continued to hike, it began to rain
   hard. We finally decided to quit because it rained _____.

4. When Jerry starts to laugh, his face turns *red*. As he continues to laugh, he gets

   _____.

5. Each term, my classes seem more *difficult*. I'm enjoying them even as they become

   _____.

6. Oscar was not *relaxed* with his children when they were younger. But as they get older,
   he's becoming _____.

7. When I got my grades, I felt very *happy*. As the evening went on, I got _____

   _____.

8. Medical insurance continues to rise. It's very *expensive* for our family. It seems that every
   year, it gets _____.

9. Snowboarding can be *dangerous*. In fact, snowboarding jumps and tricks seem to get
   _____ every year.

10. This story is so *good*. It gets _____ with every chapter.

A. Directions: Complete the sentences with double comparatives (**the more / -er . . . the more / -er**) and the words in *italics*.

Example: My science class is so *hard*. I have to study *a lot*.
The ___*harder*___ a class is, ___*the more*___ I study.

1. *Cold* drinks are *refreshing*. _____ a drink is,

_____ it tastes.

2. My fiancé gave me a *big* diamond. It was very *expensive*.

_____ a diamond is, _____

it is.

3. Our *old* car needs a lot of *repairs*. _____ a car is,

_____ it needs.

4. If it is a *hot* day, you should drink lots of *water*. _____ it is,

_____ you should drink.

5. I love *thick* steaks. They are so *good*! _____ the steak is,

_____!

B. Directions: Combine each pair of sentences. Use double comparatives (**the more / -er . . . the more / -er**) and the words in *italics*.

Example: The couple *argued*. They became *upset*.
___*The more they argued, the more upset they became*___.

1. The bus driver *sang*. The children *laughed*.

_____.

2. I *exercised*. I felt *energetic*.

_____.

3. My mom *cooks*. I *eat*.

_____.

4. It *rained*. I got *depressed*.

_____.

5. Simon works *hard*. His boss is very *happy*.

_____.

Directions: Choose the sentence in each pair that is closest in meaning to the given sentence.

Example: His bedroom has never been dirtier.
       (a.) His bedroom is dirty.   b. His bedroom isn't dirty.

1. I've never seen a better movie.
    a. I liked the movie very much.   b. I didn't like the movie much.

2. Andrey is one of the most respectful people I've ever met.
    a. Andrey is respectful.   b. Andrey isn't respectful.

3. I tried on several dresses. The black dress was the nicest, but the red one was the least expensive.
    a. The black dress cost more.   b. The red dress cost more.

4. Jim has never made spicier curry.
    a. The curry is very spicy.   b. The curry isn't spicy.

5. Kate has never been more in love.
    a. Kate is in love with someone.   b. Kate isn't in love with anyone.

6. Francesca has never been overweight.
    a. Francesca is overweight.   b. Francesca isn't overweight.

7. That is one of the least comfortable beds I've ever slept on.
    a. The bed was comfortable.   b. The bed wasn't comfortable.

8. I've never met a friendlier dog.
    a. The dog is friendly.   b. The dog isn't friendly.

9. That book was the worst book I've ever read.
    a. I liked the book a lot.   b. I didn't like the book at all.

10. My family has never been prouder of me.
    a. My family is really proud of me.   b. My family isn't proud of me.

Directions: Complete the sentences with superlatives and the appropriate word: **in, of,** or **ever.**

Example: The kitchen is (*warm*) _____the warmest_____ room ____in____ our house.

1. Those boys are (*noisy*) _____ children I've _____ taken care of.

2. Heidi is (*fast*) _____ reader _____ class.

3. There are several talented singers in our choir, but Marcos has (*beautiful*) _____ voice _____ all.

4. I had a terrible day at work yesterday. It was one of (*bad*) _____ days I've _____ had.

5. Siberia is one of (*cold*) _____ places _____ the world.

6. My ears hurt! That was (*loud*) _____ concert I've _____ been to.

7. It's frustrating. Mr. Jones works (*hard*) _____ all, but his managers don't seem to notice.

8. For their anniversary, Joanne and Ted decided to try (*expensive*) _____ _____ restaurant _____ town.

9. When I gave my speech, my knees were shaking. It was (*less/confident*) _____ _____ I've _____ felt.

10. _____ all the people in our class, Theresa is (*lazy*) _____ and (*lucky*) _____. She does very little work and always gets high grades.

A. *Directions:* Complete the sentences with *as, to, from,* or Ø.

Example: Sometimes Spiro looks like _____Ø_____ he's not listening, but actually he's just
concentrating.

1. My three-year-old son thinks that donkeys look similar _____ zebras.
   He says they look alike _____ because of their ears.

2. My new house is similar _____ my old house, but it's more updated.
   Fortunately, the appliances are different _____ my old ones. They're
   much newer.

3. A: Is the town where you grew up much different _____ this city?

   B: The size of this town is the same _____ my hometown, but the
   architecture is very different _____.

4. A panda is like _____ a bear, but they are not the same
   _____. Bears don't have thumbs, but pandas do.

B. *Directions:* Compare the size of the clouds. Use *the same (as), similar (to),*
different (from), like, or *alike*. The first one is done for you as an example.

1. Figure A is _____*the same as*_____ Figure B.

2. Figure A and Figure B are _____.

3. A and D are _____.

4. C is _____ D.

5. All of the figures are _____ each other.

6. All of the figures are _____.

Directions: Complete the sentences, using *the same, similar, different, like,* or *alike.*
More than one answer may be possible.

Example: A chipmunk looks _____*similar*_____ to a squirrel.

1. Dick likes comedy, and Sharon likes drama. Their taste in movies is very

   _____ .

2. Franz wants to marry someone who thinks _____ him and agrees
   with him on important things.

3. Tom and Will are cousins, but people think they are brothers. They have

   _____ facial features, and they talk and walk

   _____ .

4. "They're," "their," and "there" all have _____ pronunciation.

5. A: How are queen bees _____ from worker bees?
   B: A queen bee is usually the mother of all the bees in the hive.

6. I'm sorry, but we can't accept your credit card. The signature on the card and the one on
   the receipt are not _____ .

7. "Teacher, our answers on the test are _____ from each other, but
   both are correct. Why?"

8. The problems many big cities have with traffic and transportation are usually

   _____ , so city leaders can discuss solutions and learn from each

   other.

9. My twin nephews look exactly _____ . I can't tell them apart.

Directions: Correct the errors.

Example: This coffee should be ~~more~~ warmer. Could you heat it up, please?

1. The most friendliest person in our class is Julie.

2. The food at the restaurant was less good than the last time we were there.

3. The movie was very funny than we expected. We laughed the whole time.

4. Anna's dog is ugliest dog I've ever seen.

5. Grandpa's behavior is embarrassing. The older he gets, the loudly he talks.

6. I have a same bag as you. Where did you buy yours?

7. My father said that having kids was one of the best thing he ever did.

8. For Jon, the game of chess is alike an interesting math puzzle.

9. As the horse got tired, he began walking slower and more slow.

10. The driving test was hard, more than I expected.

CHAPTER 9 – TEST 1

Part A *Directions:* Complete the sentences with the comparative or superlative form of the words in parentheses.

1. Did you know that cold water is (*heavy*) _____ warm water?

2. Which is (*small*) _____: the moon or the earth?

3. In our town, December is very cold and windy. Sometimes, December is (*cold*) _____ January. Of all the months, August is (*hot*) _____ .

4. Which movies do you think are (*bad*) _____ for children: movies with violence or movies with bad language?

5. Mexico City is (*large*) _____ city in Mexico. It is also one of the world's (*populated*) _____ cities.

6. It's (*easy*) _____ to drive on State Street _____ on Park Avenue because there is less traffic.

7. Did you know that Greenland is (*big*) _____ island in the world?

8. The cheesecake was wonderful. It was one of (*delicious*) _____ cheesecakes I've ever eaten.

Part B *Directions:* Write sentences comparing the following circles. Use **big** or **small** where appropriate.

1. (*as . . . as*) _____

2. (*not as . . . as*) _____

3. (*different*) _____

4. (*the . . . -est*) _____

5. (*almost as . . . as*) _____

Part C *Directions:* Complete the sentences, using *in, of, as, to, from,* or Ø.

1. _____ all the tests we've taken, that was the most challenging.

2. White bread is not as healthy _____ whole wheat bread.

3. Who is the funniest student _____ your class?

4. I think Professor Brown's teaching methods are very different _____
   Professor Green's.

5. Mrs. Thompson thinks it's cute to dress her twins alike _____.

6. A lake is similar _____ a sea, but it is smaller.

7. The snow was not as good for sledding today _____ yesterday.

8. Henry is a fast worker, but he is the least dedicated _____ all the
   employees.

Part D *Directions:* Combine each pair of sentences. Use double comparatives (***the more** / **-er** . . .
the more** / **-er) and the words in *italics*.

1. Scott *read* many books on deep space. He got very *interested* in it.

   _____

2. Johnny made many *mistakes* on his homework. He became *upset*.

   _____

3. We hiked for a *long* time. I got *thirsty*.

   _____

4. Emily works *hard*. She earns a lot of *money*.

   _____

5. The water became *rough*. The children in the boat were *scared*.

   _____

Directions: Correct the errors.

1. Let's buy this chair. It's less expensive from that one.

2. My brother is smaller than mine.

3. Linda is in as same German class as I am.

4. I got enough sleep. I'm not as tired today than yesterday.

5. Those students are the most smartest kids in the class.

6. If you need farther assistance, please ask.

7. Please talk more quiet in the library.

8. Erin's stomachache got worser and worser as the day went on.

9. That was one of the best book I have ever read.

10. My homework isn't as difficult to yours.

CHAPTER 9 – TEST 2

Part A *Directions:* Complete the sentences with the comparative or superlative form of the words in parentheses.

1. I can read French (*good*) _____ I can speak it.

2. We learned today that light travels (*fast*) _____ sound.

3. The train trip took (*long*) _____ we expected, but it was very

   scenic. We saw some of (*lovely*) _____ sights we have ever seen.

4. Some artists prefer to paint with watercolors, but I think oils are (*pretty*)

   _____ and (*elegant*) _____ watercolors.

5. The (*big*) _____ lake in the world is the Caspian Sea.

6. Our debate topic for next month is (*bad*) " _____ person in

   history." I wish the teacher had assigned us (*famous*) " _____

   person in history."

7. How much (*far*) _____ do we have to drive? I'm getting

   hungry.

Part B *Directions:* Write sentences comparing the heights of the following trees. Use **tall** or **short** where appropriate.

```
     A          B          C          D          E
```

1. (*similar*) _____

2. (*just as . . . as*) _____

3. (*not quite as . . . as*) _____

4. (*-er . . . than*) _____

5. (*the same*) _____

Part C *Directions:* Complete the sentences, using *in, of, as, to, from,* or Ø.

1. A maple tree does not grow as tall _____ a redwood tree.

2. What is the coldest place _____ the world?

3. The public transportation system in this city is very different _____ the system in my country. My country has more subways and buses.

4. How are a duck and a goose alike _____?

5. _____ all the cities I've traveled to, Kuala Lumpur was definitely the hottest.

6. The artist who did this painting has a style similar _____ the artist in the gallery, but he is not as well known.

7. Michelle is the most talented manager _____ the company.

8. _____ the three children, Mary looks the most like her mother.

Part D *Directions:* Combine each pair of sentences. Use double comparatives (***the more** / **-er** ...* ***the more** / **-er***) and the words in *italics*.

1. The swimmer trained *hard* for the race. He felt *strong*.

   _____

2. My sister was *nervous*. She talked *fast*.

   _____

3. The baby was *hungry*. She *cried*.

   _____

4. Karen played the piano *loudly*. The dog *barked*.

   _____

5. The ideas came *fast*. The writer wrote many *pages*.

   _____

Part E *Directions:* Correct the errors.

1. These peas are delicious. I didn't know that fresh peas tasted so much better as frozen peas.

2. The flu can be a dangerous illness. It's very dangerous to have the flu than a cold.

3. Who has a more good life: a married person or a single person?

4. The clouds look dark. Let's hope it's not as rainy this afternoon that it was this morning.

5. The nine planets, Pluto is the smallest.

6. What has been a happyiest day in your life so far?

7. The kids yelled loudly and more loudly in the park.

8. A largest bird is the ostrich, but elephants are the largest land animals.

9. One of the strongest metal in the world is titanium.

10. My cell phone battery runs down more and more fast.

CHAPTER 10 The Passive

QUIZ 1 Active or Passive (Charts 10-1 and 10-2)

Directions: Decide if the sentence is active or passive. The first one is done for you.

	active	passive
1. William brought a big gift to the wedding.	✓	
2. My hair was cut by the hairdresser.		
3. The teacher is looking for errors on the test.		
4. The package was delivered by the mail carrier.		
5. Brandon posted a picture on his Web page.		
6. The cat has scratched the furniture.		
7. The flowers were eaten by deer.		
8. Emily was invited to the wedding.		
9. The movie was written by the director.		
10. The magician performs magic tricks at birthday parties.		
11. Millions of emails are sent around the world every day.		

QUIZ 2 Forms of the Passive (Charts 10-1 and 10-2)

Directions: Change the active verbs to passive by adding the correct form of the verb **be**.

Example: The boss is reading the report. The report _____*is being*_____ read by the boss.

1. Amy writes the report.

   The report _____ written by Amy.

2. The managers write reports.

   The reports _____ written by the managers.

3. Amy wrote the report.

   The report _____ written by Amy.

4. The managers wrote reports.

   The reports _____ written by the managers.

5. Amy has written the report.

   The report _____ written by Amy.

6. The managers have written reports.

   The reports _____ written by the managers.

7. Amy will write the report.

The report _____ written by Amy.

8. The managers will write reports.

The reports _____ written by the managers.

9. Amy is going to write the report.

The report _____ written by Amy.

10. The managers are going to write reports.

The reports _____ written by the managers.

Directions: Change the active verbs to the passive. Do not change the tense.

Example: The doctor examined the patient.
The patient _____*was examined*_____ by the doctor.

1. Rob drives Martha to school every day.

Every day Martha _____ to school by Rob.

2. The baseball player hit a homerun.

A homerun _____ by the baseball player.

3. The builder will fix our roof.

Our roof _____ by the builder.

4. The students clean the classrooms.

The classrooms _____ by the students.

5. The accountant has checked our tax forms.

Our tax forms _____ by the accountant.

6. Mr. Fernandez wrote two books about antiques.

Two books about antiques _____ by Mr. Fernandez.

7. Lucien ate the last piece of meat.

The last piece of meat _____ by Lucien.

8. Everyone enjoyed the parade.

The parade _____ by everyone.

9. Our gift is going to surprise you.

You _____ by our gift.

10. My boss signed the paperwork.

The paperwork _____ by my boss.

A. *Directions:* Choose the letter of the sentence that has the same meaning as the given sentence.

Example: The children were given some chocolate by their grandmother.
    a. The children gave their grandmother some chocolate.
    (b.) The grandmother gave the children some chocolate.

1. You will be told the news later.
    a. You will give someone the news.
    b. Someone will give you the news.

2. My sister was offered a new job by Mr. Crosby.
    a. My sister got a new job.
    b. Mr. Crosby got a new job.

3. The dog chased the cat by the fence.
    a. The cat was chased by the dog.
    b. The dog was chased by the fence.

4. The story has been read to the children several times.
    a. The children have read the story.
    b. Someone has read to the children.

5. Chef Daniel cooks the guests' meals by himself on Monday nights.
    a. The meals are cooked by Chef Daniel.
    b. Someone else cooks the guests' meals.

B. *Directions:* Change the sentences from passive to active. Keep the same verb tense.

Example: The email was sent by my father.
    My father sent the email.

1. Ice cream is enjoyed by children.

2. The book was discussed by the students.

3. The café's name has been changed by the new owners.

4. The game is going to be won by our team.

5. An award will be given to Mr. Reed by the city.

A. *Directions:* Change the sentences from active to passive.

SITUATION: At the Hospital

Example: The hospital will open a clinic.
_____*A clinic will be opened by the hospital.*_____

1. Volunteers greet hospital visitors.

   _____

2. Patients speak many different languages.

   _____

3. The nurse has given an injection.

   _____

4. The doctors discussed a new treatment.

   _____

5. The hospital provides excellent care.

   _____

B. *Directions:* Change the questions from active to passive.

SITUATION: Cleaning House

Example: Does your whole family clean the house?
_____*Is the house cleaned by your whole family?*_____

1. Does your mom usually clean the kitchen?

   _____

2. Are the kids going to clean the bedrooms?

   _____

3. Did Paul take out the trash?

   _____

4. Will Gary clean out the garage?

   _____

5. Has your mom given everyone a job?

   _____

Directions: Check (✓) *transitive* if the verb takes an object. Check (✓) *intransitive* if it doesn't. The first one is done for you.

	transitive	intransitive
1. Andy swam in the ocean.		✓
2. Julia met Antonio at the library.		
3. The lawyer considered the problem.		
4. The bus driver drove down the wrong street.		
5. The packages will arrive two weeks late.		
6. Gina eats eggs for breakfast every morning.		
7. Dick and Susan never agree with each other.		
8. The fish died after a week in the fish tank.		
9. The children broke the window with a ball.		
10. Mr. Park invited his parents to the theater.		
11. A storm hit the coast last night.		

Directions: Change the sentences to passive if possible. If not possible, write ***no change***.

Example: The wind blew my hat across the garden.
_____*My hat was blown across the garden by the wind.*_____

1. Jonathan was in a serious car accident last night.

_____

2. The plumber has finally fixed our sink.

_____

3. Pedro is going to leave before sunrise.

_____

4. We rode in a limousine to our wedding.

_____

5. Our neighbors will sell their car next month.

_____

6. Mr. LeBarre usually washes the dinner dishes.

_____

7. The Tangs stayed at a friend's summer house last month.

_____

8. Voicemail has recorded the message.

_____

9. Val returned the scratched DVD to the store.

_____

10. Ivan is waiting for the bus.

_____

QUIZ 8 Using the *By*-Phrase (Chart 10-4)

Directions: Change the sentences from active to passive. Use the *by*-phrase only as necessary.

Examples: Someone left his jacket on the bus.
_____*A jacket was left on the bus.*_____
Millions of people watched the Olympics on TV.
_____*The Olympics were watched on TV by millions of people.*_____

1. Someone gave me this sweater.

_____

2. Larry Page and Sergey Brin created Google.

_____

3. People check out books at a library.

_____

4. Has anyone ever lied to you?

_____

5. Picasso painted the picture.

_____

6. Someone will paint these walls tomorrow.

_____

7. The police chased the speeding car.

_____

8. When did someone first use cell phones?

_____

9. People speak French and English in Canada.

_____

10. The referee has stopped the basketball game.

_____

Directions: Complete the sentences by changing the active modals to passive.

Example: You shouldn't overcook vegetables.
Vegetables _____*shouldn't be overcooked*_____ .

1. You can reach me by phone.

   I _____ by phone.

2. Someone has to pick up Ali now.

   Ali _____ now.

3. You shouldn't eat these berries.

   These berries _____ .

4. You ought to send that letter by express mail.

   The letter _____ by express mail.

5. We have to change the date for our wedding.

   The date for our wedding _____ .

6. Someone should recycle this old TV.

   This old TV _____ .

7. If you leave the doors unlocked, someone could steal your car.

   If you leave the doors unlocked, your car _____ .

8. You must tell your parents about the accident.

   Your parents _____ about the accident.

9. Lightning might start a fire in the forest.

   A fire in the forest _____ by lightning.

10. I think we may reach an agreement today.

    I think an agreement _____ today.

Review: Passive vs. Active (Charts 10-1 → 10-5)

Directions: Choose the correct answers.

Example: My brother (*has chosen,* (*has been chosen*)) captain of the debate team.

1. Our electric bill (*has to pay, has to be paid*) today.

2. Your dog (*has eaten, has been eaten*) all of the baby's snack.

3. Shahin (*called, was called*) his uncle by mistake. He got the wrong number.

4. Look at our dirty windows! They (*should wash, should be washed*).

5. Pierre's birthday party (*will hold, will be held*) at Celebration Park.

6. Dr. Jones (*can contact, can be contacted*) at his office after the holidays.

7. Our apartment (*painted, was painted*) over the weekend.

8. The Smith's summer cabin (*built, was built*) with logs from their property.

9. I (*turned off, was turned off*) your computer.

10. The community (*must tell, must be told*) about the robberies.

Using Past Participles as Adjectives (Chart 10-6)

Directions: Complete each sentence with an appropriate preposition. More than one answer is possible.

SITUATION: Two Students

Example: Eduardo and Carlos are related ___*to*___ each other. They are cousins.

Eduardo doesn't like school. He is . . .

1. bored _____ his classes.

2. disappointed _____ his teachers.

3. never finished _____ his homework.

4. not involved _____ class projects.

5. tired _____ studying.

Carlos loves being a student. He is . . .

6. excited _____ his classes.

7. interested _____ learning.

8. always prepared _____ tests.

9. devoted _____ his studies.

10. satisfied _____ his grades.

Directions: Complete the sentences with the given words. Use the passive form and simple present or simple past. Include prepositions where necessary.

Example: excite   We _____are excited about_____ our new jobs. They begin next week.

1. engage   Angela is so happy. She _____ Yuri.

2. worry   When Elena got on the bus, she _____ being late for work.

3. scare   Why is the little girl crying? _____ she _____ the dark?

4. exhaust   The children _____ soccer and basketball practice yesterday.

5. qualify   Ibrahim _____ the job. I'm sure they will hire him.

6. relate   You look like Mr. Shiosaki. _____ you _____ him?

7. crowd   The stadium _____ fans. We couldn't find a good seat.

8. divorce   Julie _____ Fred. They haven't been together for two years.

9. compose   Canada _____ ten provinces and three territories.

10. oppose   Most people _____ higher taxes.

QUIZ 13 **Participial Adjectives: *-ed* vs. *-ing*** (Chart 10-7)

Directions: Complete the sentences with the appropriate *-ed* or *-ing* form of the words in *italics*.

Example: Adam doesn't understand the problem. It *confuses* him.
        The problem is _____confusing_____.

1. Camila watched the news. It *surprised* her.
   a. Camila was _____.
   b. The news was _____.

2. Hansa tore his pants. It *embarrassed* him.
   a. It was an _____ situation.
   b. Hansa was _____.

3. I work in a bank. The work *interests* me.
   a. It is _____ work.
   b. I am _____ in the work.
   c. The work is _____.

4. The team won the game 60 to 0. The score still *amazes* the players.
   a. The score was _____.
   b. The players are _____.
   c. It was an _____ score.

Directions: Choose the correct adjectives.

Example: Babies are (*interested*, *interesting*) in black and white objects.

1. It's very stormy outside. The children are (*frightened, frightening*) by the wind and the thunder. The noise of the storm is (*frightened, frightening*) to them.

2. Mr. Peters gave a powerful speech. The audience was (*fascinated, fascinating*) by his vision for the future.

3. Going to the dentist is (*scary, scared*) for a lot of people, but I am not usually (*scary, scared*). However, I never feel completely (*relaxed, relaxing*) at the dentist.

4. Jason's ride on the giant roller coaster was (*terrified, terrifying*). He was (*surprised, surprising*) that he didn't get sick.

5. Watching a group of gorillas is (*interesting, interested*). They seem to have a lot of actions similar to humans. I am very (*interested, interesting*) in learning more about them.

QUIZ 15 *Get* + Adjective; *Get* + Past Participle (Chart 10-8)

Directions: Complete the sentences with the appropriate forms of **get** and the words from the list.

arrest	dark	hungry	lost	rich	sunburn
confuse	fat	✓invite	nervous	serious	

Example: The Schallers are having a party. Did you _____*get invited*_____?

1. Every time the teacher explains a new problem, I _____. He needs to be clearer.

2. It took Sandy two hours to find our house. She said she _____ and had to ask for directions.

3. If you have chips and pop for breakfast every day, you will probably

   _____.

4. Before Mahmut gives a speech, he always _____. His hands shake, and his mouth gets dry.

5. It's _____ now, and soon it'll be bedtime.

6. Marcel wants to earn a lot of money and _____. He'll have to work hard.

7. Please put on some sunscreen. The last time you were in the sun, you

   _____.

8. You just had breakfast, and now you want a snack? You sure _____
quickly!

9. This situation isn't funny. We need to _____ and think of a solution.

10. The neighbor's son _____ last night for driving a stolen car.

QUIZ 16 *Be Used To/Accustomed To/Used To* (Charts 10-9 and 10-10)

A. *Directions:* Complete each sentence with the appropriate form of *be used to*, affirmative or negative.

Example: I live in Oslo. I _____ *am used to* _____ snowy winters.

1. Antonio's mom uses lots of jalapeño peppers. He _____ eating spicy food.

2. Lucia lived in Florida for years. Back then, she _____ cold weather.

3. I am usually on time for meetings. I _____ being late.

4. The Ingrahms had many Italian-speaking neighbors. They _____ hearing Italian.

5. We usually get up early. We _____ sleeping until noon.

B. *Directions:* Check (✓) the sentences that contain a completed activity or situation. The first one is done for you.

1. _✓_ I used to live by myself.

2. ____ I am used to living by myself.

3. ____ People here are used to a lot of snow.

4. ____ It used to snow more in the winter.

5. ____ Are you accustomed to the snow?

6. ____ Where did you use to live?

Directions: Complete the sentences with *used to* or the correct form of *be used to* and the verbs in parentheses.

Example: I (*live*) _____ used to live _____ in Berlin, but now I live in Munich.

1. I love learning about other cultures. When I was younger, I (*travel*) _____

   _____ a lot. When I traveled, I (*spend*) _____

   time in small cities rather than busy tourist areas.

2. My husband and I often cook ethnic foods, so we (*eat*) _____

   unusual dishes.

3. A: Where (*you, live*) _____ before you moved here?
   B: I lived in Alaska.
   A: Really? That's really different from here. (*you, live*) _____
      here now?
   B. Not really. I miss the mountains.

4. Bryan has to travel a lot for his job. He (*be*) _____ away

   from   home several times a year.

5. A: What (*your husband, do*) _____ before he became
      president of the company?
   B: He (*work*) _____ as an account executive.

6. This town (*have*) _____ lots of trees and parks, but now it

   is mostly new houses and apartments. I liked it better when it had more trees. I (*be, not*)

   _____ all this growth.

A. Directions: Make sentences with similar meanings as the given sentences. Use the correct form of *be supposed to.*

Example: The hospital expects doctors to work weekends once a month.
    <u>*Doctors are supposed to work weekends once a month*</u> .

1. The school director expects students to wear uniforms.

    _____ .

2. The phone company expects customers to pay their bills on time.

    _____ .

3. Mom told us to be on time, but we weren't. We were late.

    _____ .

4. The restaurant says customers are not expected to leave tips for service.

    _____ .

5. The weather reporter expected it to snow last night.

    _____ .

B. Directions: Check (✓) the incorrect sentences and correct them. The first one is done for you.

                    is
1. __✓__ It$_\wedge$ supposed to snow tonight.

2. _____ Drivers are suppose to drive more slowly in rainy weather.

3. _____ The new grocery store is supposed to open next week.

4. _____ You not supposed to wear shoes in the house.

5. _____ What we are supposed to do about Graciela's situation?

6. _____ Didn't you supposed to go to school early today?

Directions: Choose the correct answers.

Example: A: Where is my piece of cake?
          B: Sorry. It _____ by the dog.
          a. eating   c. ate
          (b.) got eaten   d. is eating

1. A: Are you enjoying your time in Paris?
   B: Yes, but I _____ the time change yet.
              a. wasn't used to   c. am not used to
              b. didn't use to   d. am not get used to

2. A: How was the lecture at the museum?
   B: It was terrible! I was really ____.
   - a. boring
   - b. born
   - c. boredom
   - d. bored

3. A: Where is your hometown?
   B: It ____ on the coast.
   - a. is located
   - b. located
   - c. locates
   - d. is being located

4. A: Your face is really red.
   B: I stayed in the sun so long yesterday that I ____.
   - a. was sunburn
   - b. got sunburned
   - c. was get sunburn
   - d. sunburned

5. A: Why is Martina so happy?
   B: She just ____ Nicolo.
   - a. got engaged to
   - b. got engaged with
   - c. gets engaged with
   - d. was gotten engaged to

6. A: Where's your motorcycle?
   B: At the repair shop. They ____ it.
   - a. are repaired
   - b. was repairing
   - c. are repairing
   - d. repairing

7. A: Why don't you use fresh vegetables in your cooking?
   B: I really can't tell the difference between fresh and ____ vegetables.
   - a. froze
   - b. freezing
   - c. freeze
   - d. frozen

8. A. You look like you're in hurry.
   B. I am. This project ____ done by 5:00 P.M.
   - a. has to been
   - b. will to be
   - c. has to be
   - d. must to being

9. A. Why are the police here?
   B. A car accident ____ a few minutes ago.
   - a. is happened
   - b. was happened
   - c. happens
   - d. happened

10. A. Do you want to go on a picnic?
    B. I don't think so. It ____ rain this afternoon.
    - a. is supposed
    - b. is supposed to
    - c. be supposed to
    - d. is suppose to

CHAPTER 10 – TEST 1

Part A *Directions:* Complete the sentences with the correct forms (active or passive) of the verbs in parentheses.

SITUATION: At the Pool

I. Yesterday, at the swimming pool, a young boy who didn't know how to swim (*jump*)

_____ into the deep water. He (*begin*) _____ to
  ___1___   ___2___

splash and yell when he couldn't swim to the side of the pool. He (*save*)

_____ from drowning by a lifeguard at the pool. It's lucky that he
  ___3___

(*see*) _____ by her.
              ___4___

SITUATION: A Town Hall Meeting

II. Last night at the town meeting, there (*be*) _____ a very interesting
                                                                           ___5___

discussion. People (*ask*) _____ by community leaders to discuss
                                          ___6___

several issues, but the community (*want*) _____ to discuss only one
                                                                  ___7___

issue: a huge new shopping center. Business people in the audience (*argue*)

_____ that it would bring jobs to the town. Most other people (*say*)
  ___8___

_____ it would destroy the small-town feeling of the community. The
  ___9___

discussion (*become*) _____ tense. It was clear that more time (*need*)
                                      ___10___

_____ in the future for discussion of the issue.
  ___11___

Part B *Directions:* Circle the correct answers.

1. A: What happened to the roof of your car?
   B: It _____ in the windstorm.
      a. damaged
      b. got damaged
      c. been damaged
      d. has damaged

2. A: The baby is so tired. She can hardly keep her eyes open.
   B: She _____ to bed as soon as possible.
      a. should put
      b. got put
      c. was put
      d. should be put

3. A: When does the wedding dinner begin?
   B: Dinner _____ at 7:00 P.M.
      a. served
      b. will be served
      c. will be serving
      d. is serving

4. A: My patient _____ in Room 303.
   B: Doctor, he was moved to the second floor.
      a. is supposed to be
      b. supposed to
      c. is suppose to be
      d. was suppose to be

5. A: This sculpture is beautiful.
   B: Thank you. It _____ by one of our student artists.
      a. was making
      b. is made
      c. was made
      d. has made

6. A: How do you like college?
   B: I like living in the dorm, but I _____ the food.
      a. am not use
      b. am not used to
      c. didn't used to
      d. didn't use to

Part C *Directions:* Circle the correct adjective.

1. A: That haunted house was (*thrilled, thrilling*)! Let's go again.
   B: You can go, but not me. It was too (*scared, scary*) for me. I was really (*frightened, frightening*).

2. A: I am (*disappointed, disappointing*) that the neighborhood library will close soon.
   B: Yes, that was (*surprised, surprising*) news. It's too bad they couldn't find the money to stay open. It's (*confused, confusing*) because government leaders can find money for other things, but not for the library.

1. Ben and Rachel were get engaged last month.

2. The government is opposed against lower taxes.

3. I heard my name. Who was called me?

4. Dogs in the park supposed be on a leash.

5. Your fax was come a few minutes ago. Should I get it for you?

6. Our apartment must clean before the party next week.

7. I used to running, but now I walk for exercise.

8. The fish isn't ready yet. It should be to cook a little longer.

9. We enjoyed our time in Malaysia, but we exhaust from the heat.

10. Jorge can skateboard for hours before he get tiring.

CHAPTER 10 – TEST 2

Part A *Directions:* Complete the sentences with the correct forms (active or passive) of the verbs in parentheses. More than one answer is possible.

Last night when I (*return*) _____ from my business trip, I was
1

pleasantly surprised. My husband (*decide*) _____ to present me
2

with a "welcome home" gift. The entire house (*clean*) _____.
3

The windows (*wash*) _____, the furniture (*dust*)
4

_____, and the floors (*polish*) _____.
5   6

The house had never looked so beautiful. I (*thank*) _____ him
7

for doing such a wonderful job. For a minute he (*look*) _____
8

embarrassed, and then he finally (*say*) _____: "Honey, everything
9

(*do*) _____ by a cleaning company. But I (*get*)
10

_____ a great discount!"
11

Part B *Directions:* Circle the correct answers.

1. A: Did you make your sweater?
   B: It _____ by hand, and a friend gave it to me.
   - a. made
   - b. was making
   - c. is made
   - d. was made

2. A: Did Roberto quit his job?
   B: I _____ that he took a long vacation.
   - a. telling
   - b. was told
   - c. have told
   - d. tell

3. A: When can I pick up the car?
   B. It _____ by tomorrow afternoon.
   - a. should be fixed
   - b. should fix
   - c. should have fixed
   - d. should be fixing

4. A: The weather certainly is cold here.
   B: I don't think I'll ever _____ it.
   - a. am used to
   - b. be use to
   - c. get used to
   - d. got used to

5. A: Why is there such a long line of people?
   B: All passengers _____ before boarding their airplane.
   - a. must check
   - b. must have checked
   - c. must be checking
   - d. must be checked

6. A. Who are you waiting for?
   B: My mom _____ pick me up in a few minutes.
   - a. is supposed to
   - b. will supposed to
   - c. supposed to
   - d. supposes to

Part C *Directions:* Circle the correct adjectives.

1. A: How was the movie?

   B: I was (*disappointed, disappointing*). It was supposed to have new special effects, but they weren't new. They were just (*bored, boring*).

   A: That's too bad. Would you like to try another movie tonight? I hear *Chaos* is pretty good.

   B: Let's give it a try. I'd like to see an (*excited, exciting*) movie.

2. A: I read a (*disturbed, disturbing*) article about the environment yesterday. It says that the earth is getting warmer and the environment is changing.

   B: I know the one you're talking about. I felt pretty (*depressed, depressing*) after reading it. Scientists believe the polar ice cap is melting, and oceans could rise. It's kind of (*alarmed, alarming*) to think about.

   A: We all need to change our habits to preserve the environment.

Part D *Directions:* Correct the errors.

1. The Jeffersons have been married with each other for fifty years.

2. My new boss is very interesting from my work experience.

3. My husband and I used to living on a houseboat. Now we rent an apartment downtown.

4. Dr. Barry was arrived two hours late and missed the meeting.

5. Where were you go after the movie? I couldn't find you.

6. The dog began to cross the highway, but there were so many cars that he get scare.

7. Thierry is from the French Riviera. He isn't used to live in the mountains.

8. The children are very excited for going to the aquarium.

9. Rita's wedding is today. She getting very nervous.

10. What time is the play supposed to be start?

Count/Noncount Nouns and Articles

QUIZ 1 *A* vs. *An* (Chart 11-1)

Directions: Choose the correct article: *a* or *an*. The first one is done for you.

SITUATION: Things You See in a Park

1.	a	(an)	excited child
2.	a	an	jogger
3.	a	an	interesting fountain
4.	a	an	playground
5.	a	an	bench
6.	a	an	ice cream stand
7.	a	an	bike path
8.	a	an	historic monument
9.	a	an	unusual insect
10.	a	an	lovely flower garden
11.	a	an	unique bird

QUIZ 2 *A / An* vs. *Some* (Charts 11-2 and 11-3)

Directions: Complete the phrases with *a, an,* or *some*. The first one is done for you.

SITUATION: In the Attic

Lindsay and Lee cleaned out their attic. They found a lot of stuff! They found . . .

1. _____*some*_____ dishes
2. _____ antique lamp
3. _____ old clothes
4. _____ photo album
5. _____ costume jewelry
6. _____ tennis racquets
7. _____ ugly chair
8. _____ exercise equipment
9. _____ bicycle
10. _____ ladder
11. _____ old carpet

Count and Noncount Nouns (Charts 11-2 → 11-4)

Directions: Add **-s** if necessary. Otherwise, write Ø.

Example: We need more chalk __Ø__. All the pieces are too small to use.

1. Could you mail the letter _____ on the table? They need to go out today.

2. I hope you make a lot of progress _____ on your project.

3. I don't have enough time _____ to eat breakfast. I usually just have coffee _____.

4. Winter day _____ are short. Darkness _____ comes early during the winter months.

5. I accidentally put the butter _____ in the freezer. It's completely frozen.

6. Micah has a lot of homework _____ tonight. He has assignment _____ in math, social studies, and Japanese.

7. Every anniversary, Giorgio gives his wife an expensive gift. She loves jewelry _____, but ring _____ are her favorite.

8. The lawyer asked to present several new fact _____ to the judge. He had some important information _____ about his client.

9. Knowledge _____ comes with experience.

10. It's going to rain. There are a lot of cloud _____, and it's getting dark.

QUIZ 4 *Much / Many* (Charts 11-1 → 11-5)

Directions: Complete the questions with **much** or **many**. Make the nouns plural as necessary. The first one is done for you.

SITUATION: On the Internet

1. How (much, (many)) Web site __s__ does Shelley visit?

2. How (much, many) time _____ does she spend online?

3. How (much, many) information _____ does Shelley search for?

4. How (much, many) friend _____ does she have online?

5. How (much, many) email _____ does she get?

6. How (much, many) experience _____ does Shelley have with online shopping?

7. How (much, many) money _____ does she spend on music?

8. How (much, many) game _____ does she play?

9. How (much, many) book _____ has she read online?

10. How (much, many) photo _____ of Shelley are there online?

11. How (much, many) knowledge _____ does she gain?

Directions: Complete the sentences by using *a few* or *a little* and the given nouns. Make the nouns plural as necessary.

Example: vegetable   We planted _____*a few vegetables*_____ in our garden.

1. traffic   There's _____ on the road, but it's not bad.

2. money   I gave the kids _____ to go to the movies.

3. meat   There's _____ left from dinner.

4. apple   Could you pick up _____ at the store? I need about three or four.

5. suggestion   The teacher gave her students _____ for writing topics.

6. pepper   This soup needs _____, and then it will be ready.

7. dirt   I'm sorry. I got _____ on your carpet.

8. milk   Would you like _____?

9. coin   Here are _____ old _____ for your collection. They're from the 1940s.

10. egg   I'm not very hungry. I'll just have _____ for dinner. Two should be enough.

Directions: Choose the correct words for the given nouns. More than one word may be correct.

Example: several   many   (a little)   **rain**

1. a few   much   several   **people**

2. much   many   a little   **fun**

3. some   much   a lot of   **tests**

4. several   some   many   **pollution**

5. a few   a little   a lot of   **help**

6. much   a lot of   a little   **knowledge**

7. many   several   some   **postcards**

8. several   a few   a little   **insects**

9. some   much   a little   **paint**

10. much   a few   some   **vocabulary**

QUIZ 7 Nouns That Can Be Count or Noncount (Chart 11-6)

Directions: Choose the correct answers.

Example: I had many wonderful (*experience,* (*experiences*)) living in Europe.

1. Who would like (*coffee, coffees*)? I just made a fresh pot.

2. We've had (*chicken, chickens*) every night for dinner this week. Let's have something different tonight.

3. The hotel provides (*iron, irons*) for guests who need to press their clothes.

4. Professor Chang spends a lot of (*time, times*) with his students outside of class.

5. There's a lot of (*light, lights*) in this house because there are so many windows.

6. Emma has colored her (*hair, hairs*) so often that it's starting to fall out.

7. Dennis should try wearing contact lenses for a while. He's always losing his (*glass, glasses*).

8. We need to get (*a paper, some paper*) to wrap these birthday gifts.

9. The museum exhibit has several (*work, works*) of art by Monet.

10. Professor Reed assigns a lot of (*paper, papers*) for his students to write.

QUIZ 8 Units of Measure with Noncount Nouns (Chart 11-7)

Directions: Complete each phrase with a unit of measure from the list. More than one answer is possible. The first one is done for you.

bag bottle box can jar	bowl cup glass piece slice

At the store, I bought . . .

1. a _____*can*_____ of tuna fish

2. a _____ of crackers

3. a _____ of juice

4. a _____ of honey

5. a _____ of soup

6. a _____ of rice

For a snack, I had . . .

7. a _____ of ice cream

8. a _____ of toast

9. a _____ of juice

10. a _____ of cheese

11. a _____ of tea

Directions: Complete the conversations. Use *the* or *a*.

Example: A: I'm very cold.
　　　　　B: I have __*a*__ sweater you can put on.

1. SITUATION: In a Restaurant
    A: May I take your order?
    B: Yes. I'd like _____ tuna sandwich, please.
    A: OK. What would you like to drink?
    B: I'll just have _____ glass of water.

2. SITUATION: New in Town
    A: Excuse me, I'm looking for _____ post office. I need to mail _____ package.
    B: It's right over there, across from _____ library.
    A: Thanks. And can you tell me where there's _____ dry cleaners?
    B: Sure. There's one about two blocks that way.

3. SITUATION: Coworkers
    A: Can you give me _____ ride home after work today?
    B: Sorry, I didn't drive today. I'm taking _____ bus downtown.
    A: I guess I'll ask Bill.

4. SITUATION: At Home
    A: Where's _____ newspaper? I haven't read it yet.
    B: It's on _____ kitchen table.

Directions: Check (✓) the sentences that make general statements. The first one is done for you.

1. __✓__ Insects have six legs.

2. _____ A lion is a dangerous animal.

3. _____ The book I am reading is exciting.

4. _____ Some plants blossom every year.

5. _____ Sports equipment can be expensive.

6. _____ The lemons in the basket are from my lemon tree.

7. _____ An elephant cannot jump.

8. _____ Some people are online every day.

9. _____ The new cell phone I got is very easy to use.

10. _____ An email from a loved one is always welcome.

11. _____ I saw the new *Sam Spion* movie last night.

Directions: Complete the sentences with the given nouns. Use *the* for specific statements. Do not use *the* for general statements.

Examples: flowers a. ___*Flowers*___ are a romantic gift.

b. ___*The flowers*___ in my garden are colorful.

1. sunglasses a. _____ for sale at that store are too expensive.
   b. I have to wear _____ to protect my eyes.

2. bread a. My family loves fresh _____ for breakfast.
   b. _____ my mom bakes is delicious!

3. furniture a. I don't like that apartment. _____ is old and dirty.
   b. They need to buy _____ for their living room.

4. children a. It's good for _____ to get a lot of exercise.
   b. What a nice family! _____ are very polite.

5. vocabulary a. _____ is basic to learning any language.
   b. I don't understand this story. _____ is too difficult.

Directions: Complete the sentences with *the* or Ø.

Example: ___*The*___ DVDs you got from the library last week should be returned soon.

1. Sue prefers _____ chicken to _____ fish.

2. Our water has a lot of chlorine in it. _____ water at your house tastes much better.

3. _____ bats are active at night and sleep during the day.

4. Andrew needs to change jobs. _____ work he is doing now isn't challenging.

5. I went to that new Italian restaurant last night. _____ food was very good.

6. When _____ cars were first used, they were called "horseless carriages."

7. _____ car parked behind my car is blocking my way. I need to find _____ owner.

8. _____ dolphins breathe through air holes on top of their heads.

Directions: Complete the sentences with *the* or *a*. The first one is done for you.

Yesterday, I decided to buy __a__ digital camera as ____ birthday present for my husband.
                                                                    1   2

I went to ____ store at the mall and ____ really kind salesperson helped me choose one.
                  3   4

____ camera was expensive, so I hoped my husband would be pleased with ____ present I
  5   6

had chosen. He was thrilled until he tried ____ camera and it didn't work. We went back to
                                             7

____ store to return it. Both of us felt embarrassed, however, when the salesperson showed us
  8

that we had forgotten to put in AA batteries. He gave us ____ batteries free of charge and
                                                    9

told us to have fun. We took ____ picture of ____ salesperson and told him we would. I
                          10   11

think my husband is going to enjoy taking pictures!

Directions: Complete the sentences with *a, the,* or Ø.

Example: _____The_____ air smells fresh today.

1. I prefer sleeping on ____ firm mattress.

2. Jason doesn't like ____ pickles.

3. ____ nurses need to study science.

4. It looks like ____ fruit in the bowl is spoiled.

5. Does email really help us save ____ time?

6. ____ chairs in our classroom are uncomfortable.

7. Do you have ____ pen I can borrow?

8. Does ____ success always come with hard work?

9. ____ black bear usually sleeps during the winter months.

10. Where is ____ police station?

Directions: Choose the correct completions.

Example: We plan to vacation in (*the*,(Ø)) New Zealand, but we'll visit relatives in ((*the*), Ø) Philippines first.

1. Earthquakes are common on islands in (*the*, Ø) Pacific.

2. Joel wants to climb (*the*, Ø) Mt. Kilimanjaro. He tried it last year, but failed to make it to the top.

3. Bashir and Natalya are on a two-week trip to (*the*, Ø) Europe.

4. Husam would like to visit (*the*, Ø) Abu Dhabi in (*the*, Ø) United Arab Emirates after he finishes his work in (*the*, Ø) Egypt.

5. (*The*, Ø) Caspian Sea is in (*the*, Ø) Russia.

6. I grew up in a small town in (*the*, Ø) Rocky Mountains.

7. (*The*, Ø) Professor Cloke is replacing (*the*, Ø) Dr. Roverso for the rest of the term.

8. (*The*, Ø) North America consists of (*the*, Ø) Mexico, (*the*, Ø) United States, and (*the*, Ø) Canada.

Directions: Add capital letters where necessary.

                    N   Y   A
Example: ~~n~~ew ~~y~~ears is the most important holiday in many ~~a~~sian countries.

1. theresa can't decide whether to study japanese or chinese.

2. where are you going for the summer break?

3. the alps are in switzerland, austria, and france.

4. we're reading shakespeare's *romeo and juliet* for our literature class.

5. the directions say to turn on fifth street, but this is park avenue.

6. last monday was my first day as a student at stanford university.

7. the mississippi river flows into the gulf of mexico.

8. i was supposed to be born in april, but i was a month late, so my birthday is in may.

9. which instructor do you prefer: dr. costa or professor pierce?

10. math 241 is a very high-level math class.

Directions: Choose the correct completions. The first one is done for you.

1. There are different ideas about how _____ became extinct.
   a. dinosaur
   b. a dinosaurs
   (c.) dinosaurs
   d. the dinosaurs

2. How _____ do you want, a half or a full glass?
   a. many milk
   b. much milk
   c. much milks
   d. many milks

3. I found _____ about the history of my country at the library.
   a. a little information
   b. a few information
   c. a few informations
   d. a little informations

4. Visiting the rainforest in Brazil is _____ experience.
   a. a unique
   b. unique
   c. an unique
   d. the unique

5. I have _____ to give away to charity.
   a. lots of stuffs
   b. a lot of stuffs
   c. lot of stuff
   d. a lot of stuff

6. _____ people attended the movie preview. There were no empty seats.
   a. Many
   b. A few
   c. A little
   d. Much

7. Mrs. Kim drinks _____ of hot tea with breakfast every morning.
   a. a jar
   b. a cup
   c. a can
   d. a bottle

8. I need to study _____ new vocabulary this weekend.
   a. several
   b. a
   c. some
   d. many

9. Sammy ate two _____ of chocolate ice cream.
   a. bowl
   b. bowls
   c. piece
   d. pieces

10. My parents usually give me good _____.
    a. advices
    b. informations
    c. suggestion
    d. advice

11. Busy parents sometimes don't have enough _____ with their children.
    a. time
    b. the time
    c. times
    d. the times

CHAPTER 11 – TEST 1

Part A *Directions:* Circle the correct answers.

1. I broke _____ and had to replace them.
   - a. several dishes
   - b. a little dishes
   - c. one dishes
   - d. much dish

2. We only have _____ left. I need to buy some more.
   - a. a few flours
   - b. much flour
   - c. a little flour
   - d. many flours

3. How _____ do you have for the weekend?
   - a. many homeworks
   - b. much homeworks
   - c. much homework
   - d. many homework

4. What _____! It's cooked just right.
   - a. delicious fish
   - b. delicious fishes
   - c. a delicious fishes
   - d. an delicious fish

5. Can I offer you a _____ of warm homemade bread?
   - a. glass
   - b. slice
   - c. pieces
   - d. cup

6. Mario's mother gave him _____ to buy ice cream.
   - a. a little dollars
   - b. a few dollars
   - c. few dollars
   - d. little dollars

7. I need two _____ of yellow paint for the kitchen.
   - a. jars
   - b. glasses
   - c. bottles
   - d. cans

8. Caitlin got _____ at the library.
   - a. a lot of book
   - b. lot of books
   - c. a lots of books
   - d. a lot of books

9. _____ is a quality of the heart and the human spirit.
   - a. Beauties
   - b. Beauty
   - c. A beauty
   - d. The beauty

10. _____ of other people often causes conflict in the world.
    - a. Ignorances
    - b. Some ignorances
    - c. Ignorance
    - d. Several ignorance

Part B *Directions:* Add capital letters where necessary.

1. the lake is too cold for swimming. how about going to the indoor pool at mountain view park?

2. our anatomy class will be taught by dr. jones. he's a professor, not a medical doctor.

3. maria's parents are from mexico. she speaks spanish fluently.

4. the university plans to tear down brown hall and build a new library.

5. would you be interested in going on a boat trip down the colorado river? we would see part of the grand canyon.

Part C *Directions:* Complete the sentences with *a, an, the,* or Ø.

1. Is there _____ bank near here?

2. _____ Dr. Powell called. She wants to discuss _____ results from your heart tests.

3. I hear _____ noise. Is there _____ animal outside?

4. _____ woman in the red hat has _____ question.

5. The Bakers have _____ daughter and _____ son. _____ son is away at college, but _____ daughter still lives at home.

6. Quick! Open _____ door. I'm going to drop this heavy box.

7. As I get older, I'm less excited about _____ birthdays.

8. Every day there are hundreds of _____ earthquakes around _____ world.

9. _____ Mt. Kilauea is _____ active volcano in _____ Hawaii.

10. Look at _____ fog! I can hardly see _____ road.

Part D *Directions:* Correct the errors.

1. Let's get a drink of water. I'm a thirsty.

2. A scenery in the mountains is beautiful.

3. Your hair looks great. Did you get haircut?

4. For breakfast, Thomas ordered two toasts and eggs.

5. Here's a map of United States. Do you see California?

6. I need a few more time to finish my test.

7. There are no fishes in the Dead Sea.

8. We heard that Aunt Betsy and Uncle Wes are moving to the London next month.

9. I need to have my a car checked soon.

10. Much student at Shorewood High School study Japanese.

CHAPTER 11 – TEST 2

Part A *Directions:* Circle the correct answers.

1. _____ with computer programming is necessary for this job.
   - a. Experiences
   - b. Experience
   - c. An experience
   - d. Some experiences

2. The weather forecast said there wouldn't be _____ thunder, but it was quite loud last night.
   - a. A few
   - b. several
   - c. many
   - d. much

3. Here's a _____ of hot chicken soup. It should help you feel better.
   - a. bottle
   - b. bag
   - c. cup
   - d. box

4. Dr. Rodriguez tried to give her patient _____, but she wouldn't listen.
   - a. some advices
   - b. an advice
   - c. a little advice
   - d. many advices

5. Professor Johnson encourages his students to ask _____.
   - a. questions
   - b. lot of questions
   - c. some question
   - d. several question

6. There's only _____ in our garden, so plants don't grow well.
   - a. a little sunlight
   - b. a few sunlight
   - c. a few sunlights
   - d. a little sunlights

7. Many doctors believe _____ can help an ill person heal more quickly.
   - a. the laughter
   - b. many laughters
   - c. several laughters
   - d. laughter

8. The store was almost sold out of toys. There weren't _____ left.
   - a. many
   - b. much
   - c. one
   - d. a little

9. I'm thirsty. _____ would be nice.
   - a. A glass of water
   - b. Glass of water
   - c. Glasses of waters
   - d. Some glass of water

10. _____ can come from simple pleasures in life, such as watching a sunset.
    - a. Many happinesses
    - b. Much happiness
    - c. Much happinesses
    - d. Many happiness

Part B *Directions:* Add capital letters where necessary.

1. the assignment for our literature class is to read the first chapter of shakespeare's *hamlet*.

2. i heard that my neighbors, tariq and ali, plan to visit england in may.

3. tomorrow there will be a concert at washington park, near broadway avenue. a music group from south africa will be playing.

4. there is a miami university in ohio, but miami is in florida. isn't that strange?

5. when did william begin working for the sony corporation?

Part C *Directions:* Complete the sentences with *a, an, the,* or Ø.

1. Monday is ____ holiday for ____ students and ____ government employees.

2. Oops. It looks like our waiter made ____ mistake on our bill.

3. What's ____ difference between ____ hotel and ____ motel?

4. ____ cost of gasoline could rise this summer.

5. ____ fish need ____ oxygen to breathe.

6. It can be dangerous for climbers to climb ____ mountains in ____ warm weather.

7. What brings more happiness: ____ health or ____ wealth?

8. We're lost. Let's stop at a store and get ____ map. I'm sure ____ map will have the street we're looking for.

9. We painted ____ walls of our apartment. Now we need to finish ____ ceiling.

10. ____ vitamins in this bottle have ____ iron. The others don't.

Part D *Directions:* Correct the errors.

1. I don't need a help now, but I will later on.

2. There are a little people at work who would prefer not to work with Alan.

3. The water is necessary for survival.

4. I married my a brother's best friend from college.

5. Antoine reached the top of the Mt. McKinley in Alaska yesterday.

6. Some friends bicycled through Sahara Desert last summer.

7. Nick worked on his car for a hour before he realized it needed expensive repairs.

8. Honolulu is in the Hawaii, but it is not on the island of Hawaii. It is on Oahu.

9. Carlos tried to reach his parents several time, but their phone wasn't working.

10. Adrianna has so much a homework that she doesn't know where to start.

CHAPTER 12   Adjective Clauses

QUIZ 1   Using *Who* and *That* to Describe People   (Charts 12-1 and 12-2)

A. *Directions:* Add **who** / **that** to each sentence as necessary.

Example: A photographer is someone ∧ takes pictures.
(who / that above the ∧)

1. Many tourists visit New York City enjoy going to a Broadway show.

2. The French man was in my English class had a beautiful accent.

3. Tobias thanked the nurse took care of him in the hospital.

4. I feel happy around people are optimistic about life.

5. When Maja was on the bus, she sat next to a woman was talking on her cell phone.

B. *Directions:* Change the "b" sentences to adjective clauses. Combine each pair of sentences using **who** or **that**.

Example: a. There's the little boy.   b. He lost his balloon in the wind.
            There's the little boy who lost his balloon in the wind.

1. a. I heard about a teenaged boy.   b. He takes gifts to children in hospitals.

   _____

2. a. Tomas met a marine biologist.   b. She once swam with sharks.

   _____

3. a. The people practice fire drills twice   b. They work on this boat.
       a month.

   _____

4. a. The police helped an old man.   b. He was confused and lost.

   _____

5. a. The doctor is very famous.   b. She treated me.

   _____

Directions: Complete the sentences using *who* or *whom*. Use *whom* for object pronouns.

SITUATION: We had a party in our new apartment.

Example: The neighbor _____*whom*_____ I asked for help was very friendly.

1. My sister _____ lives nearby helped us prepare the food.

2. One neighbor _____ I didn't know well asked me for my recipe for Quiche Lorraine.

3. One of the people _____ came to the party was my coworker, Pat.

4. Pat is a person _____ others like immediately.

5. The police officer _____ is moving into the apartment next to us came by for a few minutes.

6. A woman _____ we met last year brought us some flowers.

7. One of the people _____ we know told funny stories all evening.

8. The man _____ sat on the couch all night was Bob.

9. My friend _____ plays in the orchestra couldn't come. She was out of town.

10. The guests _____ we invited had a good time, and so did we.

QUIZ 3 Using *Who, That, Ø, and Whom* to Describe People (Charts 12-2 and 12-3)

Directions: Choose all the correct completions for each sentence. The first one is done for you.

1. We enjoyed the singers _____ gave the concert.
   (a.) who   (b.) that   c. Ø   d. whom

2. The children _____ attend Lake Forest Academy are very wealthy.
   a. who   b. that   c. Ø   d. whom

3. The driver _____ I helped was very upset about the accident.
   a. who   b. that   c. Ø   d. whom

4. I met the lifeguard _____ rescued my child from the water.
   a. who   b. that   c. Ø   d. whom

5. Do you trust the person _____ Mr. Wilcox hired?
   a. who   b. that   c. Ø   d. whom

6. Students _____ come to class early can get extra help from the teacher.
   a. who   b. that   c. Ø   d. whom

7. Where is the woman _____ manages this apartment building?
   a. who   b. that   c. Ø   d. whom

8. The college student _____ I take to school every morning lives next door to me.
    a. who   b. that   c. Ø   d. whom

9. The teacher _____ the students like best is creative and funny.
    a. who   b. that   c. Ø   d. whom

10. Are you the pharmacist _____ my doctor recommended?
    a. who   b. that   c. Ø   d. whom

11. I know a man _____ has nine brothers and sisters.
    a. who   b. that   c. Ø   d. whom

QUIZ 4   **Using *That* and *Which* to Describe Things**   (Chart 12-4)

A. ***Directions:*** Choose the correct completions. Both answers may be correct.

Example: I just found out that the toys _____ we saw on sale are dangerous for children.
    (a.) that/which   (b.) Ø

1. The college _____ George attends offers scholarships to 80 percent of its students.
    a. that/which   b. Ø

2. Andreas studies languages _____ are no longer spoken.
    a. that/which   b. Ø

3. My grandfather builds cabins _____ are made of logs.
    a. that/which   b. Ø

4. The furniture _____ my father designs is sold in art galleries.
    a. that/which   b. Ø

5. We're having lunch at a restaurant _____ has a breathtaking view of the city.
    a. that/which   b. Ø

B. ***Directions:*** Change the "b" sentences to adjective clauses. Combine each pair of sentences using ***which*** or ***that***.

SITUATION: Modern Technology

Example: a. I got a new laptop computer.   b. It is easy to carry.
        I got a new laptop computer which is easy to carry.

1. a. Every day I use Web sites.   b. They are great sources of information.

    _____

2. a. I have a cell phone.   b. I can use it to search the Web and send email.

    _____

3. a. Bluetooth technology is very convenient.   b. It allows me to talk on the phone while I'm washing dishes.

    _____

4. a. More hybrid cars are being developed.   b. They use both gas and electricity.

_____

5. a. Many people like technology.   b. It makes our lives easier.

_____

QUIZ 5 **Review of Adjective Clauses** (Charts 12-1 → 12-4)

Directions: Change the "b" sentences to adjective clauses. Combine each pair of sentences using **who** or **which**.

Example: a. There is the man.   b. He found our dog in the park.
_____ _There is the man who found our dog in the park._ _____

1. a. I spoke with an amazing woman.   b. She has thirteen children.

_____

2. a. Here is the new book.   b. You asked me to order it for you.

_____

3. a. The man has a broken leg.   b. He crashed into a tree.

_____

4. a. The cell phone has all the newest features.   b. I bought it yesterday.

_____

5. a. The kind man repaired my car for free.   b. He owns the gas station.

_____

6. a. I don't know the student.   b. She wrote an article for the newspaper.

_____

7. a. The biology professor is going to retire at the end of this semester.   b. I met him last year.

_____

8. a. The documentary was fascinating.   b. We watched it last night.

_____

9. a. The elderly man has no relatives.   b. He lives in the apartment next to mine.

_____

10. a. Where is the fruit?   b. It was on the counter in the kitchen.

_____

Directions: Choose the correct verbs.

Example: The students who (*studies*, (*study*)) regularly usually get higher grades.

1. The email messages that I (*gets*, *get*) from my grandfather are funny and full of news.

2. Ethan has two sons that (*enjoys*, *enjoy*) playing basketball.

3. The main character in my favorite TV series is a woman who (*writes*, *write*) for a comedy show.

4. Many people who (*works*, *work*) the night shift have sleep problems.

5. The stories that my children (*likes*, *like*) best have surprise endings.

6. Do you know the man who (*is*, *are*) waving at you?

7. The woman who (*sells*, *sell*) flowers on the corner is marrying one of her customers.

8. The house which my parents (*is*, *are*) designing is very energy-efficient.

9. I know a man that (*spends*, *spend*) every summer sailing the Pacific Ocean.

10. I hope that the people who (*calculates*, *calculate*) our taxes are honest.

Directions: Complete the sentences with appropriate prepositions. Draw brackets around the adjective clauses.

Example: The music [that we listened _to_] had a blues-jazz sound.

1. The lake that you are familiar _____ is famous for fishing.

2. The country which Marco escaped _____ is having a civil war.

3. The job Pierre is qualified _____ pays very well.

4. The book club which my mother belongs _____ sells books about knitting.

5. Don't tell me about the leak in your plumbing. The person whom you should complain _____ is the manager of your apartment building.

6. The building that your company is interested _____ is not available for rent.

7. The young man whom Mark introduced you _____ is a professor at Oxford University.

8. Ron doesn't always get along with two of the roommates that he lives _____.

9. The elderly woman whom Marta was kind _____ left her a large inheritance when she died.

10. The woman whom Blake is married _____ has both M.D. and Ph.D. degrees.

Directions: Change the "b" sentences to adjective clauses. Combine each pair of sentences. Write four different sentences for each item.

Examples: a. The taxi is coming.   b. I am waiting for it.

    The taxi that I am waiting for is coming.

    The taxi I am waiting for is coming.

    The taxi which I am waiting for is coming.

    The taxi for which I am waiting is coming.

1. a. The radio station has 24-hour news. b. We listen to it.

    _____

    _____

    _____

    _____

2. a. The manager drives a sports car. b. Sebastian works for him.

    _____

    _____

    _____

    _____

3. a. The school specializes in dance and drama instruction. b. I told you about it.

    _____

    _____

    _____

    _____

Directions: Change the "b" sentences to adjective clauses. Combine each pair of sentences using *whose*.

Example: a. I know the teacher.   b. His class is putting on a play.

          I know the teacher whose class is putting on a play.

1. a. The little girl was sad for days.   b. Her doll was taken.

      _____

2. a. I'm friends with a woman.   b. Her daughter is training to be a
                                      professional boxer.

      _____

3. a. I met a man at the park.   b. His parents know my grandparents.

      _____

4. a. I have a friend.   b. Her sailboat is also her office.

      _____

5. a. I enjoyed meeting the couple.   b. Their children go to the same school
                                        as our children.

      _____

6. a. The people are upset.   b. Their car was just hit.

      _____

7. a. The couple wants us to buy the   b. We rent their summer house.
         property next door.

      _____

8. a. I know a woman.   b. Her work involves designing houses
                                        for people in wheelchairs.

      _____

9. a. A writer spoke about his experiences. b. His new book is about mountain
                                        climbing.

      _____

10. a. The dog is being cared for by the staff.   b. His owner left him outside a restaurant.

      _____

Directions: Correct the errors.

Example: I can't stop reading the book I started ~~it~~ last night.

1. The family whose arrived late discovered they had missed the wedding.

2. A neighbor who his son works for an airline can fly around the world for free.

3. I ran into a man he was my boss twenty years ago.

4. Those are the students they volunteer to clean up parks on weekends.

5. The potatoes aren't done which I baked.

6. The woman which I see every day on the bus talks the entire time.

7. I work with a doctor which is nice to his patients but rude to the nurses.

8. Here is the magazine has the story about home theater systems.

9. Aiko and Yutaka moved into the apartment which are on the top floor.

10. The people who dog bit the delivery man had to pay the doctor bills.

CHAPTER 12 – TEST 1

Part A *Directions:* Use the "b" sentences adjective clauses. Combine the sentences using **who, whom, whose,** or **which.**

1. a. Some of the mail was addressed to our neighbor. b. He lives in the apartment downstairs.

   _____

2. a. I work with a man. b. His wife trains police dogs.

   _____

3. a. The garden is looking healthy again. b. It nearly died from lack of rain.

   _____

4. a. The pianist likes to play Chopin's *Nocturnes.* b. He plays in the hotel lobby on weekends.

   _____

5. a. The manager treats me fairly. b. I work for him.

   _____

6. a. A travel agent called. b. His name is Mike Hammers.

   _____

Part B *Directions:* Complete the sentences. Use **who, that, Ø, whose, which,** or **whom.** Write all possible choices.

1. The coin _____ Kaspar found is very valuable.

2. I met a woman _____ has two sets of twins.

3. Let's choose a movie _____ the whole family can watch.

4. I spoke with a man yesterday _____ brother is a psychologist for animals.

5. The reporter _____ I had the interview with works for the *Times.*

Part C *Directions:* Circle the correct verbs.

1. Have you met the people who (*is, are*) renting that house?

2. An astronomer is a scientist who (*studies, study*) stars and planets.

3. There are several students in my class whose families (*lives, live*) overseas.

4. The employee who (*is, are*) meeting with the supervisor is going to lose his job.

5. Those are the chairs that (*is, are*) the most comfortable.

Part D *Directions:* Complete the sentences with the appropriate prepositions.

1. President of the company is the position I am interested _____.

2. The motel that we stayed _____ was overpriced.

3. Rebecca is an employee who other workers can always depend _____.

4. Cambridge is the university that Omar graduated _____.

5. The person whom I agree _____ most often is you.

6. Josh Grobin is a singer whom I am never tired of listening _____.

Part E *Directions:* Change the "b" sentences to adjective clauses. Combine each pair of sentences. Write four different sentences for each item.

1. a. The photographs were amazing.   b. He paid a lot of money for them.

_____

_____

_____

_____

2. a. The woman was late.   b. A taxi was waiting for her.

_____

_____

_____

_____

Part F *Directions:* Correct the errors.

1. The firefighters who they put out the fire were exhausted and dirty.

2. The digital camera we ordered it still hasn't arrived.

3. The man that for I work is blind.

4. Here is the receipt which you asked.

5. The finger is healing well which I broke.

6. I studied with a professor who his books are known around the world.

7. I met a little girl whose favorite food are mushrooms.

CHAPTER 12 – TEST 2

Part A *Directions:* Use the "b" sentences adjective clauses. Combine the sentences using **who, whom, whose,** or **which.**

1. a. The earphones were defective.   b. I bought them.

   _____

2. a. The couple was surprised.   b. Their horse won the race.

   _____

3. a. Barb is an excellent supervisor.   b. People like to work for her.

   _____

4. a. We met a boy.   b. His dog can do a lot of tricks.

   _____

5. a. The actor won an Academy Award.   b. He starred in several movies last year.

   _____

6. a. The little girl picked some of the   b. They grow in my garden.
        flowers.

   _____

Part B *Directions:* Complete the sentences. Use **who, that, Ø, whose, which,** or **whom**. Write all possible choices.

1. The sandwiches _____ you made were delicious.

2. The boy _____ I asked to help me with yard work is saving for a trip
    to Nepal.

3. The book _____ you are reading has been translated into several
    languages.

4. I went to school with a man _____ software company has made him a
    multimillionaire.

5. The dress _____ Jasmine chose to wear for her wedding had a red
    sash.

Part C *Directions:* Circle the correct verbs.

1. My husband and I have a friend who (*designs, design*) jewelry for movie stars.

2. That is the bike which Michelle (*wants, want*) for her birthday.

3. Where are the socks that (*goes, go*) with those pants?

4. I study with a professor who (*speaks, speak*) several languages fluently.

5. The neighbors whose dog (*barks, bark*) all night are difficult to talk to.

Directions: Complete the sentences with the appropriate prepositions.

1. These are the jeans that everyone at school is crazy _____.

2. The man who is staring _____ me is making me nervous.

3. This is literature which all students should be familiar _____.

4. Hans is a financial advisor whom you should listen _____.

5. I'm returning the books that I borrowed _____ you.

6. M.I.T. is a school which is famous _____ its engineering program.

Part E *Directions:* Change the "b" sentences to adjective clauses. Combine each pair of sentences. Write four different sentences for each item.

1. a. My nephew lives in Argentina.   b. I told you about him.

   _____

   _____

   _____

   _____

2. a. Meg found the earrings.   b. She had been looking for them.

   _____

   _____

   _____

   _____

Part F *Directions:* Correct the errors.

1. The color of paint Sandra picked for her bedroom walls were an unusual blue.

2. The train it came through the tunnel blew its whistle several times.

3. The radio carries overseas stations which I bought.

4. The doctor whose operated on my father is very skilled.

5. I work with a woman grew up in the same neighborhood as me.

6. The ambulance driver which drove my husband to the hospital didn't turn on his siren.

7. Here's an article that you might be interested.

Verb + Gerund (Chart 13-1)

Directions: Complete each sentence with the correct form of a verb from the list. The first one is done for you.

> ✓bake   drive   get   paint   smoke   turn down
> do   find   move   run   take

1. I always enjoy _____baking_____ bread.

2. Would you mind _____ the stereo? I'm trying to sleep.

3. Hiro put off _____ his homework all week. Now he is too tired to do it.

4. My husband and I are thinking about _____ a puppy, but we're not sure yet.

5. Will took a wrong turn on the road, but he kept _____ because he didn't want his girlfriend to know he had made a mistake.

6. We finished _____ our apartment. Now we can decorate the walls.

7. The Davisons have discussed _____ closer to the city so Mr. Davison would have a shorter commute to work.

8. When did Viktor quit _____? He looks much healthier than the last time I saw him.

9. Every year we consider _____ a trip to Asia, but we haven't done it yet.

10. We are going to postpone _____ a meeting room until we know how many people will attend.

11. Katarina and Liz are talking about _____ in the city marathon next year.

Directions: Complete the sentences with the correct form of **go** and the verbs in parentheses.

Example: I (swim) _____go swimming_____ in Flathead Lake every summer.

1. Tomorrow, I (shop) _____ for new summer clothes.

2. Last weekend, we (sail) _____ in our new sailboat.

3. Let's (camp) _____ this weekend. The weather is supposed to be quite warm.

4. For Mike's seventy-fifth birthday, he (skydive) _____. His wife thought he was crazy.

5. Mr. Patrick knows a fine river nearby where we can (fish) _____.

6. To stay in shape, Janet (jog) _____ every morning before work.

7. We didn't want to spend our money, so we just (window shop) _____ _____ downtown for a while.

8. Our class (bowl) _____ next weekend to celebrate the end of the term.

9. Yesterday we (sightsee) _____ with our friends who are visiting from Spain.

10. Paolo usually (dance) _____ with his friends on Saturday nights.

Directions: Complete the sentences with the gerund or infinitive form of **work**.

Example: Martin can't stand _____working_____ at his current job. He wants to quit.

1. Hans has talked about _____ for a computer animation company.

2. Elena might consider _____ as a reporter downtown.

3. Dr. Bennett enjoys _____ in the emergency room.

4. The teenagers discussed _____ at part-time jobs during the summer.

5. The strikers refused _____ for six weeks.

6. Mari hopes _____ as a flight attendant someday.

7. The builder postponed _____ on the new bridge because of a storm.

8. Charles pretends _____ when his boss is around.

9. Mrs. Russo intends _____ until she is sixty-five.

10. My brother expected _____ last night, but he didn't have to.

Directions: Choose the correct answer. In some cases, both answers are correct.

Example: Pat hates _____ sad movies.
      (a.) to watch   (b.) watching

1. Stan offered _____ Christopher with his math.
     a. to help   b. helping

2. In the mountains, it continued _____ for a week.
     a. to snow   b. snowing

3. We have some free time before dinner. Let's go _____.
     a. to sightsee   b. sightseeing

4. From a distance, the bear appeared _____ smaller than he was.
     a. to be   b. being

5. Have you thought about _____ extra employees for the holiday season?
     a. to hire   b. hiring

6. Miroslav and Ivana have decided _____ at the same company.
     a. to work   b. working

7. Pierre began _____ English six months ago.
     a. to study   b. studying

8. Mrs. Allen can't stand _____ in icy weather.
     a. to drive   b. driving

9. We can't wait _____ our cousins on the coast.
     a. to visit   b. visiting

10. Bobby learned how _____ a computer when he was five years old.
     a. to use   b. using

Directions: Complete the sentences with the correct prepositions.

Example: He is responsible _____*for*_____ paying the bills.

1. Thank you _____ coming.

2. Jay is afraid _____ swimming in the ocean.

3. I believe _____ having money in a savings account.

4. He is nervous _____ getting married.

5. Please plan _____ coming for dinner.

6. We look forward _____ seeing you next month.

7. The kids are excited _____ flying to Los Angeles.

8. I don't feel _____ eating much today.

9. Hannaliese is good _____ drawing cartoons.

10. I apologize _____ hurting your feelings.

Directions: Complete the sentences with *by* or *with*.

Example: The package was delivered to the wrong apartment _____*by*_____ mistake.

1. We traveled around the country last summer _____ train.

2. My parents and I communicate _____ email once a week.

3. The salesperson greeted us _____ a smile.

4. The carpet installer cut the carpet _____ special scissors.

5. It's easy to get around Tokyo _____ subway.

6. The nurse took the patient's temperature _____ a thermometer.

7. Even though the Andersons are married, they live in different cities _____ choice.

8. You can pay _____ credit card, but not _____ check.

9. Marcos measured the paper _____ a ruler.

10. Young people prefer to contact each other _____ phone or text.

Directions: Complete each sentence with *by* + the correct form of a verb from the list. The first one is done for you.

change	do	✓have	paint	send	work
cut	exercise	make	promise	wash	

1. Nina's friends surprised her _____ *by having* _____ a party on her birthday.

2. You can help me _____ the windows that I can't reach.

3. We can make the apartment look better _____ the bedrooms.

4. Andy is going to earn extra money _____ the grass for his neighbors this summer.

5. Students can improve their grades _____ extra work.

6. I finally reached Julien _____ him a text message.

7. The politician won the election _____ to lower taxes.

8. The clown entertained the children _____ animals out of balloons.

9. Khalid stays in shape _____ three times a week.

10. Kwon earns extra money _____ lots of overtime at his job.

11. Maher maintains his car _____ the oil regularly.

A. *Directions:* Make sentences with the same meaning. Use a gerund as the subject.

SITUATION: Preparing for an Exam

Example: It is helpful to organize all your study materials.
<u>   Organizing all your study materials is helpful.   </u>

1. It is necessary to have a quiet place to study.

   _____

2. It is more fun to study with friends.

   _____

3. It is difficult to learn a lot of new information.

   _____

4. It is a good idea to take short breaks.

   _____

5. It is important to get a good night's sleep.

   _____

B. *Directions:* Make sentences with the same meaning. Use *It* + an infinitive. Use *for* (*someone*) as needed.

SITUATION: Taking Care of the Earth

Example: Predicting the future of life on Earth is impossible.
<u>   It is impossible to predict the future of life on Earth.   </u>

1. Recycling as much garbage as you can is important.

   _____

2. Using public transportation instead of your car is helpful.

   _____

3. Turning off lights when you leave a room is a good idea.

   _____

4. Being careful with water is good for everyone.

   _____

5. Polluting the earth is dangerous for the human race.

   _____

A. *Directions:* Add *in order* where possible.

Examples:
> Bill called the drugstore _∧ to ask a question.
>
> in order (above the ∧)
>
> Alison would prefer to stay home tomorrow. (no change)

1. Kim applied to the university for next year.

2. Judy is moving to be closer to her elderly parents.

3. Tom got new glasses to read better.

4. I have to be sure to pay my bills today.

5. Francisco practiced driving a lot to pass the driving test.

B. *Directions:* Answer the questions with the words in parentheses and *in order to*.

Example: Why did you go on a diet? (*lose weight*)
> <u>I went on a diet in order to lose weight.</u>

1. Why did you turn down the TV? (*hear you better*)

   _____

2. Why did you wear socks to bed? (*keep my feet warm*)

   _____

3. Why did you withdraw money from the bank? (*buy a car*)

   _____

4. Why did you call the doctor? (*ask if I needed a flu shot*)

   _____

5. Why did you turn off the phone? (*get some sleep*)

   _____

Expressing Purpose: *To* vs. *For* (Chart 13-9)

Directions: Complete the sentences with *to* or *for*.

Example: Last year I went to Europe _____to_____ visit a college friend.

Last weekend, I went to the mountains . . .

1. _____ ski with friends.

2. _____ a ski trip.

3. _____ have fun with friends.

4. _____ spend time away from the city.

5. _____ some fresh air and relaxation.

Yesterday, I made an appointment . . .

6. _____ my husband.

7. _____ see our lawyer.

8. _____ a meeting with our lawyer.

9. _____ speak with our lawyer.

10. _____ get some legal advice.

Using Infinitives with *Too* and *Enough* (Chart 13-10)

Directions: Complete the sentences with the correct form of the words in parentheses and *too* or *enough*.

Examples: What did you think of that movie?
        (*good*)   It was _____good enough_____ to watch again.
        (*sleepy*) I was _____too sleepy_____ to enjoy it.

1. It's hot outside. I can't work in the garden.

    (*hot*) It's _____ to work in the garden.

    (*cool*) It isn't _____ to work in the garden.

2. I can't eat plain yogurt.

    (*sour*) Plain yogurt is _____ for me to eat.

    (*sweet*) Plain yogurt isn't _____ for me to eat.

3. I'm not going to make an omelet for breakfast.

    (*eggs*) I don't have _____ to make an omelet.

    (*tired*) I'm _____ to make an omelet for breakfast.

4. The brakes on the car are bad. Don't drive it.

(*safe*) The car isn't _____ to drive.

(*dangerous*) The car is _____ to drive.

5. Your shirt still has ink spots on it. You can't wear it.

(*clean*) The shirt isn't _____ to wear.

(*dirty*) It's _____ to wear.

QUIZ 12 **Chapter Review**

Directions: Choose the correct completions. Both answers may be correct.

Example: I don't enjoy _____ to parties.
      a. to go   (b.) going

1. We plan _____ our ten-year-old car soon.
      a. to replace   b. replacing

2. Jason learned how _____ when he was three years old.
      a. to ski   b. skiing

3. Although Yasuko is fifteen, she is afraid of _____ alone in her house
when her parents are out.
      a. to stay   b. staying

4. Professor Dunn always wears a suit and tie to class _____
professional.
      a. to look   b. looking

5. I meant _____ you, but I misplaced your phone number.
      a. to call   b. calling

6. Although the teacher asked them to stop, several students continued
_____ during the art history film.
      a. to talk   b. talking

7. Tony believes in always _____ honest with people.
      a. to be   b. being

8. He's afraid _____ in elevators.
      a. to ride   b. riding

9. We'd love _____ together with you over the holidays.
      a. to get   b. getting

10. Tina doesn't mind _____ on weekends because she gets paid more.
      a. to work   b. working

11. Don't put off _____ your homework until late at night.
      a. to do   b. doing

12. Our sociology professor promised _____ extra credit to students who volunteered to work with people in the community.
    a. to give   b. giving

13. It's important for children _____ the value of money.
    a. to learn   b. learning

14. Thank you for _____ with the chemistry project. It was a lot of work.
    a. to help   b. helping

15. Kris and Sophie arrived at the theater early _____ good seats.
    a. to get   b. getting

16. Andre left the key to his house at work. He got in by _____ through an open window.
    a. climb   b. climbing

17. The students searched the Internet _____ more information for their research projects.
    a. to get   b. getting

18. It takes patience _____ young children.
    a. to teach   b. teaching

19. Geoff likes _____ to the radio at night because it helps him fall asleep.
    a. to listen   b. listening

20. Grace keeps her dog in a fenced area _____ him from running away.
    a. to stop   b. stopping

CHAPTER 13 – TEST 1

Part A   *Directions:*   Complete the sentences with the gerund or infinitive form of the verbs in parentheses. Add prepositions where necessary.

1. A young woman called (*get*) _____ help when she had car trouble on the highway.

2. I enjoy (*read*) _____ a good book when I need (*relax*) _____ .

3. My daughter promised (*call*) _____ us as soon as she gets her examination results. She hopes (*get*) _____ into medical school. She really wants (*study*) _____ oncology.

4. Joe insists (*get*) _____ to the airport at least five hours before his flight. He refuses (*arrive*) _____ any later. (*Be*) _____ in control relaxes him, and he's calmer about flying.

5. The children would like (*build*) _____ a snowman today. It began (*snow*) _____ last night, and now the snow is up to the windows. They plan (*make*) _____ a snowman as tall as the tree outside their house. School has been canceled and they are excited (*have*) _____ some time off. When they finish (*build*) _____ their snowman, they're going to go (*sled*) _____ near their house.

Part B   *Directions:*   Complete the sentences with the correct prepositions.

1. Mr. Thomas is planning _____ attending the meeting, but he'll be few minutes late.

2. Brad and Heidi hadn't seen each other since high school. They met at the airport _____ chance.

3. Carlos takes a cruise once a year because he thinks traveling _____ sea is the most interesting way to see the world.

4. After working hard all year, Alex and Donna are looking forward _____ a family vacation.

5. Mr. Jacobs ran onto the sidewalk, picked up his little boy, and stopped him _____ being hit by a runaway car.

6. The mother comforted her son _____ holding him very close for a few minutes.

7. Becky forgave her little brother _____ breaking her pearl necklace.

8. I was going to cut the lettuce _____ a knife, but my sister showed me it was faster to do it _____ a pair of scissors.

9. I'm thinking _____ studying at a private university if I can get a scholarship.

Part C *Directions:* Complete the sentences with the correct form of the words in parentheses and *too* or *enough.*

1. Jenny is sick. She can't go to school.
   a. (*sick*) Jenny is _____ to go to school.
   b. (*well*) Jenny isn't _____ to go to school.

2. Wait a few minutes before you touch the pan. It's still hot.
   a. (*cool*) The pan isn't _____ to touch.
   b. (*hot*) The pan is _____ to touch.

3. This chocolate tastes terrible. It's very bitter because it contains no sugar.
   a. (*sweet*) This chocolate isn't _____ to eat.
   b. (*bitter*) This chocolate is _____ to eat.

Part D *Directions:* Check (✓) the correct sentence of each pair.

1. a. _____ It is impossible to jump for an elephant.
   b. _____ It is impossible for an elephant to jump.

2. a. _____ We can continue discussion this topic tomorrow.
   b. _____ We can continue discussing this topic tomorrow.

3. a. _____ I enjoy walking because it is good exercise.
   b. _____ I enjoy to walk because it is good exercise.

4. a. _____ Playing golf it is a popular pastime for many people.
   b. _____ Playing golf is a popular pastime for many people.

5. a. _____ If we arrive at the resort before noon, we can go hiking in the mountains.
   b. _____ If we arrive at the resort before noon, we can go to hiking in the mountains.

6. a. _____ Toshi was surprised that the salesclerk apologized her rude behavior.
   b. _____ Toshi was surprised that the salesclerk apologized for her rude behavior.

7. a. _____ Jamie unlocked her car by the electronic key.
   b. _____ Jamie unlocked her car with the electronic key.

8. a. _____ If we hurry, we still have time to go swimming in the lake before dark.
   b. _____ If we hurry, we still have time to go to swim in the lake before dark.

9. a. _____ Helen enjoys to be the center of attention at a party.
   b. _____ Helen enjoys being the center of attention at a party.

CHAPTER 13 – TEST 2

Part A *Directions:* Complete the sentences with the gerund or infinitive form of the verbs in parentheses. Add prepositions where necessary.

1. Colin quit (*work*) _____ as a shipping clerk and expects (*start*) _____ a new job as an export broker in about a month.

2. We can't afford (*go*) _____ on a big vacation this year, so we're going camping.

3. Pedro is good (*kick*) _____ a soccer ball with his left foot even though he is right-handed. (*Play*) _____ soccer is his favorite sport.

4. Bill doesn't mind (*listen*) _____ to classical music, but he prefers rock.

5. When she gets home from work, Liz doesn't feel (*cook*) _____. She just wants (*lie*) _____ on the sofa with a good book or magazine. She often puts off (*make*) _____ dinner, but her family doesn't mind (*eat*) _____ a little later.

6. Last night I dreamt (*fly*) _____ over Paris in a hot air balloon. A tour guide told me it was the only way to go (*sightsee*) _____ in Paris, so I flew over the city for several hours. I almost touched the Eiffel Tower, but I was worried (*pop*) _____ the balloon. Suddenly I felt very cold. I tried (*cover*) _____ myself with blankets, but I couldn't. As soon as I woke up, I discovered why. My younger brother had decided (*pull*) _____ off all my blankets.

Part B *Directions:* Complete the sentences with the correct prepositions.

1. Do you believe _____ ghosts or other supernatural beings?

2. You can reach the top shelf _____ stepping on the small chair next to the table.

3. In some areas of my country, it's cheaper to travel _____ train than _____ bus.

4. Even though Mrs. Miller's children are all grown, she continues to worry _____ them.

5. We paid our electric bill _____ check, but the company has no record of it.

6. My mother-in-law made this baby blanket _____ hand.

7. Let me see if I can quickly repair your pants _____ a needle and thread.

8. New drivers are excited _____ driving, but they are sometimes afraid _____ getting in an accident.

Part C *Directions:* Complete the sentences with the correct form of the words in parentheses and *too* or *enough*.

1. I can't hear the speaker's voice. It's so soft.
   a. (*loud*) The speaker's voice isn't _____ to hear.
   b. (*soft*) The speaker's voice is _____ to hear.

2. I let my coffee sit on the table too long. Now I don't want to drink it.
   a. (*warm*) It isn't _____ to drink.
   b. (*cool*) It is _____ to drink.

3. The sun is coming in through the window. It's so bright that we can't see the picture on the TV.
   a. (*bright*) It is _____ to see the picture.
   b. (*dark*) It isn't _____ to see the picture.

Part D *Directions:* Check (✓) the correct sentence of each pair.

1. a. _____ Eating popcorn and watching a movie is a great way to relax in the evening.
   b. _____ To eat popcorn and to watch a movie is a great way to relax in the evening.

2. a. _____ I need to stop at the bank for withdrawing some money.
   b. _____ I need to stop at the bank to withdraw some money.

3. a. _____ Are you responsible for cleaning up after the party?
   b. _____ Are you responsible to clean up after the party?

4. a. _____ Is relaxing to walk barefoot in the sand on the beach.
   b. _____ It's relaxing to walk barefoot in the sand on the beach.

5. a. _____ Jeannie asked to left work early to take her children to the doctor's.
   b. _____ Jeannie asked to leave work early to take her children to the doctor's.

6. a. _____ William took photography lessons to learn how to develop his own pictures.
   b. _____ William took photography lessons for learn how to develop his own pictures.

7. a. _____ Driving in heavy traffic it requires skill and patience.
   b. _____ Driving in heavy traffic requires skill and patience.

8. a. _____ I cleaned the floor with a mop.
   b. _____ I cleaned the floor by a mop.

9. a. _____ It is sometimes scary to visit the doctor for young children.
   b. _____ It is sometimes scary for young children to visit the doctor.

QUIZ 1   Recognizing Noun Clauses   (Chart 14-1)

    A. *Directions:* <u>Underline</u> the noun clause in each sentence.

Example: The clerk asked me <u>where I live</u>.

    1. I don't know what her name is.

    2. I know where Nathan works.

    3. My son asked me if I needed help with the dishes.

    4. I know that it snowed in April last year.

    5. Do you know who lives in the big house on the corner?

    B. *Directions:* Add final punctuation – a period (.) or a question mark (?). Then circle whether it is an information question or a noun clause. The first one is done for you as an example.

1. What does Brad do for a living?	(information question)	noun clause
2. Do you know what time it is	information question	noun clause
3. When does class start	information question	noun clause
4. Please tell me. Why are you late	information question	noun clause
5. I wonder what happened	information question	noun clause
6. Did you hear what Katie said	information question	noun clause

Directions: Complete each student's response with a noun clause.

SITUATION: Questions A Student Might Hear

Example: TEACHER: What is the answer to question #3?
STUDENT: I don't know _____*what the answer to question #3 is.*_____

1. TEACHER: When did you wake up this morning?

   STUDENT: I don't remember _____

2. TEACHER: Why were you late today?

   STUDENT: I can't tell you _____

3. TEACHER: How much do you study every day?

   STUDENT: I really can't say _____

4. TEACHER: Where are you supposed to meet your study group?

   STUDENT: I don't know _____

5. TEACHER: What should you do to improve your work?

   STUDENT: I'm not sure _____

6. TEACHER: Who can help you with your homework?

   STUDENT: I wonder _____

7. TEACHER: Which class do you enjoy the most?

   STUDENT: I don't know _____

8. TEACHER: Whose dictionary did you borrow?

   STUDENT: I can't remember _____

QUIZ 3 Noun Clauses and Information Questions (Charts 5-2 and 14-2)

Directions: Complete the conversations with the correct form of the words in parentheses. Use a noun clause or an information question.

Examples: A: Where (*Harry, go*) _____did Harry go_____ on his vacation last year?
B: I'm not sure where (*he, go*) _____he went_____. He usually goes camping.

1. A: How much (*an apartment, cost*) _____ in Seattle?
   B: I don't know how much (*rent, be*) _____, but I know Seattle is an expensive place to live.

2. A: Can you tell me when (*the medical conference, start*) _____ _____?
   B: I'm not sure what (*the date, be*) _____, but we can check online.

3. A: What (*Hoang, have*) _____ for homework tonight?
   B: I'm not sure. I haven't asked him how much (*he, have*) _____ to do.

4. A: Why (*that lady, cry*) _____, Mommy?
   B: I don't know why (*she, cry*) _____, but she is very sad.

5. A: Somebody left a jacket in my car. Do you know whose jacket (*it, be*) _____?
   B: Hmmmm . . . What color (*the jacket, be*) _____?
   A: It's red.

QUIZ 4 Noun Clauses with *If* and *Whether* (Chart 14-3)

Directions: Complete the noun clause in each conversation. Use *if* to introduce the noun clause.

Example: A: Are you hungry?
B: Not really, I had a big lunch.
A: Well, please tell me _____if you are_____ hungry later.

1. A: Is Richard a lawyer?
   B: I don't know _____ a lawyer, but he works in a law office.

2. A: Are Joanna and Max rich?
   B: I wouldn't know _____ rich, but they sure spend a lot of money.

3. A: Does Oscar want french fries with his hamburger?
   B: Why are you asking me? I don't know _____ french fries with his hamburger. You need to ask him.

4. A: Are you going to the movies with us?
   B: I haven't decided _____ to the movies with you or not.

5. A: Will you have time to go shopping this afternoon?
   B: I'm not sure _____ time to go shopping. I'm pretty busy today.

6. A: Is your brother coming over this weekend?
   B: I'm sorry. What did you say?
   A: I want to know _____ over this weekend.

7. A: Did Chris take the car?
   B: I don't know. Why don't you look in the driveway to see
      _____ the car.

8. A: Does that DVD player play Blu-ray discs?
   B: I'll check to see _____ Blu-ray discs.

9. A: Has Jason finished his report yet?
   B: I haven't talked to him. You'll have to ask him _____ his
      report yet.

10. A: Do you have a phone I can use?
    B: Excuse me?
    A: I want to know _____ a phone I can use.

QUIZ 5 Noun Clauses with *That* (Chart 14-4)

Directions: Add the word ***that*** to mark the beginning of a noun clause.

that
Example: My dad doesn't think ∧ the team will win many games this season.

1. The police are trying to prove the man took the money.

2. The kindergarten children like to pretend they are lions and tigers.

3. We're disappointed you didn't believe us.

4. Did I tell you we are moving next week?

5. Our teacher really trusts us. I still can't believe she leaves the room during tests.

6. For centuries, people were convinced the earth was flat.

7. Is it true your diamond necklace is missing?

8. Can you believe it's summer already?

9. I'm positive "scissors" is spelled with "S-C" at the beginning.

10. Carlos was impressed Juan knew so much about chemistry.

Directions: Complete the conversations with **so** or **not**.

Example: A: Is it supposed to rain this weekend?
    B: I think _____so_____. (*It is probably going to rain.*)

   1. A: Are you ready for the test?
      B: I hope _____. (*I am ready.*)

   2. A: Here's a map. Do you think you can find the street the Browns live on?
      B: I think _____. (*I can find it.*)

   3. A: It's started to rain. Do you still want to go swimming?
      B: I guess _____. (*I don't want to go swimming.*)

   4. A: You have some money with you. Is it enough?
      B: I hope _____. (*It is enough money.*)

   5. A: Did you forget your wallet?
      B: I hope _____. (*I didn't forget my wallet.*)

   6. A: Is Sergei well enough to return to work?
      B: I don't think _____. (*He isn't well enough.*)

   7. A: Would you like to come with us?
      B: Oh, I guess _____. (*I would like to go with you.*)

   8. A: Have you learned the names of all your students yet?
      B: I hope _____. (*I have learned their names.*)

   9. A: Would you like another cup of coffee?
      B: I don't think _____. (*I don't want another cup.*)

  10. A: Is Amy going to visit us next month?
      B: I believe _____. (*She is going to visit us.*)

Directions: Add quotation marks, capital letters, and the correct punctuation where necessary.

Example: Josef said popcorn is my favorite snack food
___*Josef said, "Popcorn is my favorite snack food."*___

1. Carmen asked do you have money for parking

2. The doctor said stop smoking today

3. There is a mouse in the house Mickey said

4. The policeman said may I see your driver's license, please

5. Mary asked did you get the message I left for you

6. The Johnsons said we have to go now we have another party to attend tonight

7. Our teacher asked who knows the answer who would like to write it on the board

8. My mother said I won't be home until 7:00 tonight could you fix dinner

9. You speak Russian don't you asked Natasha

10. I'm so tired from the hike are you tired too Miguel asked

Directions: Punctuate the quoted speech in the conversation between a father and daughter. The first one is done for you.

1. "I don't like spiders," my daughter said.

2. Why not I asked.

3. They're quite ugly she replied.

4. Well, they might look unpleasant I said. They're not as beautiful as butterflies, but they're good to have around. They eat ants and flies that you don't want to have in your house I said. Try to think of them as a gift from nature.

5. Wow she said I didn't know spiders were so helpful.

Directions: Complete the sentences. Change the pronouns from quoted speech to reported speech.

Example: Mrs. Adams said, "My granddaughters are going to visit me in the summer."
Mrs. Adams said that ____*her*____ granddaughters were going to visit ____*her*____ in the summer.

1. Mrs. Diaz said, "My secretary is on vacation this week."

   Mrs. Diaz said that _____ secretary was on vacation this week.

2. Laura said, "The book that you lent me was really good."

   Laura said that the book that _____ had lent _____ was really good.

3. My husband said to me, "Our children want us to take them to a movie tonight."

   My husband said that _____ children wanted _____ to take

   _____ to a movie tonight.

4. Joan said, "I can come over to your house tonight and help you and your brother with the science project."

   Joan said that _____ could come over to _____ house tonight and

   help _____ and _____ brother with the science project.

5. Mr. Owens said, "I want my children to be independent and think for themselves."

   Mr. Owens said that _____ wanted _____ children to be independent

   and think for _____.

6. The woman at the bakery said, "Our customers bought all our fresh bread this morning. We're sold out."

   The woman at the bakery said that _____ customers had bought all

   _____ fresh bread this morning. _____ were sold out.

7. The teachers at the school said to the parents, "We have high standards for your children, and we will support their efforts to be successful."

   The teachers at the school said to the parents that _____ had high standards for

   _____ children, and _____ would support _____ efforts to

   be successful.

Directions: Complete the sentences using reported speech. Use formal verb forms.

Example: Teresa said, "I'm looking forward to my trip to Washington, D.C."
Teresa said that she _____*was looking*_____ forward to her trip to Washington, D.C.

1. The teacher said, "The test will be on Friday."
   The teacher said that the test _____ on Friday.

2. The mail carrier said, "There was no mail delivery on Monday because of the holiday."
   The mail carrier said that there _____ no mail delivery on Monday
   because of the holiday.

3. Marie said, "My English teacher has the flu."
   Marie said that her English teacher _____ the flu.

4. Junko said, "I don't understand the problem."
   Junko said that she _____ the problem.

5. The director said, "The actors haven't learned their lines yet."
   The director said that the actors _____ their lines yet.

6. Pedro said, "The movie is going to start in ten minutes. We need to leave."
   Pedro said that the movie _____ in ten minutes, and that they
   _____ to leave.

7. The weather reporter said, "Yesterday's weather set record cold temperatures across the
   country."
   The weather reporter said that yesterday's weather _____ record cold
   temperatures across the country.

8. The Smiths said, "We can feed your cats while you are away."
   The Smiths said they _____ our cats while we
   _____ away.

Directions: Change the quoted speech to reported speech. Use formal verb forms.

Example: My grandfather said, "I have had a wonderful life."

    My grandfather said (that) he had had a wonderful life.

1. Abdul said, "I will be twenty-five on my next birthday."

2. My parents said, "We enjoyed our trip to Costa Rica."

3. My friends said, "We want to give you a going-away party."

4. Suzanne said, "I have lived in Italy for twenty years."

5. The boy said, "The dog took my ball. He isn't coming back."

6. Dr. Wilson said, "I'm going to retire in a few years. My husband and I are planning to travel."

7. My husband said, "I can pick up the kids after school. You don't need to worry about it."

Directions: Complete the sentences with *said, told,* or *asked.*

Example: Benito ___told___ me he could take us to school.

1. The teacher _____ me if I had done my homework. I _____ her I had finished it last night.

2. The manager _____ that all employees would get extra pay for the holiday. The employees were pleased and _____ the manager that they were grateful.

3. Scott _____ his parents that he had rented an apartment. His parents _____ they were pleased that he had found one.

4. The recipe _____ to use one cup of sugar, but the children misread it and used two. They asked their mom what to do, and she _____ them to double the recipe.

5. The security guard _____ that everyone needed an I.D. card to enter the building. I _____ him that I had left mine at home. I _____ him if I could show him my driver's license. He _____, "No." He _____ me I had to go home and get it. I _____ him I would be late for work. He _____, "Sorry," but he couldn't change the rules.

Directions: Correct the errors.

Example: My sister ~~said~~ *told* me that she was going to Los Angeles for a week.

1. I don't know yet the doctor can see you tomorrow or not.

2. Please tell me what did they do.

3. Do you know whose coat on the chair is?

4. Do you know if or not the bus has come?

5. We'd like to know if the subway stop here?

6. I hope so that I can come with you tonight.

7. Leila told that she wasn't home last night.

8. I'm sorry what we have to cancel our plans.

9. The dentist said Your teeth look very healthy. You are taking good care of them.

10. The teacher isn't sure whether Liz want help or not.

CHAPTER 14 – TEST 1

Part A *Directions:* Complete Speaker B's responses with noun clauses.

 1. A: Mom, where's the milk?
   B: I don't know _____.

 2. A: Mr. Barrett, what time will we be done?
   B: I'm not sure _____.

 3. A: I'm hungry. Are there any eggs left?
   B: I don't know _____.

 4. A: Marcos, whose homework is that?
   B: I don't know _____.

 5. A: Is someone knocking at the door?
   B: I wonder _____.

 6. A: I just heard the phone ring. Who called?
   B: I'll find out _____.

 7. A: Did Kwon finish his biology lab work?
   B: Let's ask Maiko. She probably knows _____

   _____.

 8. A: What is the weather supposed to be like tomorrow?
   B: I don't know _____.
   I haven't checked the forecast.

 9. A: Has anyone met the new coach? I hear he's really nice.
   B: I'm not sure _____.
   I haven't.

 10. A: Does this assignment count a lot in our final grade for the class?
   B: I'll ask the teacher _____.

Part B *Directions:* Punctuate the quoted speech in the conversation between a mother and daughter.

 Sɪᴛᴜᴀᴛɪᴏɴ: My mom came in the bedroom and opened the curtains.

 1. What time is it I asked her.

 2. Time to get up she replied.

 3. But it's not a school day I said. Please let me sleep in I begged.

 4. You can't sleep in today she said. It's a special day.

 5. What special day I asked.

 6. It's your birthday she said.

 7. Oh my gosh! I forgot. I have to get up right away I said. I have so many things I want to do today.

Part C *Directions:* Change the quoted speech to reported speech. Use formal verb forms.

1. Julia said, "The cookies are ready."

   _____

2. The librarian said, "The library is going to close early today."

   _____

3. John asked, "How far away is the airport?"

   _____

4. The fire chief said, "It took a long time to put the fire out."

   _____

5. The clerk asked me, "Do you want paper or plastic bags?"

   _____

6. Marika said, "The flight will arrive in ten minutes."

   _____

7. The teacher said, "The test is going to be on Friday."

   _____

8. The students replied, "We don't want a test."

   _____

9. The manager said, "Computers are necessary in the modern workplace."

   _____

10. Joan asked, "Have you ever posted a video on the Internet?"

   _____

Part D *Directions:* Correct the errors.

1. My friends understand what do I like.

2. I'd like to know does this computer work?

3. The teacher told that he would be at a conference tomorrow.

4. I want to know why did they come.

5. Is a fact that exercise makes us healthier.

6. Do you know if Rick live here.

7. I'm sure, that we will have a good time together.

8. A strange man asked me "Where I live."

9. Do you know whose are these keys?

10. I'm not sure that if he wants to come or not.

CHAPTER 14 – TEST 2

Part A *Directions:* Complete Speaker B's responses with noun clauses.

1. A: What's the date today?
   B: I'm not sure _____.

2. A: Do you know the year you were born?
   B: Of course I know _____.

3. A: Did Dimitri and Irina get engaged last weekend?
   B: I have no idea _____.

4. A: That is a difficult problem. Has anyone asked for help yet?
   B: I'll see _____.

5. A: How many people knew about the problem?
   B: I'll find out _____.

6. A: Does the weather change much or stay the same in this area?
   B: I don't know _____.

7. A: I know Paula is unhappy. Did she leave the company?
   B: I haven't heard _____.

8. A: Who will be the new manager?
   B: We don't know _____.

9. A: Whose car are we taking to the mall?
   B: We haven't decided _____.

10. A: Does the copy machine work?
    B: I'll see _____.

Part B *Directions:* Punctuate the quoted speech in the conversation between a teacher and a student.

SITUATION: Last week, my teacher and I were talking about my future.

1. What do you want to do after you finish school he asked.

2. I'm not sure I said. I'd like to have a job that is interesting and pays well.

3. Everyone would like that said my teacher. Is there a specific area you see yourself working in?

4. Yes I replied. I love working with animals. Maybe I could be a veterinarian.

5. One way to find out is to work with animals first said my teacher. Volunteer at an animal shelter or zoo. See how you like it.

6. I told him I like that suggestion. Thanks!

Part C *Directions:* Change the quoted speech to reported speech. Use formal verb forms.

1. The police officer said to me, "I am giving you a warning, not a ticket."

   _____

2. My friend said, "I cleaned my apartment and did my laundry."

   _____

3. Yolanda said, "The bus will be late."

   _____

4. Joe asked, "Who took my car?"

   _____

5. The manager said, "We have decided to move our offices to a new location."

   _____

6. Brad asked, "When will the book be published?"

   _____

7. Shirley said, "I can fix that for you."

   _____

8. My parents said, "We were happy to hear about your job promotion."

   _____

9. The doctor asked me, "Have you been taking your medicine?"

   _____

10. The dancers said, "We have practiced our dance steps. We're ready for our show."

    _____

Part D *Directions:* Correct the errors.

1. Can you tell me whose coat belongs to this?

2. I felt better when the doctor said, your daughter just has a bad cold. It's nothing serious.

3. My friends asked me that. "When will you get married."

4. Did my mom ask you if or not you could come to our party?

5. Hamid asked why did I always come late?

6. Mr. Hill told to me that he was feeling ill.

7. Could you tell me where Fred work in the evenings?

8. I think so that you will enjoy being on the soccer team.

9. I know, that this will be a good opportunity for us.

10. Professor Thomas told us he will be absent yesterday.

Directions: Choose the correct completions.

Example: Maria and Tony _____ famous characters from *West Side Story*.
a. is   c. are being
(b.) are   d. has been

1. The Duncans and their son _____ dinner together on Sundays.
   a. eats usually   c. eat usually
   b. usually eats   d. usually eat

2. You _____ have a passport to travel to a foreign country.
   a. must   c. may
   b. can   d. could

3. Almost everyone in our neighborhood _____ a dog or a cat.
   a. have   c. has
   b. haves   d. is having

4. _____ is it from Barcelona to Madrid?
   a. How far   c. How long
   b. How much time   d. How often

5. You have a good job, _____ you?
   a. are   c. do
   b. aren't   d. don't

6. Some people like chocolate ice cream, but _____ prefer vanilla.
   a. other   c. the other
   b. others   d. another

7. I have been working at the same company _____.
   a. next year   c. since 2001
   b. until March   d. from now

8. Right now Marcy _____ the piano. She enjoys music.
   a. is playing   c. play
   b. plays   d. does play

9. _____ Ms. Simmons take the bus to work?
   a. Is   c. Does
   b. Are   d. Do

10. Stephan _____ coffee. He prefers tea.
    a. don't drink   c. aren't drink
    b. doesn't drink   d. isn't drink

11. Your daughter really enjoyed the ballet, _____ she?
    a. didn't   c. wasn't
    b. won't   d. can't

12. Jerry and Jennifer _____ go to Macedonia next year. They aren't sure yet.
    a. must
    b. maybe
    c. should
    d. might

13. I got a text message while I _____, so I couldn't answer it.
    a. drove
    b. drives
    c. am driving
    d. was driving

14. We have to pick up Travis in a few minutes. I have _____ address.
    a. him
    b. he's
    c. he
    d. his

15. Can you please help me? I _____ help with this heavy box.
    a. need
    b. needs
    c. am needing
    d. are needing

16. My grandparents _____ to Venice many times. They go there every year.
    a. are going
    b. has been
    c. have been
    d. was going

17. The baby _____ won't take a nap this afternoon. She had a long nap this morning.
    a. may
    b. maybe
    c. probably
    d. may be

18. Tony is moving to a new apartment tomorrow. I _____ help him move.
    a. going to
    b. am going to
    c. am
    d. will be

19. _____ does the bank open today?
    a. Where
    b. What time
    c. What
    d. Who

20. Katya and her roommate _____ together at the library last night.
    a. study
    b. was studying
    c. studied
    d. will study

21. I _____ my homework by 10:00, so I went to bed.
    a. finish
    b. was finished
    c. had finished
    d. had been finished

22. ROSA: Are you a good cook?
    MANUEL: Yes, I _____. I like to cook.
    a. am
    b. do
    c. is
    d. did

23. I have a cold. I _____ terrible yesterday, but I'm feeling better today.
    a. feel
    b. felt
    c. feels
    d. fell

24. _____ Andrew drive or take the train to London last weekend?
    a. Does
    b. Was
    c. Did
    d. Were

25. What _____ I write my essay about? I can't decide on a topic!
   a. might
   b. would
   c. should
   d. may

26. My parents _____ an old car, but now they have a new hybrid.
   a. used to drive
   b. used to driving
   c. use to drive
   b. use to driving

27. _____ when you finish checking your email?
   a. What are you do
   b. What you going to
   c. What will you do
   d. When are you going to

28. My brother _____ in ghosts, but I don't.
   a. belief
   b. believe
   c. believes
   d. is believing

29. In a few months, we _____ to Oregon.
   a. going to go
   b. will going
   c. are going
   d. going

30. I hate my new schedule! I _____ getting up at 6:30 every morning.
   a. don't used to
   b. am not used to
   c. didn't used to
   d. wasn't use to

31. When Dad _____ cooking dinner, we can eat.
   a. finish
   b. finishes
   c. will finish
   d. finished

32. _____ you please help me with my algebra? I don't understand this problem.
   a. Should
   b. May
   c. Must
   d. Would

33. _____ Ms. Carlson going to teach grammar class next semester?
   a. Is
   b. Are
   c. Does
   d. Will

34. Do you know _____ laptop computer that is?
   a. who
   b. whose
   c. who's
   d. whom

35. Freddy's soccer team _____ play in a tournament during the summer.
   a. maybe
   b. may
   c. may be
   d. be

36. As soon as my brother _____, he'll buy us some ice cream.
   a. comes
   b. will come
   c. came
   d. has come

37. My plane _____ at 10:50 Friday night.
   a. leaving
   b. has left
   c. has left
   d. leaves

38. What _____ since I saw you last summer?
   a. are you doing
   b. you are doing
   c. have you been doing
   d. you have been doing

39. Mr. Robbins has taught high school French _____.

    a. since many years   c. three years ago

    b. for fifteen years   d. last year

40. We _____ Krista since she had her baby two months ago.

    a. hasn't seen   c. didn't see

    b. haven't seen   d. wasn't seen

41. People _____ cheat on their income taxes or they will get in trouble.

    a. don't have to   c. had better not

    b. didn't have to   d. might not

42. When we arrived at the theater, the movie _____.

    a. already started   c. has already started

    b. had already started   d. is started

43. _____ lives in the house at the end of the street?

    a. Where   c. Who

    b. Whom   d. Whose

44. It's been a long time since you've seen your parents, _____ it?

    a. wasn't   c. hasn't

    b. haven't   d. isn't

45. Leila's job interview is at 1:00 P.M. _____ Thursday.

    a. on   c. in

    b. to   d. at

46. People around the world _____ the Internet to get the news.

    a. uses   c. is using

    b. use   d. has used

47. One of Beth's favorite movies is *Pretty Woman*. _____ is *My Big Fat Greek Wedding*.

    a. Other   c. Others

    b. The others   d. Another

48. When Mr. Kushner gave his presentation, people in the back of the room _____ hear him.

    a. couldn't   c. mustn't

    b. shouldn't   d. might not

49. _____ the student with the highest grade in the class?

    a. Who   c. Who's

    b. Whose   d. Whom

50. It has been snowing for two days. The skiing _____ be great.

    a. have to   c. can

    b. had better   d. must

Part A *Directions:* Complete the sentences with an appropriate form of the words in parentheses. More than one answer is possible.

Example: Helena didn't want anyone to find her diary, so she (*hide*) ___hid___ it in a shoe box in her closet.

1. When I went shopping yesterday, I (*buy*) _____ some light bulbs and a broom.

2. Every year my whole family (*get*) _____ together to celebrate my grandfather's birthday.

3. Saya (*fall*) _____ as she was getting on the bus. She (*be*) _____ so embarrassed.

4. Next September my daughter (*start*) _____ high school. She is growing up!

5. I (*be, never*) _____ to Turkey, but I think it would be an interesting place to visit.

6. By the time the chemistry lecture ended, Faisal (*take*) _____ ten pages of notes.

7. Right now the children (*draw*) _____ pictures of themselves in art class.

8. Juan (*have, not*) _____ a car. He (*take*) _____ the train to work every day.

9. Emma and Hank (*move*) _____ into their new house next weekend.

10. Vinh used to have a motorcycle, but he (*sell*) _____ it because he needed the money.

11. Mr. Smetko (*work*) _____ for the same company for twenty-nine years. Next year he (*retire*) _____.

12. Anna didn't want anyone to see her bad grade, so she (*tear*) _____ her paper into tiny pieces.

13. Brad was about to send a text to his girlfriend when he noticed that he (*get, already*) _____ a text from her.

14. After I finish taking these pictures, I (*send*) _____ them to my parents. They (*love*) _____ seeing pictures of their grandkids.

15. Many people (*cheer*) _____ when the runners crossed the finish line. The runners (*smile*) _____.

Part B *Directions:* Complete the sentences. Use *can, could, may, might, would, should, had better,* or *must*. More than one answer is possible.

Example: I used to get up at noon, but now I ____*must*____ be at work by 8:00 A.M.

1. People _____ not talk on their cell phones while driving.

2. _____ I please have a hamburger and french fries?

3. It's raining again. It _____ rain all day. I'm glad I brought my umbrella.

4. Hans is late! He _____ hurry up or he'll miss the exam.

5. Nancy has lost twenty-five pounds! She _____ feel great.

6. When I was young, I _____ not speak German, but now I speak it well.

7. _____ you please turn down your music? It's too loud.

8. I think you _____ read the new book by Paulo Coelho. It's interesting.

9. I enjoy listening to music, but I _____ not sing at all. I've got a terrible voice.

10. Children _____ be respectful when talking with adults.

Part C *Directions:* Complete the questions and answers with the correct words. More than one answer may be possible.

Examples: A: ____*Does*____ this road go through the center of town?
  B: No, ____*it doesn't*____ .

1. A: Excuse me. _____ there a good restaurant near here?
   B: Well, _____ kind of food do you want?
   A: Italian, maybe. _____ you know of any Italian restaurants in this area?
   B: Yes, _____ . There is one just up the street that's pretty good.

2. A: _____ laptop computer is that?
   B: It's mine. _____ you want to use it?
   A: Yes, _____ . _____ much memory does it have?
   B: The hard drive is 320 GB. _____ do you need to know?
   A: Because I want to download a game. _____ that OK?
   B: I guess so, but please remove it when you are finished.

3. A: You look tired. _____ you sleep well last night?
   B: No, _____ .
   A: That's too bad. _____ did you go to bed?
   B: At 1:00 A.M.
   A: Wow! _____ did you stay up so late?
   B: I had too much homework to do. _____ homework did you have?
   A: Not much. I finished it and went to bed early.

Part D *Directions:* Correct the errors.

leaves

Example: Most ~~leaf~~ are green.

1. Tom last name is Miller.

2. Tomato are good for us. They have lots of vitamin C.

3. They would rather eat Chinese food, don't they?

4. All of the actors names are listed on page six of your program.

5. Why we don't go shopping on Saturday? I need some new shoes.

6. We just moved into a four-bedrooms house.

7. My brothers started they're own gardening business last year.

8. Some children prefer to play by theirselves rather than with other kids.

9. There are two new students in class. One is from Libya, and another is from Romania.

10. When you are going on a trip, prepares your paperwork ahead of time.

Directions: Choose the correct completions.

Example: Diana _____ to her cousin's birthday party.
    a. invited   ⓒ. was invited
    b. had invited   d. invite

1. Can you please take this package to _____ post office?
    a. Ø   c. an
    b. the   d. some

2. My kids must clean their rooms _____ do laundry on Saturdays.
    a. but   c. and
    b. because   d. so

3. People should always put on _____ sunscreen lotion to protect their skin.
    a. the   c. an
    b. a few   d. Ø

4. Ted _____ horror movies, and neither does his girlfriend.
    a. doesn't like   c. don't like
    b. isn't like   d. likes

5. "Too," "two," and "to" have _____ pronunciation but different meanings.
    a. a same   c. the same
    b. like   d. alike

6. Max has a job painting houses. He _____ on a tall ladder.
    a. use to work   c. is used to working
    b. uses to work   d. was used to working

7. Babies _____ by everyone.
    a. was loved   c. loved
    b. are loved   d. have loved

8. San Francisco has many tourist attractions and _____ Los Angeles.
    a. does too   c. also does
    b. so do   d. so does

9. I'm going to go to bed early _____ I'm not feeling well.
    a. even though   c. because
    b. so   d. but

10. Willie is really good _____ computers. He can solve any computer problem!
    a. on fixing   c. fixing
    b. to fixing   d. at fixing

11. My father asked me if I _____ money for gas.
    a. needed   c. need
    b. needs   d. did need

12. My new cell phone was not _____ my old one.
    a. expensiver than   c. as expensive as
    b. more expensive as   d. more expensive

13. My sister has three kids, _____ she is very busy.
    a. because   c. or
    b. so   d. although

14. Abdul is thinking about _____ medicine, but he has to take the medical school exam first.
    a. study   c. to study
    b. studying   d. going study

15. You forgot to bring me the money you owe me, _____?
    a. don't I   c. didn't I
    b. aren't you   d. didn't you

16. The woman _____ I share my apartment with is a physician.
    a. which   c. what
    b. whom   d. whose

17. Rudy didn't have to go to the dentist, but his brother _____.
    a. does   c. would
    b. was   d. did

18. Hiromi is looking forward _____ to Hawaii on her honeymoon.
    a. going   c. to going
    b. to go   d. on going

19. The banker _____ helped us with our loan was knowledgeable and friendly.
    a. Ø   c. she
    b. who   d. whom

20. My daughter understands Italian much better than I _____.
    a. do   c. will
    b. am   d. did

21. Fiona's shoe broke while she was dancing. She was so _____.
    a. embarrassed   c. embarrassing
    b. embarrass   d. embarrasses

22. Of all the people I know, Alexis is _____.
    a. funniest   c. most funny
    b. the funniest   d. the most funny

23. German, French, and Italian _____ in different areas of Switzerland.
    a. are spoken   c. speak
    b. is spoken   d. speaks

24. The old man didn't remember where _____.
    a. he did live   c. did he live
    b. lived he   d. he lived

25. Fresh fruit and vegetables should _____ every day as part of a healthy diet.
    a. eat   c. be eaten
    b. to eat   d. eating

26. Nasrin _____ her upcoming trip to Australia.
    a. excited for   c. excites about
    b. is excited   d. is excited about

27. When I lived in London, I _____ English every day. My English got a lot better.
    a. use to speak   c. am used to speaking
    b. used to speak   d. used to speaking

28. I'm sorry, but I can't go out tonight. I have to study for _____ exam.
    a. some   c. a
    b. Ø   d. an

29. _____ in Maha's ring is 24 karats.
    a. Gold   c. Golds
    b. The gold   d. A gold

30. How _____ did George inherit when his grandfather died?
    a. many money   c. much money
    b. many monies   d. much monies

31. My parents _____ me I had to be home by midnight.
    a. said   c. told
    b. asked   d. telled

32. Anne lost her necklace. It was _____ necklace that her husband gave her on their first
    anniversary.
    a. Ø   c. the
    b. an   d. some

33. I wonder _____ this weekend. I want to go on a picnic.
    a. if it rains   c. if or not it will rain
    b. if it will rain   d. will it rain

34. Do you know the couple _____ son won the academic scholarship?
    a. their   c. whose
    b. which   d. who

35. They _____ in Chicago for ten years, and they really like it.
    a. lives   c. have lived
    b. are living   d. live

36. I had _____ in my pocket, so I gave them to the street musicians.
    a. a few coins   c. a little coins
    b. few coins   d. little coins

37. Do you know the boy _____ wearing the striped shirt?
    a. who's   c. whose
    b. he's   d. what's

38. Scientists want to do _____ research into the causes of global warming.
    a. farther   c. farthest
    b. further   d. furthest

39. My friend Shoko goes _____ every Saturday.
    a. shop   c. to shop
    b. shops   d. shopping

40. Whenever I buy plane tickets, I pay _____ credit card.
    a. by
    b. for
    c. with
    d. on

41. Hyo studied hard _____ high grades in all his classes.
    a. for getting
    b. to get
    c. on getting
    d. for get

42. The chicken is _____. I can't eat it.
    a. spicy enough
    b. to spicy
    c. too spicy
    d. spicier

43. My classes this semester aren't _____ at all. All of my professors are really good!
    a. bored
    b. bore
    c. boring
    d. bores

44. What time _____?
    a. does the movie start
    b. does start the movie
    c. the movie starts
    d. starts the movie

45. Getting my driver's license was _____ easier than I expected.
    a. more
    b. much
    c. many
    d. less

46. A: Have you ever visited Istanbul?
    B: No, I _____.
    a. didn't
    b. am not
    c. don't
    d. haven't

47. Charles can't decide _____ stay here or go back to France.
    a. should he
    b. if should he
    c. whether he should
    d. whether or not

48. Is it true _____ we only have three weeks of school left?
    a. what
    b. do
    c. if
    d. that

49. Our teacher said that we _____ to turn in our homework at the beginning of class.
    a. have
    b. had
    c. have had
    d. are having

50. _____ flowers are these? They're beautiful!
    a. Who
    b. Whom
    c. Who's
    d. Whose

Part A *Directions:* Combine the sentences with words in parentheses. Add any necessary punctuation. More than one answer may be possible.

Example: Ellis is trying to lose weight. Ellis didn't order any dessert. (because)

<u>   *Because Ellis is trying to lose weight, he didn't order any dessert.*   </u>

1. Mark wants to go to Alaska next summer. His wife would rather go to California. (*but*)

      _____

2. Mr. Meecham went to a meeting with a new client. He wore his best suit. (*when*)

      _____

3. This radio station plays lots of classic rock music. I enjoy listening to it. (*so*)

      _____

4. Chris is a great bass guitar player. Monica is a fantastic pianist. (*and*)

      _____

5. Nancy and Karen both enjoy playing tennis. They don't play together very often. (*although*)

      _____

6. We finished dinner. We had strawberry shortcake for dessert. (*as soon as*)

      _____

Part B *Directions:* Complete the sentences with a word or expression from the list. Use each word or expression one time only. The first one is done for you as an example.

> whether or not   how long   what time   ✓if   who   which   that

1. I don't care _____*if*_____ it takes you all night, I want this report finished by tomorrow.

2. Do you know _____ train goes to Sarajevo?

3. The students _____ acted in the play did a wonderful job!

4. I'm not sure _____ the concert lasts—probably about two hours.

5. It's true _____ spiders are helpful insects in the garden.

6. _____ James gets a high grade doesn't matter. He has learned a lot from writing this research paper.

7. I forgot _____ my dentist's appointment was, so I was fifteen minutes late.

Part C *Directions:* Make quoted speech. Add quotation marks, capital letters, and the correct punctuation.

Example: what is the name of the book you're looking for the clerk asked
<u>   "What is the name of the book you're looking for?" the clerk asked.   </u>

1. i'm so sorry to hear that your father is ill said margaret

2. john asked do you want to have muffins or scones for breakfast

3. could i please have a glass of water mary asked i'm really thirsty

Part D *Directions:* Change the quoted speech to reported speech. Use formal verb forms.

Example: Dora said, "I hope to travel around the world."
<u>   Dora said that she hoped to travel around the world.   </u>

1. Derek said, "Social networking Web sites are a great way to keep in touch."

   _____

2. Heidi said, "I have always dreamed of being an actress."

   _____

3. Adam asked, "Which video game do you like the best?"

   _____

4. Cole said, "I will go to college next year."

   _____

5. My friends asked, "Do you want to go to the coffee shop with us?"

   _____

Part E *Directions:* Correct the errors.

Example: Let's go to the restaurant on the corner. Their food is ~~gooder~~ *better* than the other place's.

1. Bradley is taller as his brothers.

2. I'll can help you in just a few minutes.

3. Playing the clarinet is not as difficulty as playing the oboe.

4. That is the funny joke I've heard in a long time.

5. My sisters like country-western music much better than I am. I don't enjoy listening to it.

6. If you don't fix the leak in your roof, it will cause farther water damage in your house.

7. My brother and I are twins, but I didn't see him since six years.

8. Laptop computers are usually convenienter than desktop computers.

9. How many apples you bought?

10. My classmate has as same name as me. We are both named William.

Part F *Directions:* Complete the sentences with **a, an, the**, or Ø.

Example: Will you please turn off ____the____ light?

1. I saw _____ really funny play at the theater last night.

2. _____ books that we borrowed from the library must be returned by Friday.

3. _____ alligator can weigh over 1,000 pounds.

4. It's not good for _____ children to watch too much TV.

5. Yesterday we went swimming near our house. _____ water was so cold!

Part G *Directions:* Circle the correct completions.

1. (*How far, How long*) is it from Paris to Marseille?

2. Students in Advanced English have a lot of (*homework, homeworks*) from that class.

3. Ken is allergic to (*the, Ø*) watermelon.

4. How (*much, many*) people will be at the meeting? I need to order (*a, Ø*) coffee.

5. I need (*a few, a little*) more time to prepare dinner. We'll eat in about fifteen minutes.

6. Would you like a (*piece, bowl*) of toast with your eggs?

7. Thousands of blogs (*publish, are published*) on the Internet every day.

8. (*The, Ø*) Indian Ocean touches four continents: Africa, Asia, Australia, and Antarctica.

9. Anthropologists are interested in (*to study, studying*) about ancient cultures.

10. When I was in Sicily, I went to the top of (*the, Ø*) Mt. Etna.

11. Alyssa invited (*several, much*) friends to her sixteenth birthday party.

12. I plan (*to go, going*) to the supermarket after I finish writing this email.

13. Scientists (*have been studying, have been studied*) the HIV/AIDS virus since the 1980s.

14. This umbrella isn't (*my, mine*). It belongs to Harry.

15. This camera (*gave, was given*) to me last year by my parents.

ANSWER KEY

CHAPTER 1

Quiz 1, p. 1

1. eats
2. does not/doesn't eat
3. enjoys
4. walk
5. take
6. drive
7. begins
8. rings
9. come
10. do not/don't have

Quiz 2, p. 1

walk., are walking.
walks., is walking.
walk., are walking.
walk., are walking.
walk., are walking.

Quiz 3, p. 2

A.
1. Does she
2. Does she
3. Is she
4. Does she
5. Is she

B.
1. do not/don't call
2. is not/isn't studying
3. do not/don't remember
4. are not/aren't taking
5. does not/doesn't live

Quiz 4, p. 3

A. Suggested Answers:
1. is often
2. always use
3. sometimes stops
4. always go
5. rarely see

B.
1. Does Alex *ever* go bowling?
2. We *seldom* go to the theater more than once a month.
3. Abdul is *usually* hungry at dinnertime.
4. I *never* stay out past midnight on weekends.
5. Lee doesn't *always* remember his homework.

Quiz 5, p. 4

1. is relaxing, is reading
2. comes, gets, throws
3. is ringing, is calling
4. are working, are cleaning, garden

Quiz 6, p. 4

1. need, are
2. understands
3. don't remember
4. belongs
5. am thinking
6. think
7. Are you having
8. do you know
9. don't have

Quiz 7, p. 5

1. is helping, helps
2. speaks, is speaking, need
3. is flying
4. exercises, is working, is not exercising
5. Do you like

Quiz 8, p. 5

1. A: Do your neighbors have
   B: they do, have
   A: Is he
   B: he is, loves
   A: Does he bark
   B: he does, is
   A: Are your parents
   B: they aren't

Quiz 9, p. 6

1. go, is
2. looks, Is, is, am trying
3. are having
4. Do, am leaving, don't
5. believe, own, work
6. are you doing, am sending, Do you send, don't, have
7. snows, freeze

Quiz 10, p. 7

1. usually begins, ends
2. are singing
3. is crying, is always
4. Are you watching, am,
   Do you and Sam want, don't
5. catches, walks
6. are painting
7. is, don't know, is

TEST 1, p. 8

A.
1. is coming
2. don't understand, lets
3. are watching
4. doesn't belong
5. need, is

B.
1. is getting, is coming
2. practices
3. goes, always plays, are kicking
4. works, often teaches, like, is
5. has, picks, is not, repair, are working

C.
1. do not/don't like
2. does not/doesn't want
3. is not /isn't
4. does not/doesn't see
5. am not

D.
1. The teacher **never yells** at her students. She is very patient.
2. What time **do** you leave school every day?

3. The Smiths **do not/don't** have a car. They take the bus everywhere.
4. **Does** Jonathan own an apartment or a house?
5. Wait. The sandwiches **are** ready, but not the pizza.

TEST 2, p. 10

A.
1. cuts, does
2. hear, is coming
3. reads, doesn't want
4. goes

B.
1. need
2. plays
3. is, are working, are writing, is correcting
4. own, wake, feeds, takes, have, leaves, catches, are staying, enjoying

C.
1. do not/don't have
2. is not/isn't
3. do not/don't enjoy
4. does not/doesn't taste
5. are not/aren't

D.
1. **Do** you **always** go to school by bus?
2. **I don't** like movies with sad endings.
3. Oh no, look! A rat **is playing** in the garbage can.
4. **Does** Maria go to work on Saturdays?
5. The books **are** on sale, but not the magazines.
6. Michelle **has** a beautiful engagement ring from her boyfriend.
7. Mr. Green is elderly, but he **doesn't** want to live with his children.

CHAPTER 2

Quiz 1, p. 12
1. Andrew studied for two hours yesterday.
2. Mark and Jan went to bed at 10:00 last night.
3. The alarm clock rang at 6:00 yesterday morning.
4. My grandparents visited us last month.
5. I took a nap yesterday afternoon.
6. Dr. Hughes taught medical students last Tuesday evening.
7. Victoria bought coffee on her way to work yesterday.
8. Mr. Wilson shopped at the Farmer's Market last Saturday.
9. Anne called her best friend last week.
10. It rained in Seattle last winter.

Quiz 2, p. 13
1. didn't snow
2. didn't travel
3. didn't develop
4. wasn't
5. didn't make
6. didn't write
7. didn't drive
8. weren't
9. didn't damage
10. didn't meet

Quiz 3, p. 14
1. Did
2. Were
3. Was
4. Was
5. Did
6. Were
7. Did
8. Did
9. Did
10. Was

Quiz 4, p. 15
1. Did Ben work, Ben didn't work
2. Was the restaurant, The restaurant wasn't
3. Did Julie get, Julie didn't get
4. Did the nurse take, The nurse didn't take
5. Did Nina buy, Nina didn't buy

Quiz 5, p. 16
1. A: Did Julia eat
   B: she did, ate
2. A: Did you go
   B: I didn't, was
3. A: Did a fish jump
   B: it did, jumped
4. A: Did the Warrens build
   B: they did, built
5. A: Did you sleep
   B: I didn't, heard, stayed
6. A: Did the monster movie scare
   B: it didn't, didn't scare, made

Quiz 6, p. 16
2. run
3. was
4. worked
5. weren't
6. understood
7. tied
8. had
9. cried
10. didn't yell
11. wasn't
12. hurt
13. knew
14. snored
15. cleaned
16. didn't have

Quiz 7, p. 17
1. sent
2. took
3. brought, did you buy
4. shook
5. picked
6. asked, didn't hear
7. ordered, was

Quiz 8, p. 17
2. was
3. didn't want
4. didn't tell
5. took
6. woke
7. decided
8. rode
9. got
10. wasn't
11. was
12. shopped
13. bought
14. found
15. ordered
16. walked
17. bought
18. sat
19. enjoyed
20. felt
21. was

Quiz 9, p. 18
2. /t/
3. /d/
4. /əd/
5. /t/
6. /əd/
7. /d/
8. /t/
9. /əd/
10. /d/
11. /t/

Quiz 10, p. 18

A.
- _6_ First the bird began flying.
  Then I looked out the window.
- _2_ First I ended the call.
  Then my doorbell began ringing.
- _3_ First I woke up.
  Then my mother smiled.
- _1_ First my doorbell started to ring.
  Then I ended the call.
- _5_ First I looked out the window.
  Then the bird started to fly.
- _4_ First my mother began smiling.
  Then I woke up.

B.
1. Juliette
2. Max
3. the boys
4. Jan
5. Atsushi

Quiz 11, p. 19

Possible answers:
2. Linda met with students while she was working in her office.
   Linda called her son while she was waiting for the bus.
   Linda met an old friend while she was sitting at the snack bar.
3. While Janet was working in her office, she checked her email.
   While Janet was waiting for the bus, she read a novel.
   While Janet was sitting at the snack bar, she ate some peanuts.
4. Simone answered the phone while she was working in her office.
   Simone sent a text message while she was waiting for the bus.
   Simone drank a cola while she was sitting at the snack bar.
5. While Linda was working in her office, she met with students.
   While Linda was waiting for the bus, she called her son.
   While Linda was sitting at the snack bar, she met an old friend.
6. Janet checked her email while she was working in her office.
   Janet read a novel while she was waiting for the bus.
   Janet ate some peanuts while she was sitting at the snack bar.

Quiz 12, p. 20

1. decided
2. spent, were living, studied
3. made, won
4. planned
5. ran, was traveling, tried, returned, didn't have
6. had, was blowing/blew, was howling/howled, was trying, became, hid
7. lived, spoke

Quiz 13, p. 21

3. were talking	8. was
4. joined	9. asked
5. chatted	10. wasn't
6. decided	11. pointed
7. didn't know	12. hoped

Quiz 14, p. 21

2. First: found a recipe — Second: made a shopping list
3. First: shopped — Second: had everything
4. First: finished shopping — Second: went home
5. First: got home — Second: turned on the oven
6. First: measured — Second: stirred
7. First: mixed everything — Second: poured batter
8. First: finished baking — Second: took the cake out
9. First: waited — Second: cut the cake
10. First: served — Second: began to eat
11. First: enjoyed — Second: thanked

Quiz 15, p. 22

1. After Donna got a ticket for speeding, she drove home very slowly.
2. Eric took a shower as soon as he got home.
3. While Maria and Lucio were exercising, their children played a board game.
4. Joy's parents drove her to school before she got her driver's license.
5. Rick gave the children a bath while Rachel was cooking dinner.
6. As soon as I put on my pajamas, I went to bed.
7. Until my dad got a job in Italy, my family lived in Germany.
8. Before Kevin watched a movie, he did his homework.
9. The students were nervous until the exam began.
10. Everyone started dancing after the band started to play.

Quiz 16, p. 23

2. used to swim	7. used to wake up
3. used to be	8. used to live
4. used to drink	9. used to ski
5. used to work	10. used to speak
6. used to have	11. used to chase

Quiz 17, p. 23

1. Joe **didn't** walk to work yesterday. He **took** the bus.
2. Mary **went** to the emergency room at midnight last night.
3. While Dr. Hughes **was listening** to his patient, his cell phone rang. He **didn't** answer it.
4. Marco **didn't** use to swim, but now he does because he **took** swimming lessons.
5. **After** Tua got a new job**,** he celebrated his success with his friends.
6. When the phone **rang** at 11:00 last night, I was in a deep sleep. I almost **didn't** hear it.

Quiz 18, p. 24

1. A: do you get up
   B: wake up, rises, slept, felt
2. catches, caught, was chasing, knocked
3. left, bought
4. A: are you doing
   B: am cleaning, got, were sleeping, made

5. traveled, were traveling, visited, didn't stay, enjoyed
6. watch, watched
7. stepped, was waiting
8. live, live/are living, moved, missed, am, like
9. A: Did you see
   B: didn't
   A: went

TEST 1, p. 25

A.
1. took
2. saw
3. wanted
4. left
5. found
6. hiked
7. were hiking
8. heard
9. stood
10. waited
11. were waiting
12. came
13. was eating
14. saw
15. walked
16. didn't follow
17. got

B.
A: learned
B: wasn't, taught, showed
A: Do you like
B: love

C.
1. Did, made
2. did, didn't hear
3. look, am, didn't sleep

D.
1. Bees **used to make** honey in a tree next to our house until lightning split the tree in half.
2. Carol **didn't go** to work yesterday because her son **was** sick.
3. Doug and Peter **had** a party last weekend. Everyone from our class **came**.
4. **Were** you upset with your test results yesterday?
5. After Bill **woke** up, he **got** up.

TEST 2, p. 27

A.
1. was
2. sat
3. didn't go
4. was sitting
5. watched/was watching
6. was talking
7. was trying
8. was crying
9. was eating
10. looked
11. began
12. waited
13. felt

B.
A: are you doing
B: am looking, spent
A: do they live
A: did you do
B: rented, spent, took, were walking, saw
A: did you stay
B: want

C.
1. is watching, was talking, opened, poured, added, cleaned, looks
2.
   A: did
   B: ate, had
   A: Was
   B: tasted

D.
1. Dr. Martin used to **work** in a hospital, but now she has a private practice.
2. I was home alone last night. First, I **cooked** dinner. Then, I **washed** the dishes.
3. Matt **was** busy yesterday. He **didn't** go to the party.
4. The Millers **bought** a restaurant last month. They **opened** for business last week.
5. The baby **tried** to crawl a few times, but her legs **aren't/weren't** strong enough yet.
6. Liz and Ron **planned** to get married last summer, but just before the wedding, Ron **lost** his job. Now they are waiting until next summer.
7. Professor Scott **didn't have** time to help us with our lab experiment yesterday. Maybe she can today.
8. Ernesto **built** a model train set by himself in his basement. He finished it last month.

CHAPTER 3

Quiz 1, p. 29
1. tomorrow
2. tomorrow
3. every day
4. yesterday
5. every day
6. yesterday
7. tomorrow
8. every day
9. tomorrow
10. yesterday

Quiz 2, p. 29
1. will have, are going to have
2. will meet, is going to meet
3. will return, am going to return
4. will be, are going to be
5. will leave, are going to leave

Quiz 3, p. 30
1. Will the cat catch
   Is the cat going to catch
2. Will Dr. Brown retire
   Is Dr. Brown going to retire
3. Will your family be
   Is your family going to be
4. Will our team win
   Is our team going to win
5. Will Mr. and Mrs. Bell find
   Are Mr. and Mrs. Bell going to find

Quiz 4, p. 30
1. A: are we going to leave
   B: are going to leave
2. A: Are you going to go
   B: am going to buy
3. A: is not/isn't going to visit
   B: is she going to do
   A: is going to spend
4. A: are going to go
   B: is going to perform
   A: am not going to be

Quiz 5, p. 31
1. will drive
2. will take
3. will not/won't be
4. will listen
5. will be
6. will rain
7. will bring
8. will take
9. Will we go
10. will not/won't have

Quiz 6, p. 32

1. We're
2. we'll
3. I'm
4. You're
5. aren't
6. He's
7. He'll
8. You'll
9. won't
10. We're

Quiz 7, p. 32

2. 50%
3. 90%
4. 50%
5. 100%
6. 100%
7. 100%
8. 90%
9. 50%
10. 50%
11. 90%

Quiz 8, p. 33

1. Tom will probably take/is probably going to take the cat to the vet tomorrow.
   The vet may give the cat some medicine.
2. Maybe Max will quit/is going to quit his job.
   Max's boss probably won't be/isn't going to be upset.
3. Yujung may get a job in international business.
   Maybe she will earn/is going to earn a good salary with her language skills.
4. They probably won't go/are not going to go skiing this year.
   They may spend a week on the Mediterranean.
5. They probably won't go/aren't going to go to a movie theater this weekend.
   Maybe they will watch/are going to watch a movie on DVD at home this weekend.

Quiz 9, p. 34

1. prediction
2. prior plan
3. decide/volunteer
4. prediction
5. prediction
6. prior plan
7. decide/volunteer
8. prior plan
9. prediction
10. decide/volunteer

Quiz 10, p. 35

1. will
2. is going to
3. are going to
4. will
5. will
6. are going to
7. will/are going to, will
8. is going to, are going to

Quiz 11, p. 36

1. Before the Smiths fly to Thailand, they will pick up their airplane tickets.
2. As soon as Sonya gets dressed, she will go to work.
3. Chris will stay home until he feels better.
4. Before Ellen makes lunch, she will wash her hands.
5. After Mr. Hill takes the driving test, he will get a driver's license.
6. When the Thompsons get a new phone, they will call us.
7. If Janice wins a lot of money, she will quit her job.
8. David will go home after he goes to the staff meeting.
9. Before Antonio mails the letter, he will buy a stamp at the Post Office.
10. Josh will be in bed by midnight if he finishes his homework.

Quiz 12, p. 37

A.
1. am changing
2. are remodeling
3. is joining
4. is taking
5. Are, moving

B.
1. tonight, right now, all next week
2. today, tomorrow, tonight, next week
3. today, in one hour, next week, next year
4. now, in 10 minutes, tomorrow, next week
5. tomorrow, in a few minutes, soon

Quiz 13, p. 38

A.
1. is going, is going to go
2. is visiting, is going to visit
3. leaves, is leaving, is going to leave
4. is staying, is going to stay

B.
1. starts, is starting, is going to start
2. am bringing, am going to bring

C.
1. is having, is going to have
2. opens, is opening, is going to open
3. are going, are going to go
4. closes, is closing, is going to close

Quiz 14, p. 38

2. a, c, d
3. a, b, c, d
4. a, b
5. b, c
6. a, b, c, d

Quiz 15, p. 39

1. After **I feed** the children, I will start dinner for the rest of us.
2. If I ~~will~~ have time, I will help you.
3. **You will get / You're going to get** a ticket.
4. Tina **will wash / is going to wash / is washing** the windows this afternoon.
5. Ms. Reed **intends** to help you with your expense report.
6. I plan **to** go to a conference on early childhood learning.
7. Shhh. The baby **is** about to go to sleep.
8. When are we **going to** leave?
9. In two years, I **will quit / am going to quit my job** and **sail** around the world.
10. Charlie and Kate **will get / are getting / are going to get** married next summer.

Quiz 16, p. 39

2. I am **going to hike and climb** for several days.
3. At night, when I ~~will~~ get tired, I will find a place to set up my tent.
4. I will **build** a campfire and **cook** my food.
5. Then I **will look / am going to look** at the stars through my small telescope.
6. I will probably **be** tired, so I **will go / am going to go** to bed early.
7. I **will sleep** very hard because my muscles are going **to** be very tired.
8. When I ~~will~~ wake up in the morning, I **will feel / am going to feel** much better.
9. It **is going to be / will be** a wonderful vacation.

Quiz 17, p. 40

1. clears, will take off/is going to take off, will have/are going to have/have
2. gave, were
3. am taking/am going to take, are meeting/are going to meet, finish, are going/are going to go
4. B: will check
   A: am coming
5. A: Are you going to watch/Will you watch
   B: am working/am going to work
6. B: rings
   A: will the bell ring/is the bell going to ring
7. am picking up/am going to pick up, (am) taking/(am going to) take, am going to eat, are watching/are going to watch

TEST 1, p. 41

Part A

A.

1. will help
2. will probably see
3. won't forget
4. will go, Will you get

B.

5. A: are you going to do
   B: am going to visit
   A: Are you going to stay
   B: am probably going to be, I am going to look

C.

6. will help
7. am going to make
8. am going to ask, is she going to say/will she say, she will say/she is going to say

Part B

1. is going to play/is playing
2. is going to win/will win
3. starts will start/is going to start
4. are meeting/are going to meet
5. will order/am going to order

Part C

1. A: crashed
   B: Did you lose
   A: make, will check
2. A: does your flight arrive

Part D

1. After we ~~will~~ get married, we will buy a house.
2. Correct
3. Julia will sing in the choir and ~~going to~~ play the piano at her school concert next week.
4. I **am going / will go / am going to go** downtown tomorrow with my friends.
5. My husband and I ~~are~~ will not use our credit card so much next month.
6. If Eric **calls** me, I am going tell him I am not available to work this weekend.
7. Correct
8. Tomorrow when John **gets** home, he will help you plant your vegetable garden.
9. Toshi **may** quit his job soon. / **Maybe Toshi will** quit his job soon.
10. Yoko **will cry / is going to cry** when she hears my news.

TEST 2, p. 43

Part A

A.

1. B: will rain, will be, will probably have, won't rain
   A: will bring

B.

2. A: are you going to do
   B: am going to take, put, am probably going to give
   A: are going to like

C.

3. will dry
4. am going to go, am going to swim
5. are going to sell
6. will get

Part B

1. are planting/are going to plant
2. are going to pull/are pulling
3. will dig up/are going to dig up, are going to decide/will decide
4. will die, is going to die

Part C

1. A: is buzzing, sit, will sting
   B: flew
2. A: were you
   B: was, needed
   A: Are you working/Are you going to work
   B: need, will call

Part D

1. Correct
2. The business office will **close** for one week next month.
3. Dinner is almost ready. The oven timer **is** about **to** go off.
4. Fortunately, our teacher **is not going to** give us a quiz tomorrow.
5. Next Saturday, Boris will stay home and **clean** out his garage.
6. Correct
7. Masako **is buying / is going to buy / will buy** a new truck next week. She plans to drive it to work.
8. Our electric bill **may increase** next month. **Maybe** our electric bill is going to increase next month.
9. Correct
10. Tomorrow when Pierre **gets** to work, he **will / is going to** interview several candidates for the assistant manager position.

CHAPTER 4

Quiz 1, p. 45

2. has been
3. has worked
4. has met
5. has loved
6. has visited
7. has gone
8. has eaten
9. has drunk
10. has seen
11. has traveled

Quiz 2, p. 46

2. has enjoyed
3. have been
4. has become
5. has visited
6. has written
7. has added
8. has had
9. has sewn
10. (has) stuck
11. has found

Quiz 3, p. 47

1. for
2. since
3. for
4. since
5. for
6. since
7. since
8. since
9. for
10. for

Quiz 4, p. 47

1. since, for
2. for, for
3. since, since
4. for, since
5. since, for, since

Quiz 5, p. 48

1. was
2. took
3. have been
4. received
5. has had
6. met
7. took
8. drove
9. has ridden
10. came

Quiz 6, p. 48

1. hasn't stopped
2. haven't met
3. hasn't finished
4. haven't passed
5. hasn't started
6. haven't called
7. haven't bought
8. hasn't gone
9. haven't come
10. haven't gotten

Quiz 7, p. 49

1. A: Have Cara and Jenn finished
   B: haven't, haven't finished
2. A: Have you ever gone
   B: have, have been
3. A: Has Adam ever played
   B: hasn't, has never played
4. A: Has the museum had
   B: has, have visited
5. A: Has Natalia ever made
   B: hasn't, has never tried

Quiz 8, p. 50

2. Has Miriam picked up her kids at school yet?
   No, she hasn't picked up her kids at school yet.
3. Has Miriam gone to her exercise class yet?
   Yes, she has already gone to her exercise class. OR
   Yes, she has gone to her exercise class already.
4. Has Miriam already had dinner with the Costas?
   OR Has Miriam had dinner with the Costas already?
   No, she hasn't had dinner with the Costas yet.
5. Has Miriam met with the electrician yet?
   Yes, she has already met with the electrician. OR
   Yes, she has met with the electrician already.
6. Has Miriam gotten a haircut yet?
   No, she hasn't gotten a haircut yet.

Quiz 9, p. 51

1. a
2. b
3. b
4. b
5. b
6. a
7. b
8. a
9. b
10. b

Quiz 10, p. 52

1. has drunk, didn't sleep
2. Has Oscar ever been, has, went
3. haven't eaten, wasn't
4. went, haven't had
5. won, has won

Quiz 11, p. 52

A.
2. am reading, have been reading
3. aren't working, haven't been working
4. is teaching, has been teaching
5. are dancing, have been dancing
6. isn't studying, hasn't been studying
7. are practicing, have been practicing
8. are doing, have been doing

B.
1. is doing, has been studying
2. A: are you doing
   B: am watching, have been watching
3. are you going

Quiz 12, p. 53

A.
1. has been barking
2. has been beeping
3. has been speaking
4. have been driving
5. have been downloading

B.
1. How long have you been standing here?
2. I have been working since 10:00 A.M.
3. It has been snowing for two days.
4. How long have they been studying for the test?
5. The taxi has been waiting for ten minutes.

Quiz 13, p. 54

1. has gone
2. have been combing
3. haven't talked
4. have been cooking
5. has never flown
6. have known
7. have been working
8. have heard
9. has been working
10. hasn't paid

Quiz 14, p. 55

1. a. 2nd
   b. 1st
2. a. 1st
   b. 2nd
3. a. 2nd
   b. 1st
4. a. 1st
   b. 2nd
5. a. 2nd
   b. 1st

Quiz 15, p. 56

1. had already left
2. hadn't thought
3. had already eaten
4. had already put up
5. had started
6. had already sold
7. had already paid
8. had already met
9. had already read
10. had left

Quiz 16, p. 57

1. Rita **left** two weeks ago . . .
2. She **hadn't visited** them . . .
3. Her sister and brother-in-law **have lived** . . .
4. She **has been** there many times . . .
5. Rizal Park **has** some beautiful . . .
6. . . . she has **taken** her niece . . .
7. Rita **hasn't** visited it yet.
8. . . . it **has** become Rita's favorite place . . .
9. Rita **has been/has gone** there often in the evenings.
10. Rita's parents **have** come to the U.S . . .

Quiz 17, p. 58

1. c	8. d	15. c
2. b	9. b	16. c
3. d	10. b	17. c
4. a	11. d	18. a
5. c	12. c	19. d
6. c	13. d	20. b
7. a	14. d	

TEST 1, p. 60

Part A

1. paid	6. grown
2. swum	7. left
3. known	8. cut
4. waited	9. begun
5. studied	10. eaten

Part B

1. for	4. for
2. since	5. since
3. since	6. for

Part C

1. moved, have met
2. have had, was
3. have played

Part D

1. A: Have you ever tried
   B: haven't, have made
2. A: Have you finished
   B: have
3. A: has been scratching
4. A: Has Anna driven
   B: hasn't
5. A: Have you been crying

Part E

1. a	4. b
2. b	5. b
3. a	

Part F

1. Gary **has been** at work . . .
2. Steve **has** enjoyed listening . . .
3. Nadia **hasn't** finished her dinner yet.
4. It **has rained** on my birthday every year . . .
5. I **have already decided** to major. . .

TEST 2, p. 62

Part A

1. visited	6. bought
2. spoken	7. won
3. thought	8. read
4. written	9. taught
5. stood	10. sold

Part B

1. for	4. since
2. for	5. for
3. since	6. since

Part C

1. quit, have traveled
2. have been, visited
3. have enjoyed

Part D

1. A: Have you ever worn
   B: haven't
2. A: Have you been jumping
   B: have
3. A: has been flying
4. A: Have you ever gotten
   B: have, have gotten
5. A: Have you done
   B: have

Part E

1. b	4. b
2. a	5. a
3. a	

Part F

1. Sandy **has** been trying . . .
2. Ted **hasn't** called yet.
3. Andy **has been** on vacation . . .
4. I **have known** about those problems . . .
5. Chris **has started** his Ph.D. thesis . . .

CHAPTER 5

Quiz 1, p. 64

1. Does, does	6. Have, haven't
2. Is, is	7. Are, aren't
3. Are, am	8. Will, will
4. Do, do	9. Is, is
5. Are, am	10. Do, do

Quiz 2, p. 64

1. A: Are you hungry?
   B: I'm not.
2. A: Is dinner ready?
   B: it is.
3. A: Did it rain last night?
   B: it didn't.
4. A: Is John sending a text message?
   B: he is.
5. A: Has the mail already come?
   B. it has.
6. A: Will Mr. and Mrs. Jennings be at the wedding?
   B: they won't.
7. A: Are they going to be here soon?
   B: they are.

8. A: Are you in a hurry?
   B: I am.
9. A: Has the movie started yet?
   B: it hasn't.
10. A: Did I/we already tell you that?
    B: you did.

Quiz 3, p. 65

1. a   6. a
2. b   7. c
3. a   8. a
4. c   9. c
5. b   10. a

Quiz 4, p. 66

Suggested answers:
1. Where are Sven and Erik going?
   When are Sven and Erik going to Greece?
2. What time will their flight arrive in Athens?
   When will their flight arrive in Athens?
3. Where does Sven want to go?
   Why does Sven want to go to Athens?
4. Why was Erik in Greece five years ago?
   When was Erik a student in Greece?
5. Where will Sven and Erik go on July fifteenth?
   Why will Sven and Erik return home on July fifteenth?

Quiz 5, p. 67

1. What   6. Who
2. Who   7. Who
3. What   8. What
4. Who   9. Who
5. What   10. Who

Quiz 6, p. 68

1. Who did Bill see?
2. Who saw the fox?
3. Who did Marcella pay?
4. What did Charles order?
5. Who rides a motorcycle?
6. Who came late?
7. What did Ruth bring home?
8. What broke?
9. Who did Tara call?
10. Who won a contest?

Quiz 7, p. 69

1. What do geologists do?
2. What will you do
3. What does Anne usually do
4. What did Carl do
5. What will you do
6. What is Caroline doing?
7. What are you going to do tomorrow?
8. What is David going to do this weekend?
9. What did you do
10. What do you do

Quiz 8, p. 70

1. Which   6. What
2. what   7. which
3. What   8. What
4. which   9. Which
5. what   10. What

Quiz 9, p. 71

1. Who   6. Whose
2. Who   7. Who
3. Whose   8. Who
4. Whose   9. Who
5. Who   10. Whose

Quiz 10, p. 71

A.
1. Who's   4. Whose
2. Who's   5. Who's
3. Whose

B.
1. Who's the new neighbor?
2. Whose dog always barks at the mailman?
3. Whose car is parked across the street?
4. Who's working in his garden?
5. Who's coming to the barbecue?

Quiz 11, p. 72

2. d   6. a   9. h
3. i   7. e   10. k
4. g   8. c   11. b
5. j

Quiz 12, p. 73

1. often, far, long
2. often, long, far
3. far, long, often, far

Quiz 13, p. 74

1. How long did it take to check your email?
2. How do you spell "elephant"?
3. How often do you go to the movies OR
   How many times a month do you go to the movies?
4. How did you come/get here?
5. How far away is your school?
6. How soon do we need to leave?
7. How do you pronounce "Ms."?
8. How old is Jon?
9. How are you feeling?
10. How well does Mr. Wang speak English?

Quiz 14, p. 75

A.
2. Why do you want to work here?
3. Where do you work now?
4. How long have you worked there?
5. What was your favorite project?
6. Who is your supervisor?

B.
1. Whose vacation was the most exciting?
2. How far did you ride?
3. How did it feel?
4. How often do you go to the beach?
5. When did you go to the beach?

Quiz 15, p. 76

1. aren't   6. do
2. are   7. isn't
3. don't   8. does
4. aren't   9. aren't
5. is   10. do

Quiz 16, p. 76

1. haven't
2. have
3. wasn't
4. didn't
5. did
6. aren't
7. didn't
8. have
9. aren't
10. hasn't

Quiz 17, p. 77

1. **Whose** cell phone is that, mine or yours?
2. I was right about the price of the computer, **wasn't** I?
3. What kind **of** ethnic food **do** you like to cook?
4. When **does your plane arrive** from Paris?
5. **Who** helped you prepare the dinner?
6. Why **did** you leave without me?
7. Who **did you** take to work?
8. **How often** do you see your family?
9. His name is Henri, **isn't it**?
10. How many **times** a week do you exercise?

TEST 1, p. 78

Part A

1. How
2. How long
3. Whose
4. Who
5. When / How soon
6. Which
7. Why
8. How often
9. What
10. How far

Part B

1. How often does she train / How much does she train / How long does she train
2. How far does she run / How much does she run
3. How fast does she run
4. When is she going to run in a marathon
5. Who will she run with
6. What does she plan to do
7. How does she spell her name

Part C

1. don't
2. did
3. hasn't
4. are
5. didn't
6. isn't

Part D

1. What **do** you know about the new department manager?
2. That dog is barking so loudly. **Who does it belong to? / Whose is it?**
3. What **does "besides" mean**?
4. Marta changed jobs last month, **didn't** she?
5. Which movie **did** you see last night, *Monsters* or *Dragons*?
6. **How far is it** from Paris to London? / **How long does it take to go** from Paris to London?
7. **Who told** you about the party?

TEST 2, p. 80

Part A

1. Where
2. How far
3. How long
4. Why
5. How often
6. How
7. Who
8. When / How soon
9. Which
10. Whose

Part B

1. When did Jill get a new job
2. Where does she work
3. What is she going to do for the company
4. How long does she plan to be there
5. How often does she drive to work
6. How does she go to work on the other days
7. How many hours a week does she work / How much does she work

Part C

1. didn't
2. is
3. do
4. didn't
5. isn't
6. are
7. do

Part D

1. What **does "anyway" mean**?
2. How **do** you feel about the talk you had . . .
3. **Who** left their dirty dishes . . .
4. What kind **of** soup **do** you want . . .
5. Sonya needs more time, **doesn't** she?
6. How long **does it take** to get . . .

CHAPTER 6

Quiz 1, p. 82

2. /əz/
3. /s/
4. /z/
5. /z/
6. /s/
7. /əz/
8. /s/
9. /z/
10. /s/
11. /əz/

Quiz 2, p. 82

2. mice
3. leaf
4. cities
5. tomato
6. boxes
7. women
8. deer
9. teeth
10. children
11. businesses

Quiz 3, p. 83

1. | Steve | asked | a question |
        S   V   O
2. | His question | wasn't | (none) |
        S   V   O
3. | The phone | rang | (none) |
        S   V   O
4. | I | answered | the phone |
      S   V   O
5. | Hanifa | loves | animals |
        S   V   O
6. | She | has had | many pets |
        S   V   O
7. | The police | stopped | several cars |
        S   V   O
8. | The drivers | looked | (none) |
        S   V   O
9. | My daughter | goes | (none) |
        S   V   O
10. | She | is studying | anthropology |
        S   V   O

Quiz 4, p. 84

1. N
2. V
3. V
4. N
5. V
6. N
7. N
8. V
9. V
10. N

Quiz 5, p. 84

preposition	*object of preposition*
1. during	the winter
in	the winter months
2. in	the snow
at	each other
3. with	many people
on	a snowboard
4. on	ice and snow
5. into	a frozen pond
near	their home
beneath	the ice
to	safety

Quiz 6, p. 85

2. at		7. in	
3. on		8. on	
4. on		9. in	
5. in		10. in	
6. in		11. on	

Quiz 7, p. 85

1. lives		6. use	
2. is		7. are	
3. are		8. have	
4. needs		9. Do	
5. don't		10. are	

Quiz 8, p. 86

1. new	4. hot, buttery
2. funny	5. refreshing, cold
3. comfortable	6. long, late

Quiz 9, p. 86

1. He used a tall ladder to wash the dirty windows.
2. Nan put the clean clothes into the lower drawer.
3. The interesting book told the sad story of the Great Chicago Fire of 1871.
4. The worried manager looked at the angry workers.
5. The happy child played with her new toy.

Quiz 10, p. 87

1. Your **flower** garden has many unusual flowers.
2. The mosquitos were really bad on our camping trip. I got a lot of **mosquito** bites.
3. There is **customer** parking in front of the store. The customers are happy about that.
4. I see three **spider** webs in the bathroom. I hate spiders!
5. All the **computer** printers in the library are new, but the computers are old.
6. Three people in our office are celebrating their birthdays tomorrow. There will be a lot of **birthday** cake to eat.
7. Don't throw away the **egg** cartons. We will put the hard-boiled eggs in them.
8. I love all the noodles in this soup. It's great **noodle** soup.
9. My doctor gave me an **exercise** plan. I have to do my exercises every day.
10. Collin lives in a two-**bedroom** apartment. The bedrooms are quite large.

Quiz 11, p. 88

2. them		7. We	
3. They		8. them	
4. We		9. She	
5. We		10. her	
6. us		11. her	

Quiz 12, p. 89

1. teachers'	6. woman's
2. Brown's	7. grandson's
3. wife's	8. students'
4. children's	9. hospitals'
5. theater's	10. city's

Quiz 13, p. 89

1. Mine	5. its
2. her	6. it's
3. mine	7. Their, They're, theirs, it's, their
4. your, ours	8. our, It's, it

Quiz 14, p. 90

1. himself	6. ourselves
2. yourselves	7. himself
3. herself	8. itself
4. myself	9. themselves
5. herself	10. yourself

Quiz 15, p. 90

1. another	5. the other, the other
2. another	6. another, the other
3. the other	7. another
4. another	8. the other

Quiz 16, p. 91

1. the others	6. others
2. other	7. the other
3. the others	8. the others
4. others	9. the others
5. other	10. others

Quiz 17, p. 92

1. the other	6. others
2. another	7. another
3. The others	8. the other
4. others	9. another, other
5. another	

Quiz 18, p. 93

1. There are thirty **days** in the month of April.
2. Our **apartment** manager is out of town this week.
3. The bird has brought some worms to feed **its** young.
4. She was born **on** September 8, 1993.
5. I broke my right hand, so I need to write with **the other** one.
6. The cars in the city **produce** a lot of pollution.
7. One hundred people are waiting in the rain to buy **tickets** for the concert. Everyone **seems** patient, but cold.
8. The **children's** swimming pool in the city is open to all children aged three to seven.
9. Mr. **Lee's** company recycles old computers.
10. The dancers practiced **their dance steps all morning in the studio.**

TEST 1, p. 94

A.
1. I have two children. My **children's names** are Emma and Ellen.
2. People at the lecture thought the **speaker's ideas** were fascinating
3. My new **computer isn't/computers aren't** working properly. The **instructions** aren't clear.
4. **Beth**'s computer is similar to mine. She's going to let me use hers.
5. There are several **articles** on **women** in **today's** newspaper.

B.
1. his
2. yours, Mine
3. his, her, herself
4. yours, hers
5. me, They're, their, there, It's
6. me, We

C.
1. the others
2. another
3. other
4. others
5. Another, The other

D.
1. Tony was born **on** April 2, 1998.
2. The bird's nest **has** several eggs in it.
3. Several **language** schools offer university preparation.
4. In the morning, I like to take **long walks in the park.**
5. Every **student** in the class **is** working hard and making progress.
6. The doctor is busy **at** the moment.
7. Nancy's **flower** garden has many roses in it.
8. Yesterday morning we saw three **deer** drinking water from the lake.
9. Many **words** in French **are** difficult for me to pronounce.
10. My **sister's** husband is a really funny guy. He always **tells** jokes.

TEST 2, p. 96

A.
1. Our dog had three **puppies** last night.
2. My sister has twins. Her **babies' names** are Tyler and Spencer.
3. Professor **Brown's** math **classes** are very difficult
4. The two other math **teacher's courses** are easier.
5. The **university's** main computer is having technical **problems**, so **students** cannot register at this time.

B.
1. mine
2. Your, yourself
3. its, its, It's
4. His, He, himself, him, His
5. I, his
6. there, They're

C.
1. another
2. other
3. another
4. the others
5. others
6. The other

D.
1. We rented **a cabin in the mountains for one month**.
2. What are you doing **on** Thursday evening?
3. My **apartment** building is small. It has only eleven **units**.
4. Your appointment is scheduled for Monday **in** the afternoon.
5. There **are** several **cars** in our driveway. Who do they belong to?
6. The table **has** scratches on it from the **children's** toys.
7. In the future, every **student** will need to turn in typed assignments.
8. I fell asleep **at** nine o'clock last night.
9. The wedding will be **in** May.
10. The apples in the box **were** rotten, so we didn't eat them.

CHAPTER 7

Quiz 1, p. 98

1.	Ø	6.	Ø
2.	to	7.	Ø
3.	Ø	8.	to
4.	to	9.	Ø
5.	Ø	10.	Ø

Quiz 2, p. 98

A.
1. can't, can
2. can't, can
3. can, can't
4. can't, can
5. can, can't

B.
1. could
2. wasn't able to
3. could/was able to, couldn't/wasn't able to
4. could/was able to

Quiz 3, p. 99

2.	permission	7.	permission
3.	possibility	8.	permission
4.	permission	9.	possibility
5.	possibility	10.	permission
6.	possibility	11.	possibility

Quiz 4, p. 100

1. We might go away this weekend.
2. Maybe it will snow tomorrow.
3. Maybe our baseball team will win the championship.
4. Joan might be in the hospital.
5. David may take the driving test tomorrow.
6. Sara might meet with us this afternoon.
7. Maybe James will be late for the meeting.
8. My keys may be in my backpack.
9. We may go to a movie tonight.
10. Maybe the car will be ready later this afternoon.

Quiz 5, p. 101

2.	past ability	7.	future possibility
3.	present possibility	8.	past ability
4.	past ability	9.	future possibility
5.	future possibility	10.	present possibility
6.	present possibility	11.	future possibility

Quiz 6, p. 102

Answers may vary.
1. could rain/might snow/might be sunny
2. could cook/could fix, could have/could barbecue
3. could shop/could look, might try/could go to
4. could be/might be
5. could be/might be, could be/might be
6. might go to/could watch, might stay/could stay

Quiz 7, p. 103

1. May, Could, Can
2. Could, Can, Would, Will
3. Could, Can, Would, Will
4. May, Could, Can
5. May, Could, Can
6. Could, Can, Would, Will
7. May, Could, Can
8. Could, Can, Would, Will
9. May, Could, Can
10. Could, Can, Would, Will

Quiz 8, p. 104

A.
1. should be
2. should learn
3. shouldn't expect
4. shouldn't be
5. should try

B. *Answers may vary.*
1. You should/ought to take it to the repair shop.
2. You should/ought to go to the doctor.
3. You should/ought to get something to eat.
4. He should/ought to talk to his teacher about it.
5. You should/ought get another cup of hot coffee.

Quiz 9, p. 105

A.
1. should/ought to
2. had better not
3. should/ought to
4. had better
5. had better not

B. *Answers may vary.*
1. should put cold water on it
2. should call for help
3. should call the apartment manager
4. should call his friend
5. should fix it before someone gets hurt

The above sentences can also be written with *had better* or *ought to.*

Quiz 10, p. 106

1. had to
2. had to
3. have to
4. must
5. have got to
6. have to
7. have got to
8. must
9. had to
10. has got to

Quiz 11, p. 106

1. don't have to
2. must not
3. don't have to
4. must not
5. don't have to
6. don't have to
7. doesn't have to
8. don't have to
9. must not
10. must not

Quiz 12, p. 107

2. necessity
3. logical conclusion
4. necessity
5. necessity
6. logical conclusion
7. logical conclusion
8. necessity
9. logical conclusion
10. logical conclusion
11. logical conclusion

Quiz 13, p. 107

1. must
2. must not
3. must
4. must
5. must not
6. must not
7. must
8. must
9. must not
10. must

Quiz 14, p. 108

1. don't
2. shouldn't
3. can
4. would
5. won't
6. should
7. wouldn't
8. won't
9. could
10. does

Quiz 15, p. 109

1. Prepare
2. Measure
3. Mix
4. Add
5. Pour
6. Bake
7. test
8. let
9. remove
10. decorate

Quiz 16, p. 110

1. would rather
2. likes
3. prefer
4. would rather
5. prefers
6. would rather
7. prefers
8. like
9. prefer
10. would rather

Quiz 17, p. 110

2. b	9. c	16. a
3. c	10. a	17. b
4. b	11. c	18. a
5. a	12. a	19. b
6. a	13. a	20. c
7. c	14. a	21. c
8. b	15. c	

TEST 1, p. 112

Part A
1. b
2. c
3. a
4. a
5. c
6. b
7. c
8. b
9. c
10. b

Part B
1. can
2. could/might
3. could
4. could/might
5. could

Part C
Answers will vary.
1. I had to go to work.
2. I must past a test.
3. Children shouldn't play with medicine.
4. I should rest.
5. I have to brush my teeth.

Part D

1. I'm feeling hot. I ought **to** take my temperature.
2. **Could/Can/May** I borrow your pen?
3. I don't feel like cooking. **Let's order** a pizza.
4. We'll be free on Saturday. We **could meet** then.
5. Look at the sky. It could snow tomorrow, **couldn't** it?
6. Thomas is late. He **could/might/may** have car trouble again.
7. Children **had better not/mustn't** play with matches.
8. Why **don't we** go for a walk after dinner?
9. I don't want to stay home this weekend. **I would rather** go hiking.
10. Jenny **has** to be more careful with her glasses. She has broken them twice.

TEST 2, p. 114

Part A

1. b
2. a
3. c
4. b
5. b
6. b
7. a
8. c
9. a
10. c

Part B

1. can
2. could
3. might/could
4. might
5. could

Part C

Answers will vary.

1. I must go to the dentist.
2. I should listen to my teacher.
3. People shouldn't steal.
4. I have to brush my teeth.
5. I had to pay some bills.

Part D

1. My grades are low. I **had better** study more.
2. **Can/Could/Would** you please open the window? OR **Please open the window**.
3. I want to stay home tonight. **Let's** invite some friends over.
4. We **can't come** to your party.
5. **Maybe Susan has** a solution to the problem. OR **Susan may have** a solution to the problem.
6. Jackie isn't here. She **could/might/must** be at home in bed.
7. You **mustn't walk** in mud puddles.
8. Why **don't we** go out for dinner tonight?
9. You have to study tonight, **don't** you?
10. I need to make a call. **Could/Can/May** I borrow your phone for a minute?

CHAPTER 8

Quiz 1, p. 116

1. Beth planned to serve pizza, green salad, and ice-cream at the party.
2. Sam, Jeff, and Ellen helped with the decorations. Bob picked up the pizza and drinks.
3. The party started at 6:00. **S**everal guests were late.
4. A few people talked, others played soccer, and several people danced.
5. Everyone had a wonderful time. **N**o one wanted to go home.
6. Beth thanked everyone for coming and promised to have another party. **Then** she told everyone good night.

Quiz 2, p. 116

1. B: , and
2. A: , but
   B: or
3. B: , and
   A: , but
   B: and
4. A: or
   B: and
5. B: , but/and , but

Quiz 3, p. 117

1. but
2. so
3. so
4. but
5. so
6. but
7. but
8. so
9. so
10. but

Quiz 4, p. 117

1. doesn't
2. am
3. haven't
4. won't
5. have
6. don't
7. are
8. will
9. didn't
10. do

Quiz 5, p. 118

2. doesn't
3. does
4. is
5. are
6. does
7. do
8. isn't
9. don't
10. aren't
11. is

Quiz 6, p. 118

2. will too
3. isn't either
4. is too
5. neither is
6. so does
7. doesn't either
8. does too
9. neither does
10. so has
11. is too

Quiz 7, p. 119

1. Because I had a high fever, I went to the doctor.
   I went to the doctor because I had a high fever.
2. Because Cindy didn't study, she failed the class.
   Cindy failed the class because she didn't study.
3. Because it was a beautiful day, we went to the beach.
   We went to the beach because it was a beautiful day.
4. Because my old jeans have holes in them, I need to get new jeans.
   I need to get new jeans because my old jeans have holes in them.
5. Because my car is making strange noises, I feel uncomfortable driving.
   I feel uncomfortable driving because my car is making strange noises.

Quiz 8, p. 120

A.

1. ✓ Because it was hot, I jumped in the cool water.
   ___ I jumped in the cool water, so it was hot.
   ✓ It was hot, so I jumped in the cool water.
2. ___ I took off my uncomfortable shoes, so my feet hurt.
   ___ Because my feet hurt, so I took off my uncomfortable shoes.
   ✓ My feet hurt, so I took off my uncomfortable shoes.

3. ✓ Oscar began coughing because the restaurant was smoky.
_____ The restaurant was smoky because Oscar began coughing.
✓ The restaurant was smoky, so Oscar began coughing.

B.
1. so
2. Because
3. because
4. so
5. because

Quiz 9, p. 121

A.	**B.**
1. a	1. a
2. b	2. a
3. a	3. b
4. a	4. a
5. a	5. b

Quiz 10, p. 122

1. Even though the roads were crowded, we got home on time.
2. correct
3. Because the students felt the building shake, they got under their desks.
4. correct
5. correct
6. Although this TV is new, the picture isn't very clear.
7. correct
8. Although it was raining, we stood in line to get tickets for the concert.
9. correct
10. Because my parents were celebrating twenty-five years of marriage, they had a big party.

Quiz 11, p. 122

1. I enjoy **science. My** favorite subjects are **physics, math, and** chemistry.
2. Julia doesn't participate in **sports, and neither do** her friends.
   Julia doesn't participate in **sports, and her friends don't either**.
3. Our baseball team lost the **game because** not enough players showed up.
4. The downstairs phone isn't working properly, and this one **isn't** either.
5. I wore a hat and sunglasses **because** the sun was so bright.
6. My mother is Australian, **and** my father is Brazilian.
7. Even though you're upset **now, you'll** understand our decision in a few days.
8. **Because** our parents both work, my brothers and I sometimes cook dinner.
9. I have never been to Hawaii, and **neither has** my husband.
10. The photographs turned out wonderfully, but the video **didn't.**

TEST 1, p. 123

A.
Elena decided the weather was too nice to stay at **home, so** she packed a picnic lunch and drove to the **beach. Even** though it was **crowded, she** found a place to **sit.** **She** spread out her blanket and opened her **lunch. Inside** was a **sandwich, potato chips, and** an **apple. Because** she was still full from **breakfast,** she ate only a little and saved the rest for **later. She** took out a book and opened **it. Minutes** later she was **asleep, and** she woke up just as the sun was going **down.**

B.	**C.**
1. so/and	1. so does
2. Even though	2. is too
3. but	3. isn't either
4. Because	4. neither does
5. or	5. so do
6. and	6. does too
7. Even though	7. neither has
8. or	8. will too
9. so	9. so are
10. because	10. do too

D.
1. I study hard **even though** my classes are very easy.
2. After the accident, my left arm hurt, **and so did** my right shoulder. OR
   After the accident, my left arm hurt, **and my right shoulder did too.**
3. Blackberries, strawberries, **and blueberries all** grow in our garden.
4. Because taxes were so **high, people** refused to pay.
5. We were excited about the concert, **so** we got there early to get good seats.

TEST 2, p. 125

A.
Ron needs to decide if he is going to go to graduate school, **or** if he is going to get a **job. He** will finish business school in a few **months. Although** he has enjoyed being a **student, he** wants to start earning his own **money. His** parents want him to get a Master's **degree. They** have said they will pay for **it, so** they think he should agree to stay in **school. Ron** appreciates their **generosity, but** he also wants to be more independent at this time in his **life.**

B.	**C.**
1. or	1. so is
2. Because	2. do too
3. and	3. so do
4. so	4. is too
5. Even though	5. so are
6. Because	6. so will
7. but	7. don't either
8. Even though	8. so did
9. but	9. do too
10. so	10. neither do

D.
1. People couldn't describe the **accident because** it happened so quickly.
2. **Nadia is a new student, but** she has made many friends.
   Even though Nadia is a new student, she has made many friends
3. **A storm was approaching, so** the sailors decided to go into shore.
4. You can either pay by cash **or** check. Which do you prefer?
5. Maria didn't understand the lecture. **Neither did I.**

Chapter 9

Quiz 1, p. 127

A.
2. was not as warm as
3. was almost as warm as
4. was just as warm as
5. were not as warm as
6. was not as warm as

B.
2. Maria
3. Paulo
4. Susan
5. Susan and Lacey
6. Maria

Quiz 2, p. 128

Answers may vary.
1. Light chocolate is just as delicious as dark chocolate.
2. Spring is not as colorful as fall.
3. Sending email is not as easy as text messaging.
4. A hard pillow is not as comfortable as a soft pillow.
5. A non-poisonous snake is not as scary as a poisonous snake.
6. Eating is just as important as sleeping.
7. England is not as large as China.
8. A school bus is not as fast as a sports car.
9. Basketball is not as popular as soccer.
10. The Winter Olympics are just as exciting as the Summer Olympics.

Quiz 3, p. 129

1. larger
2. healthier
3. more dangerous
4. heavier
5. longer
6. more expensive
7. easier
8. more quickly
9. more interesting
10. safer

Quiz 4, p. 130

Answers may vary.
1. Summer is warmer than winter.
2. Mexico City is bigger than New York City.
3. A holiday is more enjoyable than a work day.
4. Rocks are heavier than air.
5. Snow is softer than ice.
6. Ice cream is tastier than lemons.
7. A book is more expensive than a newspaper.
8. Vegetables are healthier than butter.
9. A DVD is cheaper than a DVD player.
10. A year is longer than a month.

Quiz 5, p. 131

1. further
2. farther/further
3. farther/further
4. further
5. farther/further
6. further
7. farther/further
8. farther/further
9. farther/further
10. further

Quiz 6, p. 132

2. I am, they are
3. mine/ours
4. they can
5. hers
6. he can
7. we did
8. he is
9. they do

Quiz 7, p. 133

1. very
2. much/a lot/far
3. very
4. much/a lot/far
5. much/a lot/far
6. very
7. very
8. much/a lot/far, much/a lot/far
9. much/a lot/far

Quiz 8, p. 133

1. not as sweet as
2. both
3. both
4. both
5. not as fast as
6. both
7. not as soft as
8. both
9. both
10. not as hard as

Quiz 9, p. 134

1. more water
2. faster
3. more time
4. more difficult
5. sunnier
6. more miles
7. easier
8. more rain
9. better
10. more quietly

Quiz 10, p. 135

1. hotter and hotter
2. more and more confused
3. harder and harder
4. redder and redder
5. more and more difficult
6. more and more relaxed
7. happier and happier
8. more and more expensive
9. more and more dangerous
10. better and better

Quiz 11, p. 136

A.
1. The colder, the more refreshing
2. The bigger, the more expensive
3. The older, the more repairs
4. The hotter, the more water
5. The thicker, the better

B.
1. The more the bus driver sang, the more the children laughed.
2. The more I exercised, the more energetic I felt.
3. The more my mom cooks, the more I eat.
4. The more it rained, the more depressed I got.
5. The harder Simon works, the happier his boss is.

Quiz 12, p. 137

1. a
2. a
3. a
4. a
5. a
6. b
7. b
8. a
9. b
10. a

Quiz 13, p. 138

1. the noisiest, ever
2. the fastest, in
3. the most beautiful, of
4. the worst, ever
5. the coldest, in
6. the loudest, ever

7. the hardest of
8. the most expensive, in
9. the least confident, ever
10. Of, the laziest, the luckiest

Quiz 14, p. 139

A.
1. to, Ø
2. to, from
3. A: from
   B: as, Ø
4. Ø, Ø

B.
Answers may vary.
2. the same/alike
3. different
4. different from
5. similar to
6. similar

Quiz 15, p. 140

Answers may vary.
1. different
2. the same as/like
3. similar/the same; the same/alike
4. the same
5. different
6. the same/alike
7. different
8. similar/the same
9. alike/the same

Quiz 16, p. 141

1. **The friendliest** person in our class is Julie.
2. The food at the restaurant was **worse** than the last time we were there.
3. The movie was **funnier** than we expected. We laughed the whole time.
4. Anna's dog is **the** ugliest dog I've ever seen.
5. Grandpa's behavior is embarrassing. The older he gets, The **more** loudly he talks
6. I have **the** same bag as you. Where did you buy yours?
7. My father said that having kids was one of the best **things** he ever did.
8. For Jon, the game of chess is **like** an interesting math puzzle.
9. As the horse got tired, he began walking **more and more slowly**.
10. The driving test was **harder** than I expected.

TEST 1, p. 142

Part A
1. heavier than
2. smaller
3. colder than, the hottest
4. worse
5. the largest, most populated
6. easier, than
7. the biggest
8. the most delicious

Part B
Answers may vary.
1. B is as big as D.
2. A is not as big as C.
3. E and C are different.
4. E is the smallest. OR C is the biggest.
5. E is almost as big as A.

Part C
1. Of
2. as
3. in
4. from
5. Ø
6. to
7. as
8. of

Part D
1. The more books Scott read, the more interested he got.
2. The more mistakes Johnny made on his homework, the more upset he became.
3. The longer we hiked, the thirstier I got.
4. The harder Emily works, the more money she earns.
5. The rougher the water became, the more scared the children were.

Part E
1. Let's buy this chair. It's less expensive **than** that one.
2. My brother is smaller than **I am / me**.
3. Linda is in **the** same German class as I am.
4. I got enough sleep. I'm not as tired today **as** yesterday.
5. Those students are **the smartest** kids in the class.
6. If you need **further** assistance, please ask.
7. Please talk more **quietly** in the library.
8. Erin's stomachache got **worse and worse** as the day went on.
9. That was one of the best **books** I have ever read.
10. My homework isn't as difficult **as** yours.

TEST 2, p. 145

Part A
1. better than
2. faster than
3. longer than, the loveliest
4. prettier, more elegant than
5. biggest
6. The worst, The most famous
7. farther/further

Part B
1. A and B are similar.
2. A is just as short as E.
3. C is not quite as tall as D.
4. C is taller than B.
5. A and E are the same.

Part C
1. as
2. in
3. from
4. Ø
5. Of
6. to
7. in
8. Of

Part D
1. The harder the swimmer trained, the stronger he felt.
2. The more nervous my sister was, the faster she talked.
3. The hungrier the baby was, the more she cried.
4. The more loudly Karen played the piano, the more the dog barked.
5. The faster the ideas came, the more pages the writer wrote.

1. These peas are delicious. I didn't know that fresh peas tasted so much better **than** frozen peas.
2. The flu can be a dangerous illness. It's **more** dangerous to have the flu than a cold.
3. Who has a **better** life: a married person or a single person?
4. The clouds look dark. Let's hope it's not as rainy this afternoon **as** it was this morning.
5. **Of** the nine planets, Pluto is the smallest.
6. What has been **the happiest** day in your life so far?
7. The kids yelled **more and more loudly** in the park.
8. **The** largest bird is the ostrich, but elephants are the largest land animals.
9. One of the strongest **metals** in the world is titanium.
10. My cell phone battery runs down **faster and faster**.

CHAPTER 10

Quiz 1, p. 148

2.	passive	7.	passive
3.	active	8.	passive
4.	passive	9.	passive
5.	active	10.	active
6.	active	11.	passive

Quiz 2, p. 148

1.	is	6.	have been
2.	are	7.	will be
3.	was	8.	will be
4.	were	9.	is going to be
5.	has been	10.	are going to be

Quiz 3, p. 149

1. is driven
2. was hit
3. will be fixed
4. are cleaned
5. have been checked
6. were written
7. was eaten
8. was enjoyed
9. are going to be surprised
10. was signed

Quiz 4, p. 150

A.

1.	b	4.	b
2.	a	5.	a
3.	a		

B.

1. Children enjoy ice cream.
2. The students discussed the book.
3. The new owners have changed the café's name.
4. Our team is going to win the game.
5. The city will give an award to Mr. Reed.

Quiz 5, p. 151

A.

1. Hospital visitors will be greeted by volunteers.
2. Many different languages are spoken by patients.
3. An injection has been given by the nurse.
4. A new treatment was discussed by the doctors.
5. Excellent care is provided by the hospital.

B.

1. Is the kitchen usually cleaned by your mom?
2. Are the bedrooms going to be cleaned by the kids?
3. Was the trash taken out by Paul?
4. Will the garage be cleaned out by Gary?
5. Has everyone been given a job by your mom?

Quiz 6, p. 152

2.	transitive	7.	intransitive
3.	transitive	8.	intransitive
4.	intransitive	9.	transitive
5.	intransitive	10.	transitive
6.	transitive	11.	transitive

Quiz 7, p. 152

1. no change
2. Our sink has finally been fixed by the plumber.
3. no change
4. no change
5. The car will be sold next month by our neighbors.
   OR
   Our neighbors' car will be sold next month.
6. The dinner dishes are usually washed by Mr. LeBarre.
7. no change
8. The message has been recorded by voicemail.
9. The scratched DVD was returned to the store by Val.
10. no change

Quiz 8, p. 153

1. This sweater was given to me. OR I was given this sweater.
2. Google was created by Larry Page and Sergey Brin.
3. Books are checked out at a library.
4. Have you ever been lied to?
5. The picture was painted by Picasso.
6. These walls will be painted tomorrow.
7. The speeding car was chased by the police.
8. When were cell phones first used?
9. French and English are spoken in Canada.
10. The basketball game has been stopped by the referee.

Quiz 9, p. 154

1.	can be reached	6.	should be recycled
2.	has to be picked up	7.	could be stolen
3.	shouldn't be eaten	8.	must be told
4.	ought to be sent	9.	might be started
5.	has to be changed	10.	may be reached

Quiz 10, p. 155

1.	has to be paid	6.	can be contacted
2.	has eaten	7.	was painted
3.	called	8.	was built
4.	should be washed	9.	turned off
5.	will be held	10.	must be told

Quiz 11, p. 155

1.	with/by	6.	about
2.	with/in	7.	in
3.	with	8.	for
4.	in	9.	to
5.	of	10.	with

Quiz 12, p. 156

1. is engaged to
2. was worried about
3. Is, scared of
4. were exhausted from
5. is qualified for
6. Are, related to
7. was crowded with
8. is divorced from
9. is composed of
10. are/were opposed to

Quiz 13, p. 156

1. a. surprised
   b. surprising
2. a. embarrassing
   b. embarrassed
3. a. interesting
   b. interested
   c. interesting
4. a. amazing
   b. amazed
   c. amazing

Quiz 14, p. 157

1. frightened, frightening
2. fascinated
3. scary, scared, relaxed
4. terrifying, surprised
5. interesting, interested

Quiz 15, p. 157

1. get confused
2. got lost
3. get fat
4. gets nervous
5. getting dark
6. get rich
7. got sunburned
8. get hungry
9. get serious
10. got arrested

Quiz 16, p. 158

A.
1. is used to
2. wasn't used to
3. am not used to
4. were used to
5. aren't used to

B.
2. _____ I am used to living by myself.
3. _____ People here are used to a lot of snow.
4. ✓ It used to snow more in the winter.
5. _____ Are you accustomed to the snow?
6. ✓ Where did you use to live?

Quiz 17, p. 159

1. used to travel, used to spend
2. are used to eating
3. did you use to live, Are you used to living
4. is used to being
5. did your husband use to do, used to work
6. used to have, am not used to

Quiz 18, p. 160

A.
1. Students are supposed to wear uniforms.
2. Customers are supposed to pay their bills on time.
3. We were supposed to be on time, but we weren't.
4. Customers are not supposed to leave tips for service.
5. It was supposed to snow last night.

B.
2. Drivers are **supposed** to drive more slowly in rainy weather.
3. correct
4. You **are** not supposed to wear shoes in the house.
5. What **are we** supposed to do about Graciela's situation?
6. **Weren't/Aren't** you supposed to go to school early today?

Quiz 19, p. 160

1. c
2. d
3. a
4. b
5. a
6. c
7. d
8. c
9. d
10. b

TEST 1, p. 162

Part A
I. 1. jumped
    2. began
    3. was saved
    4. was seen
II. 1. was
    2. were asked
    3. wanted
    4. argued
    5. said
    6. became
    7. will be needed

Part B
1. b
2. d
3. b
4. a
5. c
6. b

Part C
1. A: thrilling
   B: scary, frightened
2. A: disappointed
   B: surprising, confusing

Part D
1. Ben and Rachel **got** engaged last month.
2. The government is opposed **to** lower taxes.
3. I heard my name. Who **called** me?
4. Dogs in the park **are supposed to be** on a leash.
5. Your fax **came** a few minutes ago. Should I get it for you?
6. Our apartment **must be cleaned** before the party next week.
7. I used to **run**, but now I walk for exercise.
8. The fish isn't ready yet. It **should be cooked** a little longer.
9. We enjoyed our time in Malaysia, but **we were exhausted** from the heat.
10. Jorge can skateboard for hours before he **gets tired**.

TEST 2, p. 165

Part A
1. returned
2. decided/had decided
3. was cleaned/had been cleaned
4. were washed/had been washed
5. was dusted/had been dusted
6. were polished/had been polished

7. thanked
8. looked
9. said
10. was done
11. got

Part B

1. d	4. c
2. b	5. d
3. a	6. a

Part C
1. B: disappointed, boring
   B: exciting
2. A: disturbing
   B: depressed, alarming

Part D
1. The Jeffersons have been married **to** each other for fifty years.
2. My new boss is very **interested in** my work experience.
3. My husband and I used to **live** on a houseboat. Now we rent an apartment downtown.
4. Dr. Barry **arrived** two hours late and missed the meeting.
5. Where **did** you go after the movie? I couldn't find you.
6. The dog began to cross the highway, but there were so many cars that he **got scared**.
7. Thierry is from the French Riviera. He isn't used to **living** in the mountains.
8. The children are very excited **about** going to the aquarium.
9. Rita's wedding is today. She **is getting** very nervous.
10. What time is the play **supposed to start?**

CHAPTER 11

Quiz 1, p. 167

2. a	7. a
3. an	8. a
4. a	9. an
5. a	10. a
6. an	11. a

Quiz 2, p. 167

2. an	7. an
3. some	8. some
4. a	9. a
5. some	10. a
6. some	11. an

Quiz 3, p. 168

1. letters	6. Ø, assignments
2. Ø	7. Ø, rings
3. Ø, Ø	8. facts, Ø
4. days, Ø	9. Ø
5. Ø	10. clouds

Quiz 4, p. 168

2. much time	7. much money
3. much information	8. many games
4. many friends	9. many books
5. much email	10. many photos
6. much experience	11. much knowledge

Quiz 5, p. 169

1. a little traffic	6. a little pepper
2. a little money	7. a little dirt
3. a little meat	8. a little milk
4. a few apples	9. a few, coins
5. a few suggestions	10. a few eggs

Quiz 6, p. 169

1. a few, several	6. much, a lot of, a little
2. much, a little	7. many, several, some
3. some, a lot of	8. several, a few
4. some	9. some, much, a little
5. a little, a lot of	10. much, some

Quiz 7, p. 170

1. coffee	6. hair
2. chicken	7. glasses
3. irons	8. some paper
4. time	9. works
5. light	10. papers

Quiz 8, p. 170

2. bag, box	7. bowl, cup
3. bottle, box, can, jar	8. piece, slice
4. bottle, can, jar	9. cup, glass
5. can, box	10. piece, slice
6. bag, box	11. cup, glass

Quiz 9, p. 171

1. a, a
2. the, a, the, a
3. a, the
4. the, the

Quiz 10, p. 171

Checked sentences are 2, 4, 5, 7, 8, 10.

Quiz 11, p. 172

1. a. The sunglasses
   b. sunglasses
2. a. bread
   b. The bread
3. a. The furniture
   b. furniture
4. a. children
   b. The children
5. a. Vocabulary
   b. The vocabulary

Quiz 12, p. 172

1. Ø, Ø	5. The
2. The	6. Ø
3. Ø	7. The, the
4. The	8. Ø

Quiz 13, p. 173

2. a	7. the
3. a	8. the
4. a	9. the
5. The	10. a
6. the	11. the

Quiz 14, p. 173

1.	a	6.	The
2.	Ø	7.	a
3.	Ø	8.	Ø
4.	the	9.	A
5.	Ø	10.	the

Quiz 15, p. 174

1.	the	5.	The, Ø
2.	Ø	6.	the
3.	Ø	7.	Ø, Ø
4.	Ø, the, Ø	8.	Ø, Ø, the, Ø

Quiz 16, p. 174

1. **T**heresa can't decide whether to study **J**apanese or **C**hinese.
2. **W**here are you going for the summer break?
3. **T**he **A**lps are in **S**witzerland, **A**ustria, and **F**rance.
4. **W**e're reading **S**hakespeare's *Romeo and Juliet* for our literature class.
5. **T**he directions say to turn on **F**ifth **S**treet, but this is **P**ark **A**venue.
6. **L**ast **M**onday was my first day as a student at **S**tanford **U**niversity.
7. **T**he **M**ississippi **R**iver flows into the **G**ulf of **M**exico.
8. **I** was supposed to be born in **A**pril, but **I** was a month late, so my birthday is in **M**ay.
9. **W**hich instructor do you prefer: **D**r. **C**osta or **P**rofessor **P**ierce?
10. **M**ath 241 is a very high-level math class.

Quiz 17, p. 175

2.	b	7.	b
3.	a	8.	c
4.	a	9.	b
5.	d	10.	d
6.	a	11.	a

TEST 1, p. 176

Part A

1.	a	6.	b
2.	c	7.	d
3.	c	8.	d
4.	a	9.	b
5.	b	10.	c

Part B

1. **T**he lake is too cold for swimming. **H**ow about going to the indoor pool at **M**ountain **V**iew **P**ark?
2. **O**ur anatomy class will be taught by **D**r. **J**ones. **H**e's a professor, not a medical doctor.
3. **M**aria's parents are from **M**exico. **S**he speaks **S**panish fluently.
4. **T**he university plans to tear down **B**rown **H**all and build a new library.
5. **W**ould you be interested in going on a boat trip down the **C**olorado **R**iver? **W**e would see part of the **G**rand **C**anyon.

Part C

1.	a	6.	the
2.	Ø, the	7.	Ø
3.	a, an	8.	Ø, the
4.	The, a	9.	Ø, an, Ø
5.	a, a, The, the	10.	the, the

Part D

1. Let's get a drink of water. **I'm thirsty**.
2. **The scenery** in the mountains is beautiful.
3. Your hair looks great. Did you **get a haircut**?
4. For breakfast, Thomas ordered **two slices/pieces of toast** and eggs.
5. Here's a map of **the United States**. Do you see California?
6. I need **a little more time** to finish my test.
7. There are no **fish** in the Dead Sea.
8. We heard that Aunt Betsy and Uncle Wes are moving **to London** next month.
9. I need to have **my car** checked soon.
10. **Many students** at Shorewood High School study Japanese.

TEST 2, p. 178

Part A

1.	b	6.	a
2.	d	7.	d
3.	c	8.	a
4.	c	9.	a
5.	a	10.	b

Part B

1. **T**he assignment for our literature class is to read the first chapter of **S**hakespeare's *Hamlet*.
2. **I** heard that my neighbors, **T**ariq and **A**li, plan to visit **E**ngland in **M**ay.
3. **T**omorrow there will be a concert at **W**ashington **P**ark, near **B**roadway **A**venue. **A** music group from **S**outh **A**frica will be playing.
4. **T**here is a **M**iami **U**niversity in **O**hio, but **M**iami is in **F**lorida. **I**sn't that strange?
5. **W**hen did William begin working for the **S**ony **C**orporation?

Part C

1. a, Ø, Ø
2. a
3. the, a, a
4. The
5. Ø, Ø
6. Ø, Ø
7. Ø, Ø
8. a, the
9. the, the
10. The, Ø

Part D

1. I don't **need help** now, but I will later on.
2. There are **a few people** at work who would prefer not to work with Alan.
3. **Water** is necessary for survival.
4. I married **my brother's** best friend from college.
5. Antoine reached the top of **Mt. McKinley** in Alaska yesterday.
6. Some friends bicycled through **the Sahara Desert** last summer.
7. Nick worked on his car **for an hour** before he realized it needed expensive repairs.
8. Honolulu is **in Hawaii**, but it is not on the island of Hawaii. It is on Oahu.
9. Carlos tried to reach his parents **several times**, but their phone wasn't working.
10. Adrianna has **so much homework** that she doesn't know where to start.

CHAPTER 12

Quiz 1, p. 180

A.
1. Many tourists **who/that** visit New York City enjoy going to a Broadway show.
2. The French man **who/that** was in my English class had a beautiful accent.
3. Tobias thanked the nurse **who/that** took care of him in the hospital.
4. I feel happy around people **who/that** are optimistic about life.
5. When Maja was on the bus, she sat next to a woman **who/that** was talking on her cell phone.

B.
1. I heard about a teenage boy who/that takes gifts to children in hospitals.
2. Tomas met a marine biologist who/that once swam with sharks.
3. The people who/that work on this boat practice fire drills twice a month.
4. The police helped an old man who/that was confused and lost.
5. The doctor who/that treated me is very famous.

Quiz 2, p. 181

1. who	6. whom
2. whom	7. whom
3. who	8. who
4. whom	9. who
5. who	10. whom

Quiz 3, p. 181

2. a, b	7. a, b
3. a, b, c, d	8. a, b, c, d
4. a, b	9. a, b, c, d
5. a, b, c, d	10. a, b, c, d
6. a, b	11. a, b

Quiz 4, p. 182

A.
1. a, b
2. a
3. a
4. a, b
5. a

B.
1. Everyday I use Web sites which/that are great sources of information.
2. I have a cell phone which/that I can use to search the Web and send email.
3. Bluetooth technology which/that allows me to talk on the phone while I'm washing dishes is very convenient.
4. More hybrid cars which/that use both gas and electricity are being developed.
5. Many people like technology which/that makes our lives easier.

Quiz 5, p. 183

1. I spoke with an amazing woman who has thirteen children.
2. Here is the new book which you asked me to order for you.
3. The man who crashed into a tree has a broken leg.
4. The cell phone which I bought yesterday has all the newest features.
5. The kind man who owns the gas station repaired my car for free.
6. I don't know the student who wrote an article for the newspaper.
7. The biology professor who I met last year is going to retire at the end of this semester.
8. The documentary which we watched last night was fascinating.
9. The elderly man who lives in the apartment next to mine has no relatives.
10. Where is the fruit which was on the counter in the kitchen?

Quiz 6, p. 184

1. get	6. is
2. enjoy	7. sells
3. writes	8. are
4. work	9. spends
5. like	10. calculate

Quiz 7, p. 184

1. The lake [that you are familiar **with**] is famous for fishing.
2. The country [which Marco escaped **from**] is having a civil war.
3. The job [Pierre is qualified **for**] pays very well.
4. The book club [which my mother belongs **to**] sells books about knitting.
5. Don't tell me about the leak in your plumbing. The person [whom you should complain **to**] is the manager of your apartment building.
6. The building [that your company is interested **in**] is not available for rent.
7. The young man [whom Mark introduced you **to**] is a professor at Oxford University.
8. Ron doesn't always get along with two of the roommates [that he lives **with**].
9. The elderly woman [whom Marta was kind **to**] left her a large inheritance when she died.
10. The woman [whom Blake is married **to**] has both M.D. and Ph.D. degrees.

Quiz 8, p. 185

1. The radio station that we listen to has 24-hour news.
   The radio station we listen to has 24-hour news.
   The radio station which we listen to has 24-hour news.
   The radio station to which we listen has 24-hour news.
2. The manager that Sebastian works for drives a sports car.
   The manager Sebastian works for drives a sports car.
   The manager who/whom Sebastian works for drives a sports car.
   The manager for whom Sebastian works drives a sports car.
3. The school that I told you about specializes in dance and drama instruction.
   The school I told you about specializes in dance and drama instruction.
   The school which I told you about specializes in dance and drama instruction.
   The school about which I told you specializes in dance and drama instruction.

Quiz 9, p. 186

1. The little girl whose doll was taken was sad for days.
2. I'm friends with a woman whose daughter is training to be a professional boxer.
3. I met a man at the park whose parents know my grandparents.
4. I have a friend whose sailboat is also her office.
5. I enjoyed meeting the couple whose children go to the same school as our children.
6. The people whose car was just hit are upset.
7. The couple whose summer house we rent wants us to buy the property next door.
8. I know a woman whose work involves designing houses for people in wheelchairs.
9. A writer whose new book is about mountain climbing spoke about his experiences.
10. The dog whose owner left him outside a restaurant is being cared for by the staff.

Quiz 10, p. 187

1. The family **who/that** arrived late discovered they had missed the wedding.
2. A neighbor **whose** son works for an airline can fly around the world for free.
3. I ran into a man **who/that** was my boss 20 years ago.
4. Those are the students **who/that** volunteer to clean up parks on weekends.
5. The potatoes **which/that I baked** aren't done.
6. The woman **who/that/whom** I see on the bus every day talks the entire time.
7. I work with a doctor **who/that** is nice to his patients but rude to the nurses.
8. Here is the magazine **which/that** has the story about home theater systems.
9. Aiko and Yutaka moved into the apartment which **is** on the top floor.
10. The people **whose** dog bit the delivery man had to pay the doctor bills.

TEST 1, p. 188

Part A
Answers may vary.
1. Some of the mail was addressed to our neighbor who lives in the apartment downstairs.
2. I work with a man whose wife trains police dogs.
3. The garden which nearly died from lack of rain is looking healthy again.
4. The pianist who plays in the hotel lobby on weekends likes to play Chopin's *Nocturnes*.
5. The manager whom I work for treats me fairly
   The manager for whom I work treats me fairly.
6. A travel agent whose name is Mike Hammers called.

Part B
1. which, that, Ø
2. who, that
3. which, that, Ø
4. whose
5. who, whom, that

Part C
1. are
2. studies
3. live
4. is
5. are

Part D
1. in
2. at/in
3. on
4. from
5. with
6. to

Part E
1. The photographs that he paid a lot of money for were amazing.
   The photographs which he paid a lot of money for were amazing.
   The photographs he paid a lot of money for were amazing.
   The photographs for which he paid a lot of money were amazing.
2. The woman who the taxi was waiting for was late.
   The woman whom the taxi was waiting for was late.
   The woman the taxi was waiting for was late.
   The woman for whom the taxi was waiting was late.

Part F
1. The firefighters **who put out** the fire were exhausted and dirty.
2. The digital camera **we ordered** still hasn't arrived.
3. The man **that/who/whom/Ø I work for** is blind.
4. Here is the receipt which you **asked for**.
5. The **finger which/that I broke** is healing well.
6. I studied with a professor **whose** books are known around the world.
7. I met a little girl whose favorite food **is** mushrooms.

TEST 2, p. 190

Part A
Answers may vary.
1. The earphones which I bought were defective.
2. The couple whose horse won the race was surprised.
3. Barb is a supervisor whom people like to work for.
   Barb is a supervisor for whom people like to work.
4. We met a boy whose dog can do a lot of tricks.
5. The actor who starred in several movies last year won an Academy Award.
6. The little girl picked some of the flowers which grow in my garden.

Part B
1. which, that, Ø
2. who, whom, that, Ø
3. which, that, Ø
4. whose
5. which, that, Ø

Part C
1. designs
2. wants
3. go
4. speaks
5. barks

Part D
1. about
2. at
3. with
4. to
5. from
6. for

Part E
1. My nephew whom I told you about lives in Argentina.
   My nephew that I told you about lives in Argentina.
   My nephew I told you about lives in Argentina.
   My nephew about whom I told you lives in Argentina.
2. Meg found the earrings which she had been looking for.
   Meg found the earrings that she had been looking for.
   Meg found the earrings she had been looking for.
   Meg found the earrings for which she had been looking.

Part F
1. The color of paint Sandra picked for her bedroom walls **was** an unusual blue.
2. The **train that/which came** through the tunnel blew its whistle several times.

3. The **radio that/which I bought** carries overseas stations.
4. The doctor **who** operated on my father is very skilled.
5. I work with a woman **who** grew up in the same neighborhood as me.
6. The ambulance driver **who** drove my husband to the hospital didn't turn on his siren.
7. Here's an article which you might be interested **in.**

CHAPTER 13

Quiz 1, p. 192

2. turning down
3. doing
4. getting
5. driving
6. painting
7. moving
8. smoking
9. taking
10. finding
11. running

Quiz 2, p. 193

1. will go/am going to go/am going shopping
2. went sailing
3. go camping
4. went skydiving
5. go fishing
6. goes jogging
7. went window shopping
8. will go/is going to go/is going bowling
9. went sightseeing
10. goes dancing

Quiz 3, p. 193

1. working
2. working
3. working
4. working
5. to work
6. to work
7. working
8. to work
9. to work
10. to work

Quiz 4, p. 194

1. a
2. a and b
3. b
4. a
5. b
6. a
7. a and b
8. a and b
9. a
10. a

Quiz 5, p. 195

1. for
2. of
3. in
4. about
5. on
6. to
7. about
8. like
9. at
10. for

Quiz 6, p. 195

1. by
2. by
3. with
4. with
5. by
6. with
7. by
8. by, by
9. with
10. by

Quiz 7, p. 196

2. by washing
3. by painting
4. by cutting
5. by doing
6. by sending
7. by promising
8. by making
9. by exercising
10. by working
11. by changing

Quiz 8, p. 197

A.
1. Having a quiet place to study is necessary.
2. Studying with friends is more fun.
3. Learning a lot of new information is difficult.
4. Taking short breaks is a good idea.
5. Getting a good night's sleep is important.

B.
1. It is important to recycle as much garbage as you can.
2. It is helpful to use public transportation instead of your car.
3. It's a good idea to turn off lights when you leave a room.
4. It is good for everyone to be careful with water.
5. It is dangerous for the human race to pollute the earth.

Quiz 9, p. 198

A.
1. no change
2. Judy is moving **in order** to be closer to her elderly parents.
3. Tom got new glasses **in order** to read better.
4. no change
5. Francisco practiced driving a lot **in order** to pass the driving test.

B.
1. I turned down the TV in order to hear you better.
2. I wore socks to bed in order to keep my feet warm.
3. I withdrew money from the bank in order to buy a car.
4. I called the doctor in order to ask if I needed a flu shot.
5. I turned off the phone in order to get some sleep.

Quiz 10, p. 199

1. to
2. for
3. to
4. to
5. for
6. for
7. to
8. for
9. to
10. to

Quiz 11, p. 199

1. too hot, cool enough
2. too sour, sweet enough
3. enough eggs, too tired
4. safe enough, too dangerous
5. clean enough, too dirty

Quiz 12, p. 200

1. a
2. a
3. b
4. a
5. a
6. a, b
7. b
8. a
9. a, b
10. b
11. b
12. a
13. a
14. b
15. a
16. b
17. a
18. a
19. a, b
20. a

TEST 1, p. 202

Part A
1. to get
2. reading, to relax
3. to call, to get, to study
4. on getting, to arrive, Being
5. to build, to snow/snowing, to make/on making, about having/to have, building, sledding

Part B
1. on
2. by
3. by
4. to
5. from
6. by
7. for
8. with, with
9. about

Part C
1. a. too sick
   b. well enough
2. a. cool enough
   b. too hot
3. a. sweet enough
   b. too bitter

Part D
1. b
2. b
3. a
4. b
5. a
6. b
7. b
8. a
9. b

TEST 2, p. 204

Part A
1. working, to start
2. to go
3. at kicking, Playing
4. listening
5. like cooking, to lie, making, eating
6. of/about flying, sightseeing, about popping, to cover, to pull

Part B
1. in
2. by
3. by, by
4. about
5. by
6. by
7. with
8. about, of

Part C
1. a. loud enough
   b. too soft
2. a. warm enough
   b. too cool
3. a. too bright
   b. dark enough

Part D
1. a
2. b
3. a
4. b
5. b
6. a
7. b
8. a
9. b

CHAPTER 14

Quiz 1, p. 206

A.
1. I don't know what her name is.
2. I know where Nathan works.
3. My son asked me if I needed help with the dishes.
4. I know that it snowed in April last year.
5. Do you know who lives in the big house on the corner?

B.
2. Do you know what time it is? noun clause
3. When does class start? information question
4. Please tell me. Why are you late? information question
5. I wonder what happened. noun clause
6. Did you hear what Katie said? noun clause

Quiz 2, p. 207
1. when I woke up this morning.
2. why I was late today.
3. how much I study every day.
4. where I am supposed to meet my study group.
5. what I should do to improve my work.
6. who can help me with my homework.
7. which class I enjoy the most.
8. whose dictionary I borrowed.

Quiz 3, p. 208
1. A: does an apartment cost
   B: rent is
2. A: the medical conference starts
   B: the date is
3. A: does Hoang have
   B: he has
4. A: is that lady crying
   B: she is crying
5. A: it is
   B: is the jacket

Quiz 4, p. 208
1. if Richard is
2. if Joanna and Max are
3. if Oscar wants
4. if I am going
5. if I will have
6. if your brother is coming
7. if Chris took
8. if that DVD player plays
9. if he has finished
10. if you have

Quiz 5, p. 209
1. The police are trying to prove **that** the man took the money.
2. The kindergarten children like to pretend **that** they are lions and tigers.
3. We're disappointed **that** you didn't believe us.
4. Did I tell you **that** we are moving next week?
5. Our teacher really trusts us. I still can't believe **that** she leaves the room during tests.
6. For centuries, people were convinced **that** the earth was flat.
7. Is it true **that** your diamond necklace is missing?
8. Can you believe **that** it's summer already?
9. I'm positive **that** "scissors" is spelled with "S-C" at the beginning.
10. Carlos was impressed **that** Juan knew so much about chemistry.

Quiz 6, p. 210

1. so	6. so
2. so	7. so
3. not	8. so
4. so	9. so
5. not	10. so

Quiz 7, p. 211

1. Carmen asked, **"D**o you have money for parking**?"**
2. The doctor said, **"S**top smoking today.**"**
3. "There is a mouse in the house," Mickey said.
4. The policeman said, **"M**ay I see your driver's license, please**?"**
5. Mary asked, **"D**id you get the message I left for you**?"**
6. The Johnsons said, **"W**e have to go now. We have another party to attend tonight.**"**
7. Our teacher asked, **"W**ho knows the answer? Who would like to write it on the board**?"**
8. My mother said, **"I** won't be home until 7:00 tonight. Could you fix dinner**?"**
9. "You speak Russian, don't you?" said Natasha.
10. "I'm so tired from the hike. **A**re you tired too**?"** Miguel asked.

Quiz 8, p. 211

2. "Why not?" I asked.
3. "They're quite ugly," she replied.
4. "Well, they might look unpleasant," I said. "They're not as beautiful as butterflies, but they're good to have around. They eat ants and flies that you don't want to have in your house," I said. "Try to think of them as a gift from nature."
5. "Wow," she said. "I didn't know spiders were so helpful."

Quiz 9, p. 212

1. her
2. I, her
3. our, us, them
4. she, my/our, me, my
5. he, his, themselves
6. their, their, They
7. they, their, they, their

Quiz 10, p. 213

1. would be
2. had been
3. had
4. didn't understand
5. hadn't learned
6. was going to start, needed
7. had set
8. could feed, were

Quiz 11, p. 214

1. Abdul said (that) he would be twenty-five on his next birthday.
2. My parents said (that) they had enjoyed their trip to Costa Rica.
3. My friends said (that) they wanted to give me a going-away party.
4. Suzanne said (that) she had lived in Italy for twenty years.
5. The boy said (that) the dog had taken his ball and that he wasn't coming back.
6. Dr. Wilson said (that) she was going to retire in a few years and that she and her husband were planning to travel.
7. My husband said (that) he could pick up the kids after school and that I didn't need to worry about it.

Quiz 12, p. 215

1. asked, told
2. said, told
3. told, said
4. said, told
5. said, told, asked, said, told, told, said

Quiz 13, p. 215

1. I don't know yet **if/whether** the doctor can see you tomorrow or not.
2. Please tell me what **they did.**
3. Do you know whose coat **is** on the chair?
4. Do you know if the bus has come **or not**?
5. We'd like to know if the subway **stops here.**
6. I **hope that** I can come with you tonight.
7. Leila **said/told me** that she wasn't home last night.
8. I'm sorry **that** we have to cancel our plans.
9. The dentist said, **"** Your teeth look very healthy. You are taking good care of them.**"**
10. The teacher isn't sure whether Liz **wants** help or not.

TEST 1, p. 216

Part A

1. where the milk is
2. what time we will be done
3. if/whether there are any eggs left
4. whose homework that is
5. if/whether someone is knocking at the door
6. who called
7. if/whether Kwon finished his biology lab work
8. what the weather is supposed to be like
9. if/whether anyone has met him
10. if/whether this assignment counts a lot in our final grade

Part B

1. **"W**hat time is it?**"** I asked her.
2. "Time to get up," she replied.
3. "But it's not a school day," I said. "Please let me sleep in," I begged.
4. "You can't sleep in today," she said. "It's a special day."
5. "What special day?" I asked.
6. "It's your birthday," she said.
7. "Oh my gosh! I forgot. I have to get up right away," I said. "I have so many things I want to do today."

Part C

1. Julia said (that) the cookies were ready.
2. The librarian said (that) the library was going to close early today.
3. John asked how far away the airport was.
4. The fire chief said (that) it had taken a long time to put the fire out.
5. The clerk asked me if/whether I wanted paper or plastic bags.
6. Marika said (that) the flight would arrive in ten minutes.

7. The teacher said (that) the test was going to be on Friday.
8. The students replied (that) they didn't want a test.
9. The manager said (that) computers were necessary in the modern workplace.
10. Joan asked if/whether I had ever posted a video on the Internet.

Part D
1. My friends understand **what I like**.
2. I'd like to know **if/whether this computer works**.
3. The teacher **said/told us** that he would be at a conference tomorrow.
4. I want to know why **they came**.
5. **It is** a fact that exercise makes us healthier.
6. Do you know if Rick **lives** here?
7. **I'm sure that** we will have a good time together.
8. A strange man asked me **where I lived**.
   A strange man asked me, **"Where do you live?"**
9. Do you know whose **keys these are**?
10. I'm not **sure if** he wants to come or not.

TEST 2, p. 218

Part A
1. what the date today is
2. the year I was born
3. if/whether Dimitri and Irina got engaged last weekend
4. if anyone has asked for help yet
5. how many people knew about the problem
6. if/whether the weather changes much or stays the same in this area
7. if/whether Paula left the company
8. who the new manager will be
9. whose car we are taking to the mall
10. if/whether the copy machine works

Part B
1. "What do you want to do after you finish school?" he asked.
2. "I'm not sure," I said. "I'd like to have a job that is interesting and pays well."
3. "Everyone would like that," said my teacher. "Is there a specific area you see yourself working in?"
4. "Yes," I replied. "I love working with animals. Maybe I could be a veterinarian."
5. "One way to find out is to work with animals first," said my teacher. "Volunteer at an animal shelter or zoo. See how you like it."
6. I told him, "I like that suggestion. Thanks!"

Part C
1. The police officer said (that) he was giving me a warning, not a ticket.
2. My friend said (that) he/she had cleaned his/her apartment and done his/her laundry.
3. Yolanda said that the bus would be late.
4. Joe asked who had taken his car.
5. The manager said that they had decided to move their offices to a new location.
6. Brad asked when the book would be published.
7. Shirley said (that) she could fix that for me/us.
8. My parents said (that) they had been happy to hear about my promotion.
9. The doctor asked me if/whether I had been taking my medicine.
10. The dancers said that they had practiced their dance steps and were ready for their show.

Part D
1. Can you tell me **whose coat this is**?
   Can you tell me **who this coat belongs to**?
2. I felt better when the doctor said, **"Your** daughter just has a bad cold. It's nothing **serious."**
3. My friends asked me, **"When will you get married?"**
   My friends asked **me when I would get married.**
4. Did my mom ask you **if** you could come to our party **or not**?
5. Hamid asked why **I always came** late.
6. Mr. Hill **said to/told me** that he was feeling ill.
7. Could you tell me where Fred **works** in the evenings?
8. I **think that** you will enjoy being on the soccer team.
9. **I know that** this will be a good opportunity for us.
10. Professor Thomas told us he **would** be absent yesterday.

MIDTERM EXAM 1, p. 220

1. d	11. a	21. c	31. b	41. c
2. a	12. d	22. a	32. d	42. b
3. c	13. d	23. b	33. a	43. c
4. a	14. d	24. c	34. b	44. c
5. d	15. a	25. c	35. b	45. a
6. b	16. c	26. a	36. a	46. b
7. c	17. c	27. c	37. d	47. d
8. a	18. b	28. c	38. c	48. a
9. c	19. b	29. c	39. b	49. c
10. b	20. c	30. b	40. b	50. d

MIDTERM EXAM 2, p. 224

Part A
1. bought
2. gets
3. fell, was
4. is going to start/will start/is starting
5. have never been
6. had taken
7. are drawing
8. doesn't have, takes
9. are going to move/will move/are moving
10. sold
11. has worked/has been working, will retire/is going to retire
12. tore
13. had already gotten
14. will send/am going to send, love/will love/are going to love
15. cheered/were cheering, smiled/were smiling

Part B
1. can/may/should/had better/must
2. Can/Could/May
3. could/may/might
4. should/had better/must
5. must
6. could
7. Can/Could/Would
8. should
9. can
10. should/had better/must

Part C
1. Is, what, Do, I do
2. Whose, Do, I do, How, Why, Is
3. Did/Didn't, I didn't, When/What time, Why, How much

Part D

1. **Tom's** last name is Miller.
2. **Tomatoes** are good for us. They have lots of vitamin C.
3. They would rather eat Chinese food, **wouldn't** they?
4. All of the **actors'** names are listed on page six of your program.
5. Why **don't we** go shopping on Saturday? I need some new shoes.
6. We just moved into a four-**bedroom** house.
7. My brothers started **their** own gardening business last year.
8. Some children prefer to play by **themselves** rather than with other kids.
9. There are two new students in class. One is from Libya, and **the other** is from Romania.
10. When you are going on a trip, **prepare** your paperwork ahead of time.

FINAL EXAM 1, p. 227

1. b	11. a	21. a	31. c	41. b
2. c	12. c	22. b	32. c	42. c
3. d	13. b	23. a	33. b	43. c
4. a	14. b	24. d	34. c	44. a
5. c	15. d	25. c	35. c	45. b
6. c	16. b	26. d	36. a	46. d
7. b	17. d	27. b	37. a	47. c
8. d	18. c	28. d	38. b	48. d
9. c	19. b	29. b	39. d	49. b
10. d	20. a	30. c	40. a	50. d

FINAL EXAM 2, p. 231

Part A

1. Mark wants to go to Alaska next summer, but his wife would rather go to California.
2. When Mr. Meecham went to a meeting with a new client, he wore his best suit.
3. This radio station plays lots of classic rock music, so I enjoy listening to it.
4. Chris is a great bass guitar player, and Monica is a fantastic pianist.
5. Although Nancy and Karen both enjoy playing tennis, they don't play together very often.
6. As soon as we finished dinner, we had strawberry shortcake for dessert.

Part B

2. which
3. who
4. how long
5. that
6. Whether or not
7. what time

Part C

1. **"I'm** so sorry to hear that your father is ill**,"** said Margaret**.**
2. John asked**, "D**o you want to have muffins or scones for breakfast**?"**
3. **"**Could **I** please have a glass of water**?"** Mary asked. **"**I'm really thirsty.**"**

Part D

1. Derek said that social networking Web sites were a great way to keep in touch.
2. Heidi said that she had always dreamed of being an actress.
3. Adam asked which video game I liked the best.
4. Cole said (that) he would go to college next year.
5. My friends asked if I wanted to go to the coffee shop with them.

Part E

1. Bradley is **taller than** his brothers.
2. **I'll help/I can help** you in just a few minutes.
3. Playing the clarinet is not **as difficult as** playing the oboe.
4. That is **the funniest** joke I've heard in a long time.
5. My sisters like country-western music much better than **I do.** I don't enjoy listening to it.
6. If you don't fix the leak in your roof, it will cause **further** water damage in your house.
7. My brother and I are twins, but I **haven't seen him in/for** six years.
8. Laptop computers are usually **more convenient than** desktop computers.
9. How many apples **did you buy?**
10. My classmate has **the same** name **as** me. We are both named William.

Part F

1. a
2. The
3. An
4. Ø
5. The

Part G

1. How far
2. homework
3. Ø
4. many, Ø
5. a little
6. piece
7. are published
8. The
9. studying
10. Ø
11. several
12. to go
13. have been studying
14. mine
15. was given